"*Les Fleurs du mal* is full of bea[...]
are notoriously difficult to ren[...]
grateful that Nathan Brown, a scholar of such rigor
and sensitivity, has taken the plunge and translated
this ever-living masterpiece, and by a novel and
much-needed approach: with nimble fidelity to the
line, with a commitment to "hear" the poem and
be out of its way, to let Baudelaire speak to us, as
directly as he can, through the prism of a new mind."
Rachel Kushner, author of *The Flamethrowers*

"I've never been able to read any translations of Baudelaire
except the plain prose versions in Francis Scarfe: the
verse always sounded too lofty in English. But Nathan
Brown somehow manages to stay true to *Les Fleurs
du mal*'s darkness and cheap thrills—and to what old
Eric Auerbach called its essential 'aesthetic dignity'."
T. J. Clark, author of *If These Apples
Should Fall: Cézanne and the Present*

"There is no complete English translation available as
good as Nathan Brown's. Brown is extremely adept with
his lexical choices, deftly finding words which at once
preserve the nineteenth-century context but also are
striking in tone and nuance. His versions do a fine job
of maintaining the cutting edge of the original, and he
avoids preciosity and literariness throughout, without
falling into either a drab tonality of 'translatorese' or
overcompensating in the other direction with forced
and inappropriate renderings. This accounts for one
of the book's most notable and precious virtues:
versions which are painstakingly literal without being
bland—a truly outstanding feature of his renderings."
Daniel Katz, editor of *Be Brave to Things: The
Uncollected Poetry and Plays of Jack Spicer*

The Flowers of Evil

Charles Baudelaire

Translated by Nathan Brown

VERSO

London • New York

First published by Verso 2024
An earlier version of this translation was published by
MaMa — Multimedijalni institut (Zagreb); Kontrapunkt
(Skopje); and Anteism Books (Montréal) 2021
Translation © Nathan Brown 2021
Introduction © Nathan Brown 2024

1 3 5 7 9 10 8 6 4 2

Verso
UK: 6 Meard Street, London W1F 0EG
US: 388 Atlantic Avenue, Brooklyn, NY 11217
versobooks.com

Verso is the imprint of New Left Books

ISBN-13: 978-1-80429-660-8
ISBN-13: 978-1-80429-661-5 (UK EBK)
ISBN-13: 978-1-80429-662-2 (US EBK)

British Library Cataloguing in Publication Data
A catalogue record for this book is available from the British Library

Library of Congress Cataloging-in-Publication Data

Names: Baudelaire, Charles, 1821-1867, author. | Brown, Nathan, 1978-
translator. | Baudelaire, Charles, 1821-1867. Fleurs du mal. |
Baudelaire, Charles, 1821-1867. Fleurs du mal. English.
Title: The flowers of evil / Charles Baudelaire ; translated by Nathan
Brown.
Description: First edition paperback. | London ; New York : Verso Books,
2024. | Includes bibliographical references. | Parallel text in French
and English.
Identifiers: LCCN 2024038392 (print) | LCCN 2024038393 (ebook) | ISBN
9781804296608 (paperback) | ISBN 9781804296622 (ebk)
Subjects: LCSH: Baudelaire, Charles, 1821-1867--Translations into English.
| LCGFT: Poetry.
Classification: LCC PQ2191.F6 E5 2024b (print) | LCC PQ2191.F6 (ebook)
|
 DDC 841/.8--dc23/eng/20240826
LC record available at https://lccn.loc.gov/2024038392
LC ebook record available at https://lccn.loc.gov/2024038393

Printed and bound by CPI Group (UK) Ltd, Croydon CR0 4YY

This translation is for Alexi Kukuljevic—
connoisseur of the void, cormorant of the concept

Contents

PARISIAN TABLEAUX

WINE

LES

FLEURS DU MAL

PAR

CHARLES BAUDELAIRE

SECONDE ÉDITION

AUGMENTÉE DE TRENTE-CINQ POÈMES NOUVEAUX

ET ORNÉE D'UN PORTRAIT DE L'AUTEUR

DESSINÉ ET GRAVÉ PAR BRACQUEMOND

PARIS

POULET-MALASSIS ET DE BROISE, ÉDITEURS

97, RUE DE RICHELIEU, ET PASSAGE MIRÈS, 36

—

1861

Introduction:
The Poetics of Contradiction
in *The Flowers of Evil*

At the core of *The Flowers of Evil*, in the center of Baudelaire's great poem "The Swan," we find the poet anchored amid the flux of modernity:

> Paris changes! But nothing in my melancholy
> Has stirred! new palaces, scaffoldings, blocks,
> Old neighborhoods, for me everything becomes allegory,
> And my cherished memories more weighty than rocks.

Mood, which might seem evanescent, is unchanging, while Paris undergoes the transformations of Baron Haussmann's renovation of the city in the 1850s at the behest of Napoleon III: the demolition of proletarian neighborhoods and narrow medieval streets, the displacement of old theaters and cafés, the construction of wide boulevards, vast squares, and grand monuments, the refurbishing and reconstruction of the Tuileries and the Palais du Justice, the annexation of the suburbs.[1] The material process of this transformation

---

1   It was Walter Benjamin's influential writings on Baudelaire, contextualizing his poetry within the transformations of nineteenth-century Paris, that established his reception as the foremost poet of the modern city and the capitalist commodity form. See Benjamin, *Charles Baudelaire: A Lyric Poet in the Era of High Capitalism*, trans. Harry Zohn (London: Verso, 1973). See also the important correspondence between Benjamin and Theodor Adorno concerning these writings, collected in *Aesthetics and Politics*, Theodor Adorno, Walter Benjamin, Ernst Bloch, Bertolt Brecht, and Georg Lukács (London: Verso, 1977).

becomes allegory—comes to represent something other than itself, undergoing a figuration of History by imagination —while intangible memories take on a massive solidity outweighing the stones of the city. The stanza constructs a conceptual and emotional chiasmus of mutability and stasis, of matter and memory, concretely situated in space and time: standing before the Louvre after crossing the new Place du Carrousel, here in the middle of the nineteenth century, the poet is "oppressed by an image."

It is a double image. Earlier in the poem, the speaker recalled a swan that had escaped its cage, once encountered near an old menagerie that had occupied the Place du Carrousel prior to its reconstruction. Thinking of this escaped yet homeless captive—parched and dragging its wings across the ground, "heart full with the beautiful lake of his birth"—the speaker thinks as well of Andromache, the Trojan widow of Hector held as "lowly chattel" by the Greek Pyrrus, mourning her dead husband while standing "bowed in a trance beside an empty tomb." The nineteenth-century displacement of medieval Paris recapitulates the fall of Troy and also the displacement of antiquity by modernity, while the double image of Andromache and the swan symbolizes the exilic melancholia of "whoever has lost what cannot be found." On the one hand, the poem is dedicated to Victor Hugo, living in exile in Guernsey since the institution of the Second Empire by the coup d'état of Napoleon III in 1851 (the poem was written in 1859). On the other hand, the thinking of the poem extends to those exiled *within* Paris by the displacements of colonialism and slavery:

> I think of the negress, gaunt and consumptive,
> Trudging in sludge, and seeking, eyes haggard,
> The absent palms of splendid Africa
> Behind the immense barrier of fog.

We will return to the colonial imaginary of *The Flowers of Evil*, but, here, the displaced African woman is drawn into the poem, along with "starving orphans parched as flowers," as a figure of the dispossessed and the downtrodden, wandering the grey metropole as it is rebuilt in the image of imperial power. Before the stately edifice of the Louvre, the poet is oppressed by an image of suffering, historically compound and geographically complex, as he thinks "Of the captives, of the vanquished! . . . and of many more!" In this final line of the poem, the imagination strains toward the innumerable, toward the many, as historical determination opens onto its indeterminate scope. "Thus in the forest of my mind's exile," Baudelaire writes in the last stanza, "An ancient Memory sounds a full-throated horn!" In "The Swan," *memories* of an earlier Paris are gathered, through an allegorical apotheosis of melancholic recollection, into *Memory*, exceeding the psyche of the individual, sounding from an ancient world within a modern spirit exposed to its own exteriority. Exile is the concept and the feeling of this exposure.

In his essay "The Painter of Modern Life," Baudelaire will famously coin the term "modernity" to denote "the transient, the fleeting, the contingent" which is "one half of art, the other being the eternal and immovable."[2] In "The Swan" it is melancholy that is immovable, while the city changes. Far beyond its registration of subjective sadness, yearning, and guilt, that melancholy is also the objective registration of modernity as a history of social dispossession and alienation, such that "the ephemeral, the fleeting forms of beauty in the life of our day" are fused with the implacable wrong, the illness and the evil that Baudelaire's title designates as *mal*.[3] The substance of that contradiction is the soil from which his flowers grow.

---

2   "The Painter of Modern Life" in *Charles Baudelaire: Selected Writings on Art and Literature*, trans. and ed. P. E. Charvet (New York: Penguin, 1972), 403.

3   Ibid., 435.

Modernity, Revolution, *Mal*

Baudelaire was born in 1821 and died in 1867. His life and work thus took place during the turbulent period of French history between the French Revolution, beginning in 1789, and the Paris Commune of 1871—years marked by cycles of restoration and revolution, and also by the emergence of romanticism as the vanguard of French painting, music, and literature. It was a year after Baudelaire's birth, at the Salon of 1822, that Eugène Delacroix exhibited *The Barque of Dante*, a work that established him as the representative figure of romanticism in painting, as Victor Hugo would be in literature.[4] Delacroix's canvas depicts Dante standing unbalanced upon a small craft crossing the River Styx with Phlegyas at the oars and the city of Dis aflame in the background. The pallid bodies of the damned rise from the water, surrounding the boat and trying to climb in while Virgil extends a steadying hand, calmly balancing Dante amid the chaotic scene. Dante is the modern poet in the *Divine Comedy*, steadied by his ancient predecessor. But, five hundred years later, amid the heaving instability of post-revolutionary France, who would steady Baudelaire's lyric speaker as he makes his way through the quotidian inferno of modern Paris? Perhaps it bespeaks the historical compression of cultural transformation in the nineteenth century that, for Baudelaire, his contemporary elders, Delacroix and Hugo, would be as Virgil to his Dante. Or perhaps that is not quite right. Since there were no classical guides that would suffice for navigating this new terrain, it is rather as though these contemporary elders were at the oars of the barque, propelling it into stormy waters, while those of the younger generation worked to sustain and

---

4   Baudelaire revered Delacroix and would champion his work in reports on the Salons of 1845, 1846, and 1859, as well as in his memorial tribute, "The Life and Work of Eugène Delacroix" in *Charles Baudelaire: Selected Writings on Art and Literature*, 358–89.

exacerbate the disequilibrium in which they found themselves. This treacherous voyage would be the passage from romanticism to modernism, from Hugo through Baudelaire to Verlaine, Rimbaud, Mallarmé, Apollinaire, Artaud, and Césaire.

Consider "The Seven Old Men," the second in a suite of three poems dedicated to Hugo in the 1861 edition of *The Flowers of Evil*:

> Swarming city, city full of dreams,
> Where the specter in broad daylight seizes the passerby!
> Mysteries seep everywhere like sap
> Through the pinched arteries of the mighty colossus.

The poem opens onto an urban dreamscape populated by ghosts who no longer need the cover of darkness. The phantasmic underworld has risen to the surface of everyday life and that representative figure of nature, the tree, has morphed into the stony arborescence of city streets wherein mysteries flow rather than sap, with the uncanny vitality of the undead. When an old man appears—the sort of figure who might offer some words of wisdom or a guiding hand—he instead multiplies into an "infernal procession" of replicas, seven simulacral copies pushing the speaker to the brink of madness as he flees back to his room:

> Vainly my reason tried to take the helm;
> The beguiling tempest baffled its efforts,
> And my soul danced, danced, old barge
> Without sails, upon a monstrous and unbounded sea!

When Hugo received a manuscript of the poem, he famously replied that the younger poet had created "a new shiver" (*un frisson nouveau*). The torch is passed from romanticism to what will be called modernism, but modernism is itself so new that it is barely emergent, still on the very cusp of its incipience: unreason takes the helm, sustaining the instability of unrest, yet the form of the poem, impeccably crafted in rhyming alexandrines, remains more or less traditional, though constructed through ever more intricate grammatical and narrative suspensions.

Baudelaire's verse thus marks a point of saturation where the old must pass over into the new. Here is Gautier's discerning description of its cultural position:

> The poet of *Fleurs du Mal* loved what is improperly called the style of decadence, and which is nothing other than art arrived at that point of extreme maturity at which aging civilizations are delimited by oblique rays of their setting suns: a style ingenious, complicated, knowing, full of nuances and researches, forever expanding the limits of language, borrowing from all technical vocabularies, taking its colors from all palettes, notes from all keyboards, striving to render the thought within that which is most ineffable, and the form in those most vague and most fleeting contours, listening in order to translate the subtle confidences of the neurotic, the avowals of aged passion that depraves and the bizarre hallucinations of the idée fixe giving rise to madness. This style of decadence is the last word of the Word summoned to express everything and carried to extreme excess.[5]

Gautier rightly grasps that it is poetic maturity and complexity, not the impatience of an enfant terrible, that is characteristic of Baudelaire's style, even at its most provocative.

The last poem of the Hugo suite, "The Little Old Ladies," is perhaps Baudelaire's most mature and complicated work. Here again, we find the flâneur wandering through Paris,

---

5   Théophile Gautier, *Préface aux Oeuvres complètes* (1868) in André Guyaux, ed., *Baudelaire: Un demi-siècle de lectures des Fleurs du mal (1855–1905)* (Paris: Presses du l'Université Paris-Sorbonne, 2007), 476–7. My translation.

though now he does find guidance "across the chaos of teeming cities":

> In the sinuous folds of old capitals,
> Where all, even horror, turns to enchantment,
> I spy, obeying my fatal humors,
> Certain singular beings, decrepit and charming.

The horror of the "The Seven Old Men" turns to the enchantment of the fragile old women the speaker follows, meditating upon the hardships of their lives, their "stoic and uncomplaining" persistence, the metaphysical riddles of their destiny, and the mortal community they portend:

> Ruins! my family! o congenerous brains!
> I bid you each evening a solemn adieu!
> Where will you be tomorrow, octogenarian Eves,
> Upon whom presses God's fearsome claw?

Note how the materialism of "congenerous brains" meets the mythic register of "octogenarian Eves," as well as the wry humor of mingling such dry terminology with an invocation of the biblical archetype. Baudelaire's mind is incessantly agile, never shorn of irony even in its most sincere expressions of devotion, here to the kinship of ruin and finitude. As Ronjaunee Chatterjee has argued, the "singular beings" Baudelaire's speaker follows through the sinuous folds of the city suggest a complex evocation of "feminine singularity" specific to yet also displaced within modernity, wherein gendered existence becomes incipiently ungrounded from stable political and social foundations.[6]

---

6   See Ronjaunee Chatterjee, *Feminine Singularity: The Politics of Subjectivity in Nineteenth-Century Literature* (Palo Alto: Stanford University Press, 2002), 56–89. On the temporality of representations of the feminine in Baudelaire, see Elissa Marder, *Dead Time: Temporal Disorders in the Wake of Modernity (Baudelaire and Flaubert)* (Stanford: Stanford University Press, 2001).

The "modernity" of Baudelaire's work has to be approached through the irony and complexity of its relation to his historical context. No poet, except perhaps Eliot, has been so overburdened with standing as representative of "the modern." Yet one might just as well argue that Baudelaire is an antimodern poet. When he refers to "the transient, the fleeting, the contingent" which is "one half of art, the other being the eternal and the immovable," he immediately emphasizes that "there was a form of modernity for every painter of the past."[7] That is: by "modernity" Baudelaire does not necessarily refer to a specific historical epoch, but rather to what is new at any given time. Nevertheless, what is new in the moment at which Baudelaire lives is modernity understood as that epoch in which the new itself becomes a historically specific ideal—i.e., what is new is the hegemony of the new. What is at issue here is not merely an incipient avant-garde, but an epoch structured by the economic and social relations of the capitalist mode of production, traversing those political ruptures amid and in the wake of which Baudelaire lived, suffusing the lived experience of the metropole and spiraling out into and back from the brutal domination and commercial exploits of colonialism and slavery at the periphery.

All this enters into *The Flowers of Evil*, though at a level deeper than programmatic intention. Baudelaire is an antimodern poet insofar as what he considers "eternal and immovable" is not only the other half of beauty but also the whole of evil, the permanence of original sin. In an essay on Edgar Allan Poe, of whom he remains the preeminent French translator, Baudelaire states his position on this question in no uncertain terms while polemicizing against the moral optimism of utopian socialism:

> But for the moment I want to take account only of the great forgotten truth—the primeval perversity of man —and not without a very real sense of satisfaction do I see

7 Baudelaire, "The Painter of Modern Life," 403.

a few fragments of ancient wisdom floating back to us from a country whence they were not expected [i.e. Poe's America]. How good it is that a few old-fashioned truths should thus explode in the faces of all these flatterers of humanity, all these mollycoddlers and opiate-pedlars who never stop repeating, with every possible variation of tone, "I am born good, and you too, and all of us, we're all born good!", quite forgetting—no! pretending to forget, nonsensical egalitarians that they are—that we are all born branded with the mark of evil![8]

Evil is the mark of original sin, manifest in our primeval perversity, and it will not be alleviated by putting our faith in progress. According to Baudelaire, "civilized man invents the philosophy of progress to console himself for his abdication and decline."[9] But if evil, sin, and damnation are eternal and immovable, Baudelaire's polemic against utopian socialism nevertheless sets the significance of the eternal in the political context of the present. It seems that the problem of evil marks, in a new way, the problem of modernity: the latter thinks it can solve the former, but Baudelaire is not persuaded. The irrational perversity of man is too evident, too omnipresent, for the prospective social overcoming of *mal* to seem compelling.

Yet when it mattered most, Baudelaire had been on the side of socialism. He gravitated toward the radical circles of Gustave Courbet prior to the revolution of 1848, and he was in the streets during the insurrectionary struggles of February 22–24. According to the account of Charles Toubin, Baudelaire was armed and on the barricades on the 24th, calling for the assassination of his stepfather, General Aupick, who was then commander of the L'École Polytechnique military academy. With Toubin and Jules Champfleury, he started a revolutionary newspaper, *Le Salut public*; he joined Auguste

---

8   Charles Baudelaire, "Further Notes on Edgar Poe" in *Charles Baudelaire: Selected Writings on Art and Literature*, 192.

9   Baudelaire, "Further Notes on Edgar Poe," 195.

Blanqui's Central Republican Party; he was a feverish participant in the bloody uprisings of the June Days; he wrote to and met with Proudhon, whom he admired.[10] Later he would refer to "my inebriation in 1848" and ask himself, "What was the nature of this inebriation?" His reply: "Thirst for revenge. Taking *natural* pleasure in demolition. Drunk on literature; memory of books read."[11] Baudelaire retrospectively sees his revolutionary engagement as both literary and Luciferian; perhaps our "primeval perversity" includes an appetite for destruction and a proclivity for getting drunk on reading. He describes his feverish insurrectionary zeal as a type of *mal*, and if what is called "evil" or "sin" is not on the side of "progress," it may well be on the side of revolt and revolution. Walter Benjamin writes that the "irreplaceable value of class hatred consists precisely in its affording the revolutionary class a healthy indifference toward speculations concerning progress."[12] Baudelaire did not belong to the revolutionary class of workers, but he certainly did belong among those who hate the bourgeoisie.

My point is that we are not dealing with two Baudelaires —one a reactionary, antimodern theologian of original sin, the other a revolutionary poet of the modern city. Driven by a Luciferian spirit of revolt, Baudelaire's political engagement was at once a fleeting passion and the expression of what he considered an eternal tendency. That tendency aligned him, for a time, with the socialist class politics of his contemporaries. In a poem that may have been written during the years of 1847–1851,[13] Baudelaire bitterly contrasts

10   See the account of Baudelaire's activities in and around 1848 in Claude Pichois, *Baudelaire*, trans. Graham Robb (London: Hamish Hamilton, 1989), 155–78.

11   Charles Baudelaire, "My Heart Laid Bare" in *Late Fragments*, trans. and ed. Richard Sieburth (New Haven: Yale University Press, 2022), 114.

12   Walter Benjamin, *The Arcades Project*, trans. Howard Eiland and Kevin McLaughlin (Cambridge: Harvard University Press, 1999), 339.

13   Claude Pichois conjectures that the poem may have

the poverty and suffering of the "Race of Cain" with the blessings accorded to the "Race of Abel":

> Race of Abel, sleep, eat and drink;
> God smiles on you complacently.
>
> Race of Cain, in filth
> Crawl and perish miserably.
> ...
> Race of Abel, see how your seeds
> And your cattle prosper;
>
> Race of Cain, your entrails
> Howl with hunger like a dog.

The poem's blasphemous conclusion is at once a declaration of membership in the Devil's party and a materialist battle cry for the revolutionary class to take up arms and depose their masters:

> Ah! race of Abel, your carrion
> Will fat the steaming soil!
>
> Race of Cain, your work
> Is not yet done;
>
> Race of Abel, here is your shame:
> The iron is vanquished by the spear!
>
> Race of Cain, ascend to heaven,
> And cast God down to earth.

---

been composed during Baudelaire's "period of socialist fervor," noting that in French literature, "toward 1850 the myth [of Cain and Abel] tends to be transformed into an image of class struggle." See Pichois' editorial note in *Baudelaire: Oeuvres complète*, Vol. I (Paris: Gallimard, 1975), 1081. My translation.

Even if he would come to admire the counterrevolutionary thinker Joseph de Maistre after his political disengagement (following the coup d'état of 1851), at the height of his lyric powers, in "The Swan," Baudelaire continued to identify not with the powerful but with the exiles, the captives, and the vanquished—with "those who drink their own tears."

Spleen and Ideal

"The Swan" was written in 1859, two years after the first edition of Les Fleurs du mal was published and then prosecuted for offence to public decency in July 1857. Baudelaire's Luciferian blasphemies in "Saint Peter's Denial," "Abel and Cain," and "The Litanies of Satan" were deemed admissible, but six of the poems found to depict deviant and explicit sexuality were banned, remaining so in France until 1949. The banned poems were "The Jewels," "Lethe," "To She Who Is Too Gay," "Lesbos," "Damned Women," and "Metamorphoses of the Vampire"; these are included here and placed after the poems they followed in the 1857 edition. The succès de scandale occasioned by the trial is less important than its effect on the substance of Baudelaire's book. Baudelaire emphasized in his defense that the book must be understood as a whole, and having six of one hundred poems excised from a painstakingly composed volume would be bad enough, but the thematic and structural damage of these exclusions was disproportionate to their quantity.

In the 1857 edition, "The Jewels" was the twentieth poem of the book, marking the transition from an opening section focused primarily upon the spiritual tribulations of the poet to a suite of poems focused on the agonies and ecstasies of eros. "Lethe" had linked these two groups by associating erotic damnation with the stygian realm of "Don Juan in Hell." Likewise, "Metamorphoses of the Vampire" returns, much later in the volume (in the section titled "Fleurs du Mal"), to the mistress "writhing like a snake" addressed in

"The Dancing Serpent" and "With her wavering and pearly gowns ...", a figure introduced in "The Jewels." When, in a statement prepared for the trial, Baudelaire's friend Jules Barbey d'Aurevilly insisted upon the structural necessity of each poem to the volume by famously referring to its "secret architecture," such unmarked transitions and implicit thematic bonds were no doubt at issue.

"To She Who Is Too Gay" belongs to a group of poems inspired by Apollonie Sabatier, bohemian hostess of a notable salon. "All of the poems included between page 84 and page 105 belong to you," Baudelaire writes when he sends her his book.[14] "Remember that someone thinks of you, that his thought is never trivial, and that he resents you a little for your malicious gaiety."[15] Baudelaire recalls the sound of her voice, greeting him on a previous occasion as he had tried to slink away unnoticed: *"Bonjour, Monsieur! With that beloved voice whose timbre enchants and rends."* Thus, "To She Who Is Too Gay" concerns the most intimate element of Sabatier's impression on Baudelaire, the rending gaiety of her voice, apparently registered as "malicious" in its contrast with the *mal* afflicting the poet and his "sickly flowers" (*fleurs maladives*).[16] The poem ends with one of the book's most notorious passages:

> Sometimes in a beautiful garden
> Where I would drag my atony,
> I have felt, like an irony,
> The sun rend my breast;

---

14 In the present edition, the group of poems to which Baudelaire refers is numbered XXXIX–XLIX (from "I give you these verses ..." to "Poison").

15 Charles Baudelaire to Apollonie Sabatier, August 18, 1857, in *Baudelaire: Correspondance*, Vol. 1, ed. Claude Pichois (Paris: Gallimard, 1973), 423. My translation.

16 The phrase is from Baudelaire's dedication of *The Flowers of Evil* to Théophile Gautier.

And the spring and the verdure
So humiliated my heart,
That I punished a flower
For the insolence of Nature.

Thus would I, one night,
When the sensual hour sounds,
Towards the treasures of your person,
Like a coward, creep silently,

To chasten your joyous flesh,
To bruise your pardoned breast,
And to carve in your unsuspecting side
A wide and hollow wound,

And, vertiginous softness!
Through those novice lips,
More gleaming and more beautiful,
To infuse my venom, my sister!

Baudelaire insists that it is not syphilis but spleen that is the phantasmic venom referred to in the final line, absorbing a mood exterior to the volume (his resentment of Sabatier's "malicious gaiety") into the internal logic and symbolic determinations of the book. Transforming the highly self-conscious recrimination of his letter into the artifice of a poem, "Too She Who Is Too Gay" confesses the sadistic fantasy of infusing spleen into a feminine ideal associated with the insolent beauty of an allegorized Nature.

Yet, two poems later, in "Confession," we find a very different relation to the same figure. Here we move from fantasy to abrupt realism, as "she who is too gay" now articulates her disenchantment with the idealizations of gender:

Suddenly, amid the easy intimacy
            Hatched by the milky light,
From you, rich and sonorous instrument where vibrates
            Only radiant cheer,

From you, clear and joyous as a fanfare
            In the sparkling morning air,
A plaintive note, a strange note
            Escaped, faltering

Like a sickly, horrible, dark, dirty child
            Who would make her family blush,
And had long since, hidden from the world,
            Been kept in a secret cellar.

Poor angel, she sang, your piercing note:
            "How nothing on earth is certain,
And however carefully made up, always,
            Human egoism betrays itself;

"What hard work it is to be a beautiful woman,
            And how banal the labor
Of the cold and demented dancer who swoons
            In her machinic smile;

"How stupid it is to take things to heart;
            How things fall apart, love and beauty,
Until Oblivion throws them in his sack
            To give them back to Eternity!"

I have often recalled that enchanted moon,
            That languor and that silence,
And that horrible whispered confidence
            At the confessional of the heart.

Sustaining ideals of feminine beauty is hard work; the labor of dancing for money is banal; the smile put on to assuage masculine insecurity is machinic; romantic faith is stupid; love and beauty are prone to worldly dissolution. Allegory itself—Baudelaire's cherished device, here conferring proper names upon Oblivion and Eternity—amounts to returning the refuse of broken promises to their source in an untrue denial of finitude. Baudelaire is certainly not a feminist, but "Confession" is a feminist poem, and this discrepancy speaks to the differential ground of poetry, which subsumes, exceeds, transfigures, complicates, and sometimes contradicts the subjective attitudes of those who produce it. Poetry makes a place for the discrepancy that we are and to which writing testifies, wherein strange notes pierce the consistency of voice.

In "Heauton Timorumenos," the disharmony of identity recoils upon the speaker as a predatory Irony from which he cannot escape, however he attempts to displace its violence:

> Am I not a false chord
> In the divine symphony,
> Thanks to the voracious Irony
> That shakes me and sinks in its teeth?

The "I" is a disharmony internal to the Ideal, "a false chord / In the divine symphony," and Spleen is the self-lacerating registration of the Irony that stalks our ability to think and desire the Ideal at all. "I am the wound and the knife!" declares the speaker. Love and sex are infected by this Irony, the inseparability of Spleen and Ideal, and this is one of the senses of *mal*. In "Confession," the gendered asymmetry of this sickness is exposed by the speaking muse; in "Heauton Timorumenos," its violence turns back upon the speaker and hunts him down with devouring inevitability. The intricate significance of such relations among the moods, styles, and subjective postures of discrepant poems is why the excision of a poem like "To She Who Is Too Gay" would have seriously compromised the complex unity of *The Flowers of Evil*. The violence of that poem is required to realize the irony of its phantasmic sadism and to prepare the deflationary realism of "Confession," from which it is separated only by a poem titled "Reversibility."

There is a poem titled "Ideal" in the volume, and the ironic relation of this term to Spleen is perhaps best approached through that sonnet:

> Never will these beauties in vignettes,
> Debased products, born of a miscreant century,
> These feet in buskins, these fingers in castanets,
> Know how to satisfy a heart like mine.
>
> I leave to Gavarni, poet of chlorosis,
> His chirping flock of hospital belles,
> For I cannot find among these pale roses
> One flower resembling my ideal red.
>
> Profound as an abyss, what this heart requires
> Is you, Lady Macbeth, soul equal to the crime,
> Dream of Aeschylus hatched in stormwinds;
>
> Or you, great Night, Michelangelo's daughter,
> Who peacefully twists in exotic pose
> Your charms fashioned in the mouths of Titans!

The octave rejects idealized representations of fainting femininity, adorned in antique costume and rendered in pale colors. After the volta, the sestet posits a counterpoint to these "pale roses": an "ideal red" whose depth and power exceeds the "debased products" of a "miscreant century." The blood red ideal will be ancient, criminal, abyssal, relayed from Clytemnestra to Lady Macbeth. Of Titanic origin, of the Night, it twists in stasis. If there is a false ideal and a true Ideal, the criterion of the latter is its dialectical intimacy with Spleen, which lends it depth and irony.

Spleen may thus be considered an attunement to the disharmony at the root of the Ideal, inhabiting the body as both desire and disease. At once ancient and modern, it installs the clinamen of Luciferian revolt within a historical epoch subsequent to the decapitation of the Great Chain of Being. In "The Irremediable," Baudelaire's Satan descends into the abyss from a void that opens in the heavens:

> An Idea, a Form, a Being
> Parted the azure and fell
> In a murky and leaden Styx
> Where no eye of Heaven penetrates

In Immanuel Kant's *Critique of Pure Reason* (1781), Soul, World, and God are ideas of reason we cannot help but think, even if they cannot become objects of knowledge, and faith in their possible harmony allows us to align morality with divine providence. In *The Flowers of Evil*, a chasm fractures the harmony of ideas, a void wherein Satan appears as the *diable* within "L'Irrémédiable": an "ironic beacon" of "the conscience within evil." For Baudelaire, the Devil is "An Idea, a Form, a Being" that may be expelled from Heaven and may be disavowed on Earth, but which ultimately cannot be expelled from the "I," since the severance of mortal subjectivity from divine perfection entails an ineradicable intimacy with *mal*.

All of the banned poems are integral to establishing the double bind of this intimacy, in a mode blending the thwarted desire of the courtly love poem and troubadour lyric with the explicit eroticism of libertine culture. In "The Jewels," the sexually direct mistress dislodges the soul of the reserved speaker from its fortress of solitude:

> And her arms and her legs, and her thighs and her loins,
> Polished as if with oil, undulating like a swan,
> Passing before my eyes clairvoyant and serene;
> And her belly and breasts, grapes on my vine,

Advanced, more coaxing than malicious Angels,
To trouble the nest where my soul took rest,
And dislodge it from the crystal rock
Where, calm and alone, it had set itself.

In "Metamorphoses of the Vampire," seduction gives way to sexual disgust and hallucinatory horror, as the body of the mistress is transformed into

the remnants of a skeleton
Which among themselves issued the shriek of a weathervane
Or of a sign, hung from an iron nail,
That sways in the wind during winter nights.

In "Lethe," this morbid entanglement of sex and death is figured as a fatalistic drama of dialectical determination, wherein damnation is not only accepted but willed as the inevitable outcome of desire:

To engulf my sated sobs
Nothing compares to the abyss of your bed;
Potent oblivion inhabits your mouth,
And Lethe flows in your kisses.

My destiny, hereafter my delight,
I shall obey as a predestination;
Docile martyr, condemned innocent,
Whose fervor fuels the ordeal,

I will suck, to drown my rancor,
Nepenthe and beneficent hemlock
At the lovely tips of your pointed breast,
Which has never imprisoned a heart.

Erotic oblivion enables a forgetting of ennui, but only by way of suicidal devotion to the traditional poetic figure of a cruel mistress who embodies the duplicity of Spleen and Ideal.

"Lesbos" and "Damned Women" also dramatize this sexual fatalism. These poems seem to have been so central to Baudelaire's conception that he initially planned to title his book *The Lesbians*. In "Lesbos," the death of Sappho turns the idealized Greek island into a figure of melancholic torment, of eternal lamentation unappeased by the honors paid to it by the tradition. In "Damned Women," erotic obsession opens an abyss within the hearts of its classical figures, Delphine and Hippolyta, who descend "the path of eternal hell." "May our closed curtains divide us from the world!" Hippolyta cries. Prior to Sappho's death, Lesbos is presented as a sensuous paradise of "endlessly inexhaustible refinements," indifferent to the dour gaze of Platonic rationalism. But neither the classical island nor the sumptuous enclosures of modern bohemia can hold out against the incursions of sexual despair. The fantasy of "the lesbian" seems to have interested Baudelaire as a figure binding social transgression with inevitable destruction, and if this does not distinguish these poems from his representations of heterosexual torment, it may be that figuring a possible "outside" to that torment offered a way of negating its specificity. The figure of the lesbian seems to offer an idealized, utopian escape from the impasses of heterosexual desire, such that the inevitable lapse of this fantasy may also figure the *inescapable* binding of eros to damnation.

Colonial Synesthesia

Fantasies of others and elsewheres, and the disenchantment of those fantasies, are central to *The Flowers of Evil*. If "Damned Women" sutures the classical paradise of "Lesbos" to the fallen sexuality of bohemian modernity, the poems associated with Jeanne Duval, Baudelaire's mixed-race lover of French and Haitian ancestry, figure the inextricability of sexual ambivalence and colonial desire. Baudelaire's evocations of balmy islands and perfumed breezes draw the geographic distance of the colonies into the grey world of the metropole, while the erotic agonies of these poems reverse that trajectory: within the intimacy of the boudoir, "oriental allure" ("A Phantom") opens a portal to far off places and foreign pleasures. In "Exotic Perfume," for example:

> When, with eyes shut, on a warm autumn eve,
> I breathe the scent of your balmy breast,
> I see the unfolding of fortunate shores
> Dazzling in the flames of a monotonous sun;
>
> An indolent island where nature offers
> Curious trees and savory fruits;
> Men of slender and vigorous build,
> And women with eyes of startling candor.
>
> Guided by your scent toward pleasant climes,
> I see a port replete with sails and masts
> Still wearied by the tossing sea,
>
> While the perfume of green tamarinds,
> That circles in the air and swells in the nostril,
> Mingles in my soul with the mariners' song.

I breathe the scent of your breast, I see with my eyes closed, and finally I hear the silent song of imagined sailors: the mingling of these sensations makes synesthesia a key trope of orientalist fantasy in *The Flowers of Evil*, affording a fleeting metaphysical unity of body and soul, a fusion of presence and absence. The poem goes so far as to venture the rhyme of *marine* (sea) with *narine* (nostril) in order to foreground the corporeal interiorization of an exotic else- where through the evocative intimacy of what is sensed here and now. The mediating figure of this tropological transit is the port, with its "sails and masts / still wearied by the tossing sea" suggesting the indolence of postcoital fatigue.

In 1841, in order to interrupt what his family saw as the downward spiral of Baudelaire's bohemian life in the Latin Quarter, his stepfather arranged to send him off on a sea voyage to India, departing from Bordeaux on June 4. Baudelaire's father had died in 1827, when Baudelaire was six years old. His mother then married Jacques Aupick in 1828, a former soldier in Napoleon's army whose military career had traced a meteoric rise from aide-de-camp to major, colonel, and general, with a litany of honors and distinctions along the way. Baudelaire would remain on good terms with his stepfather through his childhood and adolescence, but the disciplinary voyage of 1841 marked the onset of hostilities that would characterize their relationship until Aupick's death in April 1857, two months before the publication of the first edition of *The Flowers of Evil*.

Baudelaire would not make it to India. Following a nearly catastrophic storm around the Cape of Good Hope, the ship required repairs over six weeks in Mauritius and Réunion, and Baudelaire refused to reembark from the latter on October 19, remaining on the island until November 4, when he sailed back to Bordeaux on a different ship, arriving on February 15. The first poem Baudelaire published in his own name, "To a Creole Lady," was addressed to Madame Autard de Bragard, the wife of a wealthy plantation owner whose acquaintance he made in Mauritius:

> In a perfumed land caressed by the sun,
> I knew, beneath a canopy of crimson trees
> And palms that rain idleness upon the eyes,
> A creole lady of unrecognized charms.
>
> Her hue is pale and warm; brown enchantress
> Whose neck bears noble manners;
> Tall and svelte in stride like a huntress,
> Her smile is tranquil and her eyes assured.

Should you go, Madame, to the true land of glory,
Upon the banks of the Seine or the verdant Loire,
Beauty fit to ornament venerable manors,

You would, within an arbor of reclusive shadows,
Germinate a thousand sonnets in the hearts of the poets,
Whom your wide eyes would make more submissive than
    your blacks.

The inception of Baudelaire's poetic career is thus linked to a figure of mediating racialization, appended to a tropical idyll enabled by the social relations of slavery. The pale and warm hue of the creole lady, of European descent but born in the colony, renders her a "brown enchantress" presiding over black slaves who serve as figural models for the submission she would inspire in "the hearts of poets," should she journey to the metropole. Baudelaire's voyage to the tropics inscribes this complex in his psyche and his work, where it will be played out primarily through figural transmutations of Jeanne Duval.

These figural transmutations are expressive of a colonial and orientalist ideology that saturates much of nineteenth-century French literature and art,[17] the cultural ubiquity of which makes it a matter not only of unconscious cathexis but also of reflexive recognition and self-conscious representation. In the late poem "Hair" ("La Chevelure"), the psychosexual intoxication of synesthetic exoticism achieves so systematic an articulation that it takes on the reflexive character of a poetically compressed theoretical summa. The fleecy curls of the exotic mistress, in their perfumed recesses, are an "ebony sea" opening onto whole continents fading into the mists of time:

---

17   See Edward W. Said, *Orientalism* (New York: Pantheon, 1978) and Christopher L. Miller, *Blank Darkness: Africanist Discourse in French* (Chicago: Chicago University Press, 1985).

Languorous Asia and feverish Africa,
A whole distant world, absent, nearly extinguished,
Lives in your depths, fragrant forest!
As other spirits drift upon music,
My own, o my love! swims upon your perfume.

I shall go where trees and men, brimming with sap,
Swoon at length in the atmosphere's ardor;
Powerful tresses, be the swell that carries me away!
You contain, ebony sea, a dazzling dream
Of sails, of oarsmen, of flames and masts:

A resounding port where my soul may drink
In great waves the scent, the sound and the hue;
Where the vessels, gliding in gold and moiré,
Spread their vast arms to embrace the glory
Of a pure sky shimmering with eternal heat.

Delirious as they are, these stanzas are also an exacting
presentation of the colonies' role in the masculine psychic
economy of European modernity. The absent presence of
the colonies opens the distance of another world, which
is simultaneously overcome through the sensual delights
it makes available to the metropole. Primitivist represen-
tation produces an anachronistic temporality, wherein the
tropics are imagined as both prior to and simultaneous
with modernity, thus preserving another time that has been
nearly extinguished by the accelerated pace of spatial and
historical transformation. The vigorous potency of "trees
and men, brimming with sap" assures the persistent survival
of natural fecundity beyond the degeneracy of urban ennui.
The "resounding port"—likewise charged with homoerotic
desire in "a dazzling dream / Of sails, of oarsmen, of flames
and masts"—is the switching point at which the capitalist
core accesses an apparent exterior that is in fact its con-
dition of possibility. The port harbors vessels that carry

weary city-dwellers away on exotic adventures while bringing back the colonial cargo requisite to reproduce not only their economy but also their pleasures. The circuitous curls of a mistress's "twisted locks" are the synecdoche of these paradoxical entanglements, gathering them into a topos of synesthetic transport.

If "The Swan" mournfully registers the destitution of a consumptive African woman displaced amid colonial modernity, how does the pathos of that representation affect our understanding of the idealizing exoticism on display in "Hair," written in the same year? To what extent should the implicit irony so often at issue in the relation between different poems and moods, at the level of Baudelaire's book, determine our reading of individual poems and their ideological entailments? To what extent is such irony self-consciously active in the process of composition? Is "Hair" a deliriously orientalist poem or a poem about orientalist delirium? Can it be both? These remain open questions, and we become better readers of *The Flowers of Evil* when we consider them carefully.

Baudelaire's "Invitation to the Voyage" is perhaps *the* orientalist poem, its formal perfection and aural beauty inscribing the "there" of its refrain within the "here" of its articulation:

> Là, tout n'est qu'ordre et beauté,
> Luxe, calme et volupté.

> There, all is order and beauty,
> Pleasure, calm, and luxury.

The poem evokes a distant land whose "oriental splendor" "would speak / To the soul in secret / its soothing native tongue." Yet consider how self-consciously the final stanza connotes the economic and psychological ground of colonial geography:

See on these canals
These ships asleep
Whose humor is to wander;
It's to satisfy
Your least desire
That they come from the ends of the earth.
—The setting suns
Adorn the fields
The canals, the city entire,
With hyacinth and gold;
The world drifts off
Amid warm illumination.

"It's to satisfy / Your least desire / That they come from the ends of the earth": here orientalist desire is not directly articulated but reflexively thematized in its connection to the maritime economy, its connection to the actual voyages the poem transforms into a fantasy of the Voyage. Then the poetic sunset puts that knowledge to sleep, as "The world drifts off / Amid warm illumination." Is this a critique of orientalist ideology so intimate with that ideology as to be indistinguishable from it? Again, it is poetry that enables that sort of ambiguity, that sort of ambivalence, that sort of irony.

However we assess this subtle complicity of ideological fantasy and self-conscious critique, we can note that by the time Baudelaire composes "The Voyage" in 1859, as the last poem of his volume, he can inscribe this not-so-subtle quatrain:

Bitter knowledge, that one draws from the voyage!
The world, monotonous and small, today,
Yesterday, tomorrow, always, makes us see our own image:
An oasis of horror in a desert of ennui!

This is the bitter knowledge *The Flowers of Evil* draws from the colonial fantasies it propagates. At the end of Baudelaire's book, that knowledge turns us back upon the mystical synesthesia of an apparently apolitical poem like "Correspondences," with its evocation of "infinite things, / Like amber, musk, benjamin, and incense, / That sing the transports of spirit and sense." These are also transports of colonial cargo, which deliver not only the mirage of *something other* but also the same old thing: the image of that "least desire" that resolves into an oasis of horror.

The Blooming of the Invisible

The addition of "The Voyage" to the 1861 edition of *The Flowers of Evil* is exemplary of the profound transformation of Baudelaire's book by the thirty-five new poems written after the censorship of the original 1857 edition. The section titled "Parisian Tableaux" was added in 1861 (though some of the poems it contains were included in the first edition), marking Baudelaire's deepening attention to the poetics of urban modernity. The great poetic memento mori, "Danse Macabre," was written at the end of 1858; the suite of poems dedicated to Hugo—"The Swan," "The Seven Old Men," and "The Little Old Ladies"—was composed in 1859 along with "The Voyage," "The Mask," "Song of Autumn," and "Hair," all masterpieces of French poetry; and the iconic poem of *flânerie*, "To a Passerby," was written in early 1860.[18] Though it may have been written earlier, the important allegory of Baudelaire's aesthetic principles, "Hymn to Beauty," was first published in *L'Artiste* in 1860 and then included in the second edition of 1861. These additions make the 1861 edition the definitive statement of Baudelaire's poetic achievement.

---

18 On the remarkable flourishing of Baudelaire's poetic powers in 1859, see Richard D. E. Burton's study, *Baudelaire in 1859: A Study in the Sources of Poetic Creativity* (Cambridge: Cambridge University Press, 1988).

The final two stanzas of "Hymn to Beauty" return us to Baudelaire's understanding of the beautiful as a synthesis of the transient and the eternal:

> That you come from heaven or hell, who cares,
> Oh Beauty! enormous, frightening, ingenuous monster!
> If your eye, your smile, your foot, opens the door
> Of an Infinite that I love and have never known?
>
> From Satan or from God, who cares? Angel or Siren,
> Who cares, if you render,—velvet-eyed fairy,
> Rhythm, fragrance, glimmer, o my unique queen!—
> The universe less hideous and the instants less heavy?

Beauty is manifest in the transience of fleeting qualities —rhythm, fragrance, glimmer—and these open the door "Of an Infinite that I love and have never known." Perhaps the presentation of *the* Infinite, grasped as a whole, would obliterate the particularity of contingent qualities, so here we have the finite appearing of "your eye, your smile, your foot." Yet these nevertheless present more than themselves, an opening to an unknown Infinite that is never attained but ardently desired.

It is a matter of indifference whether the allegorical figure of Beauty comes from heaven or hell, derives from Satan or God. That is, the singular aesthetic presentation of the beautiful cannot be aligned with the moral polarities of good or evil, not because it is amoral but because it is irreducibly complex:

> Do you fall from the heavens or rise from the abyss,
> O Beauty? your gaze, infernal and divine,
> Pours confusedly beneficence and crime,
> And in this one may compare you to wine.

Again, we encounter the implacable dialectical irony of Spleen and Ideal: each would seem to negate the other, but each generates and sustains their duality as a condition of mutual possibility. Beauty makes "the universe less hideous and the instants less heavy," but its devotees are compared to the "dazzled ephemerid" winging toward a flame that will devour it, or to the "panting lover" swooning over his beloved like "a moribund caressing his tomb."

The beauty of Baudelaire's flowers is indivisible from their sickness unto death, yet it indomitably flares up from the poems through the intricacy of their intelligence, the subtlety of their irony, the pathos of their devotion, and the revelatory seeing of their perspectivalism. Let me close with an example of this seeing, perhaps the most important of Baudelaire's poetic capacities. In "Voyaging Gypsies," the form of the sonnet foregrounds the ruptural emergence, within the field of the visible, of visionary poiesis:

> The prophetic tribe with ardent eyes
> Set out yesterday, bearing their babies
> Upon their back, or offering to their haughty appetites
> The ever-ready treasure of pendant breasts.
>
> The men go by foot beneath gleaming weapons
> Beside the wagons where their kin are crouched,
> Scanning the sky with eyes weighed down
> By dreary longing for absent chimeras.
>
> Deep in his sandy lair, the cricket,
> Watches them pass, redoubles his song;
> Cybele, who loves them, quickens her green,
>
> Makes the rocks flow and flowers the desert
> Before these voyagers, for whom unfolds
> The familiar empire of tenebrous futures.

This is an ekphrastic poem, responding to a series of etchings by Jacques Callot with the title *Les Bohémiens* (1621–31). We begin in the register of description accompanied by adjectival flourishes of imagination: the tribe is prophetic, the appetites of the babies are haughty, the eyes of the men are weighed down by their longing for absent chimeras. At the volta, however, the poem departs from depicting the etching and enters more fully into the world of the imagination, as if through the portal of the chimeras' absence. The poem's omniscient speaker sees the cricket, though it is "deep in his sandy lair," and the cricket watches the passage of the tribe—as we have been doing. The cricket "redoubles his song" as if in celebration, or alarm, at the tribe's entrance into its field of vision, and as it does so "Cybele, who loves them, quickens her green." We have moved from the plane of the horizontal—the passage of the tribe from left to right in the etching, or across the imaginary landscape of the poem— to the plane of the vertical: cricket below, Cybele above.

It is at the crux of this intersection that the poem blooms into fantasy, the realism of landscape dissolving into symbol as the goddess "makes the rocks flow and flowers the desert." The stability of the visual image pours into the mutability of imagination, and the world of the poem bursts into fecundity in the mind's eye, as the tribe travels into what we cannot see: "the familiar empire of tenebrous futures." "Familiar" and "tenebrous" are key words in *The Flowers of Evil*, wherein the familiar is always uncanny, and shadowy darkness ever invites us into its foreboding atmosphere. Meanwhile, the cricket sings, a figure of the poet—subterranean, observant, laudatory—watching those who pass without seeing him but, perhaps, while hearing the redoubled song that resounds in silence for those who read. The tribe moves on, departing the imaginary frame, and we are left to contemplate the cricket's song diminishing from celebration of the event (the poem) into the continuity of his own furtive existence, persisting amid past and future passages. Baudelaire's sonnet is a subtly redoubled, reflexive study of observation as it passes into imagination, and this is the locus of his singular poetic gift. "Have you noticed" (*Avez-vous observé*), he asks in "The Little Old Ladies," and what we are asked to notice is at once observable fact and beguiling symbol, a metaphysical puzzle hiding in plain sight for those with eyes to see.

Baudelaire sees as no one before or since. Yet, as we read, the tenebrous futures of his book are also our own. And we read not only in order to see, but also to sense the blooming of the invisible.

Translator's Statement

Translators often consider competing claims of semantic accuracy and poetic license. I prefer to think in terms of precision. A precise translation is one that renders the sense of the original as closely as possible while conveying its tone and meticulously sustaining its figurative and rhetorical devices. The goal of this translation is to provide a version of *Les Fleurs du mal* that is precise enough to be taught in the classroom, to be quoted by critics, and to give the general reader confidence that the sense of the English text corresponds as closely as possible to that of Baudelaire's French. Moreover, I aim to produce English poems that are formally precise—rhythmically cohesive, structurally exacting, and aurally compelling—without forcing the transposition of rhyme schemes and metrical patterns that can never be adequately rendered in English.

In pursuing these aims I have followed several principles. First, I have translated the poems "line by line," taking the poetic line as a unit of sense that should be translated as a unit, such that the reader may refer to a line in French and find that line translated into English on the facing page. With only several exceptions throughout the volume, I avoid shifting any material from one line to another, so that the line remains a formal constraint in the production of meaning, thus preserving its contribution to the relation between form and content in the construction of the poem.

Second, I have taken care to preserve Baudelaire's punctuation, such that its production of caesurae, rhythmic and syntactical relationships, and its regulation of line endings is maintained wherever possible. This may seem a minor point, but while I have found this principle seldom observed in translations of poetry, I have also found it highly productive in conveying poetic effects of the original. Punctuation functions as a constraint that is preserved relatively easily in translation; obeying that constraint forces a certain fidelity to the rhythms and mood of the original. Baudelaire's use of punctuation is particularly vital to the *suspense* of his poems: he frequently pursues long, hypotactic sentences that defer and complicate semantic resolution. Consider, for example, a poem that is among his simplest, at the level of content, and among his most complex in its grammatical articulation:

Je n'ai pas oublié, voisine de la ville,
Notre blanche maison, petite mais tranquille;
Sa Pomone de plâtre et sa vieille Vénus
Dans un bosquet chétif cachant leurs membres nus,
Et le soleil, le soir, ruisselant et superbe,
Qui, derrière la vitre où se brisait sa gerbe,
Semblait, grand œil ouvert dans le ciel curieux,
Contempler nos dîners longs et silencieux,
Répandant largement ses beaux reflets de cierge
Sur la nappe frugale et les rideaux de serge.

—

I have not forgotten, next to the city,
Our white house, little but tranquil;
Its plaster Pomona and its elderly Venus
In a meager copse hiding their naked members,
And the sun, in the evening, streaming down and superb,
Which, behind the pane where its sheaf would shatter,
Seemed, great open eye in the curious sky,
To contemplate our long and silent dinners,
Spreading widely its beautiful candle reflections
Upon the frugal cloth and the serge curtains.

Here the time of the "not forgotten," unfolding across a single sentence, is rejoined through grammatical suspensions which become the medium of the poem's content: the illuminating refractions of memory. I have tried to preserve such structures of grammatical subordination and semantic deferral in English. This is what I mean by "structurally exacting."

Third, I have sought to convey a sense of poetic formality not through regular rhyme and meter, but rather through assonance, alliteration, internal rhyme and occasional end rhyme, and by frequently preserving structures of grammatical inversion. It is relations not only among sounds but also among meanings that are established by rhyme, and which lend it its peculiar power in the hands of a master like Baudelaire. But the relations among sounds and meanings established by rhyme cannot be captured in translation, since the *words* that rhyme will be different, even if the pattern of rhyme is the same. This is why rhyme in translation so often feels lifeless and more formally arbitrary than unrhymed lines: the bond between form and content, which makes the poem, has been broken. The content is already there, in the poem being translated, and it is now fitted to rhyme in translation. But this is never the case in the composition of the original, where the relation between rhyme, rhythm, and meaning is felt at every instant of contemplation and composition, shaping diction and the determination of meaning as the content of the poem comes into being.

The same is true of metrical regularity. Baudelaire writes in regular meters, most often in the traditional French alexandrine. But an effort to capture Baudelaire's metrical formality through twelve syllable lines or the transposition of the alexandrine into pentameter lines loses the intimate bond between form and content in the original, which can be better sustained by allowing the sense of the poem to dictate the line break. Yet this also means this is not a "free verse" translation, since free verse also relies upon a feeling for how the line should be established as the poem is composed. In translation, the sense of the line is already there; if I sustain a precise rendering of that sense within the line, I cannot decide where to break it. Therefore my principle is that the composition of the poetic line should emerge from the sense of the original rather than attempting to regulate it through pre-established patterns, since the content of a translated poem cannot be genuinely co-produced by rhyme and meter while sustaining semantic precision.

Conversely, this is why the criterion of formal precision in this translation is obedience to the poetic line and to structures of punctuation: in these cases, the relation between content and form *can* be replicated in translation. Consider the famous opening quatrain of Baudelaire's book, comparing popular translations by James McGowan and Richard Howard to my own:

> La sottise, l'erreur, le péché, la lésine,
> Occupent nos esprits et travaillent nos corps,
> Et nous alimentons nos aimables remords,
> Comme les mendiants nourrissent leur vermine.

McGowan: Folly and error, stinginess and sin
Possess our spirits and fatigue our flesh.
And like a pet we feed our tame remorse
As beggars take to nourishing their lice.

Howard: Stupidity, delusion, selfishness and lust
torment our bodies and possess our minds,
and we sustain our affable remorse
the way a beggar nourishes his lice.

Dropping two commas in the first line and adding conjunctions, McGowan loses the four part rhythm of the line and the difference between its grammatical structure and that of the second line. In the fourth line, the declarative, driving force of the quatrain is compromised by both translations in order to accommodate a ten-syllable meter, such that the concision and sharpness of the original is diminished by metrical filler ("take to"; "the way a"). Moreover, McGowan interprets and explicates a possible figurative implication in the third line ("like a pet"), introducing a simile where none is offered, rather than sustaining the *implicit* evocation —and this decision also seems intended to fill out a metrical pattern.

In translating the quatrain, I attempt semantic exactitude (why "delusion" for "l'erreur"? why "lust" for "le péché"?), replicate punctuation, seek tonal precision, and pursue opportunities for aural coherence through alliteration rather than rhyme:

> Stupidity, error, sin, thrift,
> Worry our minds and work our bodies,
> And we feed our friendly regrets,
> Like beggars nourish their lice.

The effort is to allow grammatical parallelism and rhythms of punctuation to carry the formality of the poem, while retaining its abrupt and incisive tone through poetic concision. This is a relatively simple quatrain to render in English; one has only to get out of the way, allowing sense and syntax to guide the composition. Throughout, I try to achieve rather than complicate such simplicity.

Finally, where I do allow myself poetic license, it is in response to what *cannot* be achieved without it. Thus, in "Song of Autumn," the line "J'aime de vos longs yeux la lumière verdâtre," becomes "I love the greenish light of your almond eyes." The phrase "long eyes" does not quite come off in English, and "almond eyes," by melding their greenish light with a warm brown, conveys something of the autumnal warmth suggested by the rhyme between "verdatre" and "l'atre" (hearth), which cannot be rendered directly in English. My principle is that creative inspiration should derive from and answer to *impossibilities* of translation, rather than to the whim of the translator. Poetic license should solve problems rather than introduce them, and it should thus be relatively infrequent.

I hope that this translation of Baudelaire's singular volume finds adequate, appropriate solutions to such problems, varying from the semantic determinations of the original only where there are precise reasons and sound explanations for doing so. And I hope it will provide English readers with a sure guide, line by line and phrase by phrase, to the subtlety, precision, and beauty of Baudelaire's French. The work has been a labor of love. Translation is an act of devotion.

In my view, translation is also a task inseparable from scholarly study and deep conceptual reflection. Research at Vanderbilt's W. T. Bandy Center for Baudelaire and Modern French Studies was pivotal to my understanding of Baudelaire, and I thank Yvonne Boyer for her assistance with the collections. My work at the Bandy Center and the opportunity to study collections and artworks in Paris and Montpellier was enabled by a sabbatical leave from Concordia University and by the resources of the Canada Research Chair in Poetics. Invitations to present lectures on Baudelaire from Audrey Wasser (Miami University, Ohio), Tracy McNulty and Aaron Schuster (Cornell University), Daniel Katz (University of Warwick), and Iskra Geshoska (Kontrapunkt, Skopje) enabled me to think more deeply about *Les Fleurs du mal*, and I thank the audiences at those events for their questions and contributions.

Working with Verso on this edition has been a pleasure. Thanks to Sebastian Budgen, Mark Martin, Nick Walther, and Michael Gordon for their assistance and to the readers for press, who offered many helpful suggestions. This translation was published in an earlier edition by MaMa (Zagreb) with the support of Kontrapunkt (Skopje) and Anteism (Montreal). I am grateful to Petar Milat for the opportunity to produce that volume in a matching edition with my critical book *Baudelaire's Shadow: An Essay on Poetic Determination* (2021). Thanks as well to Dejan Dragosavac Ruta, whose design has been retained in this edition.

I am indebted to Marianne Costa—French translator of Anne Waldman and Lawrence Ferlinghetti—for her meticulous attention to the complete manuscript; I have incorporated many of her insights. Zoe Lambrinakos-Raymond offered suggestions at an earlier stage, and Nora Fulton proofread the complete manuscript. Stephen Ross provided essential assistance with "Franciscae Meae Laudes," and his friendship and encouragement have been an enabling condition of my work on Baudelaire. I am also indebted to many people who read these translations and supported this project, including Alexis Briley, Ronjaunee Chatterjee, Willy Claflin, Robyn Creswell, Jacqueline Darrigrand, Greg Ellermann, Peter Gizzi, Martin Hägglund, Daniel Katz, Naomi Levine, Cynthia Mitchell, Omri Moses, Marjorie Perloff, Jed Rasula, Kim Rodgers, and Aaron Schuster. In particular, I want to acknowledge the constitutive importance of conversations about Baudelaire with Alexi Kukuljevic, to whom this translation is dedicated.

Finally, thanks to the brilliant students in my graduate seminar on Baudelaire in the winter of 2021, with whom I had the opportunity to test these translations in the classroom and discuss the poems in detail. Their observations and suggestions helped me to make improvements in the final stages of my work on the manuscript.

Note on the Text

I have followed the 1975 Pléiade text of the 1861 edition of
Les Fleurs du mal, established by Claude Pichois. The six
banned poems ("Les Bijoux," "Le Léthé," "À celle qui est trop
gaie," "Les Métamorphoses du vampire," "Lesbos," "Femmes
damnées") have been restored to positions following the
poems after which they were included in the 1857 edition.
In order to preserve the canonical numbering of the poems
in the 1861 edition, the banned poems are left unnumbered
in this translation.

Les Fleurs
du Mal

The Flowers of Evil

AU POÈTE IMPECCABLE

AU PARFAIT MAGICIEN ÈS LETTRES FRANÇAISES
À MON TRÈS CHER ET TRÈS VÉNÉRÉ

MAÎTRE ET AMI

THÉOPHILE GAUTIER

AVEC LES SENTIMENTS
DE LA PLUS PROFONDE HUMILITÉ

JE DÉDIE
CES FLEURS MALADIVES

C.B.

TO THE IMPECCABLE POET

TO THE PERFECT MAGICIAN OF FRENCH LETTERS
TO MY VERY DEAR AND HIGHLY VENERATED

MASTER AND FRIEND

THÉOPHILE GAUTIER

WITH SENTIMENTS
OF THE MOST PROFOUND HUMILITY

I DEDICATE
THESE SICKLY FLOWERS

C.B.

AU LECTEUR

La sottise, l'erreur, le péché, la lésine,
Occupent nos esprits et travaillent nos corps,
Et nous alimentons nos aimables remords,
Comme les mendiants nourrissent leur vermine.

Nos péchés sont têtus, nos repentirs sont lâches;
Nous nous faisons payer grassement nos aveux,
Et nous rentrons gaiement dans le chemin bourbeux,
Croyant par de vils pleurs laver toutes nos taches.

Sur l'oreiller du mal c'est Satan Trismégiste
Qui berce longuement notre esprit enchanté,
Et le riche métal de notre volonté
Est tout vaporisé par ce savant chimiste.

C'est le Diable qui tient les fils qui nous remuent!
Aux objets répugnants nous trouvons des appas;
Chaque jour vers l'Enfer nous descendons d'un pas,
Sans horreur, à travers des ténèbres qui puent.

Ainsi qu'un débauché pauvre qui baise et mange
Le sein martyrisé d'une antique catin,
Nous volons au passage un plaisir clandestin
Que nous pressons bien fort comme une vieille orange.

Serré, fourmillant, comme un million d'helminthes,
Dans nos cerveaux ribote un peuple de Démons,
Et, quand nous respirons, la Mort dans nos poumons
Descend, fleuve invisible, avec de sourdes plaintes.

TO THE READER

Stupidity, error, sin, thrift,
Worry our minds and work our bodies,
And we feed our friendly regrets,
Like beggars nourish their lice.

Our sins are stubborn, our repentance slack;
We pay ourselves fatly for our confessions,
And we blithely return to muddy paths,
Believing vile tears wash away all our stains.

On the pillow of evil Satan Trismegistus
Slowly lulls our enchanted minds,
And the precious metal of our will
Is vaporized by this cunning chemist.

It's the Devil who pulls the strings that move us!
In repugnant things we discover charms;
Each day toward Hell we descend a step,
Bereft of horror, through shades of stench.

Like a debauched wretch who sucks and slurps
The martyred breast of an aging whore,
We snatch in passing a clandestine pleasure
That we squeeze as hard as a wizened orange.

Tight, swarming, like a million helminths,
In our brains a nation of Demons carouse,
And, when we breathe, Death into our lungs
Descends, invisible stream, with muffled moans.

Si le viol, le poison, le poignard, l'incendie,
N'ont pas encor brodé de leurs plaisants dessins
Le canevas banal de nos piteux destins,
C'est que notre âme, hélas! n'est pas assez hardie.

Mais parmi les chacals, les panthères, les lices,
Les singes, les scorpions, les vautours, les serpents,
Les monstres glapissants, hurlants, grognants, rampants,
Dans la ménagerie infâme de nos vices,

Il en est un plus laid, plus méchant, plus immonde!
Quoiqu'il ne pousse ni grands gestes ni grands cris,
Il ferait volontiers de la terre un débris
Et dans un bâillement avalerait le monde;

C'est l'Ennui! l'œil chargé d'un pleur involontaire,
Il rêve d'échafauds en fumant son houka.
Tu le connais, lecteur, ce monstre délicat,
— Hypocrite lecteur, — mon semblable, — mon frère!

If rape, poison, arson, the knife,
Have not yet embellished with their pleasing designs
The banal canvas of our piteous destinies,
It's just that our soul, alas! lacks sufficient life.

But among the jackals, the panthers, the bitches,
The apes, the scorpions, the vultures, the serpents,
The monsters shrieking, howling, growling, creeping,
In the infamous menagerie of our vices,

There is one most ugly, most vicious, impure!
Though expending neither great gestures nor cries,
It willingly makes of the earth a waste
And swallows the world within its yawn;

It's Ennui! Eye brimming with an involuntary tear,
He dreams of the scaffold and smokes his hookah.
You're acquainted, reader, with this delicate monster,
—Hypocrite reader, —my likeness, —my brother!

SPLEEN ET IDÉAL

SPLEEN AND IDEAL

I

BÉNÉDICTION

Lorsque, par un décret des puissances suprêmes,
Le Poète apparaît en ce monde ennuyé,
Sa mère épouvantée et pleine de blasphèmes
Crispe ses poings vers Dieu, qui la prend en pitié:

— « Ah! que n'ai-je mis bas tout un nœud de vipères,
Plutôt que de nourrir cette dérision!
Maudite soit la nuit aux plaisirs éphémères
Où mon ventre a conçu mon expiation!

« Puisque tu m'as choisie entre toutes les femmes
Pour être le dégoût de mon triste mari,
Et que je ne puis pas rejeter dans les flammes,
Comme un billet d'amour, ce monstre rabougri,

« Je ferai rejaillir ta haine qui m'accable
Sur l'instrument maudit de tes méchancetés,
Et je tordrai si bien cet arbre misérable,
Qu'il ne pourra pousser ses boutons empestés! »

Elle ravale ainsi l'écume de sa haine,
Et, ne comprenant pas les desseins éternels,
Elle-même prépare au fond de la Géhenne
Les bûchers consacrés aux crimes maternels.

Pourtant, sous la tutelle invisible d'un Ange,
L'Enfant déshérité s'enivre de soleil,
Et dans tout ce qu'il boit et dans tout ce qu'il mange
Retrouve l'ambroisie et le nectar vermeil.

I

BENEDICTION

When, by decree of supreme powers,
The Poet appears in this tired world,
His appalled and blasphemous mother
Clenches her fists at God, who regards her with pity:

—"Ah! better to plop out a whole knot of vipers,
Than to suckle this derision!
Cursed be the night of ephemeral pleasures
When my womb conceived my expiation!

"Since you've chosen me of all women
To be the bane of my sorry husband,
And since I'm unable to cast into the flames,
Like a love note, this shriveled monster,

"I'll splash the hate you've poured on me
Upon the accursed instrument of your spite,
And so thoroughly will I twist this miserable tree,
It will never push out its fetid buds!"

Thus she ravins down the foam of her hate,
And, not comprehending eternal designs,
She herself prepares in the depths of Gehenna
The pyre consecrated to maternal crimes.

Yet, under the invisible tutelage of an Angel,
The disinherited Child is intoxicated by the sun,
And in all that he drinks and all that he eats
Discovers ambrosia and vermillion nectar.

Il joue avec le vent, cause avec le nuage,
Et s'enivre en chantant du chemin de la croix;
Et l'Esprit qui le suit dans son pèlerinage
Pleure de le voir gai comme un oiseau des bois.

Tous ceux qu'il veut aimer l'observent avec crainte,
Ou bien, s'enhardissant de sa tranquillité,
Cherchent à qui saura lui tirer une plainte,
Et font sur lui l'essai de leur férocité.

Dans le pain et le vin destinés à sa bouche
Ils mêlent de la cendre avec d'impurs crachats;
Avec hypocrisie ils jettent ce qu'il touche,
Et s'accusent d'avoir mis leurs pieds dans ses pas.

Sa femme va criant sur les places publiques:
« Puisqu'il me trouve assez belle pour m'adorer,
Je ferai le métier des idoles antiques,
Et comme elles je veux me faire redorer;

« Et je me soûlerai de nard, d'encens, de myrrhe,
De génuflexions, de viandes et de vins,
Pour savoir si je puis dans un cœur qui m'admire
Usurper en riant les hommages divins!

« Et, quand je m'ennuierai de ces farces impies,
Je poserai sur lui ma frêle et forte main;
Et mes ongles, pareils aux ongles des harpies,
Sauront jusqu'à son cœur se frayer un chemin.

« Comme un tout jeune oiseau qui tremble et qui palpite,
J'arracherai ce cœur tout rouge de son sein,
Et, pour rassasier ma bête favorite,
Je le lui jetterai par terre avec dédain! »

He plays with the wind, chats with the cloud,
And elatedly sings the way of the cross;
And the Spirit who follows his pilgrimage
Weeps to see him as gay as the birds in the trees.

All those he would love regard him with fear,
Or else, emboldened by his tranquility,
Look for ways to pick on him,
And make him the measure of their ferocity.

In the bread and wine destined for his mouth
They blend in ashes with filthy spit;
Hypocritically they reject what he touches,
And accuse one another of treading his path.

His wife proclaims in public squares:
"Since he finds me worthy of adoration,
I'll take up the role of ancient idols,
And have myself regilded as I please;

"I'll inundate myself with nard, incense, and myrrh,
With genuflections, with meat and with wine,
To see if within a doting heart
I can usurp divine devotions for a laugh!

"And, when I'm tired of impious farces,
I'll set on him my frail and heavy hand;
And my nails, like the nails of harpies,
Will know just the way to his heart.

"Like a fledgling bird that trembles and flutters,
I'll tear out that heart all red with his blood,
And, to sate the hunger of my favorite beast,
Disdainfully throw it upon the ground!"

Vers le Ciel, où son œil voit un trône splendide,
Le Poète serein lève ses bras pieux,
Et les vastes éclairs de son esprit lucide
Lui dérobent l'aspect des peuples furieux:

— « Soyez béni, mon Dieu, qui donnez la souffrance
Comme un divin remède à nos impuretés
Et comme la meilleure et la plus pure essence
Qui prépare les forts aux saintes voluptés!

« Je sais que vous gardez une place au Poète
Dans les rangs bienheureux des saintes Légions,
Et que vous l'invitez à l'éternelle fête
Des Trônes, des Vertus, des Dominations.

« Je sais que la douleur est la noblesse unique
Où ne mordront jamais la terre et les enfers,
Et qu'il faut pour tresser ma couronne mystique
Imposer tous les temps et tous les univers.

« Mais les bijoux perdus de l'antique Palmyre,
Les métaux inconnus, les perles de la mer,
Par votre main montés, ne pourraient pas suffire
À ce beau diadème éblouissant et clair;

« Car il ne sera fait que de pure lumière,
Puisée au foyer saint des rayons primitifs,
Et dont les yeux mortels, dans leur splendeur entière,
Ne sont que des miroirs obscurcis et plaintifs! »

Toward Heaven, where his eye sees a splendid throne,
The serene Poet lifts his pious arms,
And vast flashes of lightning from his lucid spirit
Spare him the sight of the furious masses:

—"Blessed be thou, my God, who offers suffering
Like a divine remedy for our impurities
And like the finest and purest essence
Which prepares the strong for holy pleasures!

"I know thou hold a place for the Poet
In the blessed ranks of the holy Legions,
And invite him to the eternal celebration
Of Thrones, of Virtues, of Dominations.

"I know that pain is the sole nobility
Neither earth nor hell can corrode,
And to wreathe my mystic crown it must
Rule all of time and space.

"But the vanished jewels of ancient Palmyra,
The unknown metals, the pearls of the sea,
By your own hand set, could never suffice
For this beautiful diadem dazzling and clear;

"For it will be made of pure light,
Drawn from the holy hearth of primitive rays,
Of which mortal eyes, in all their splendor,
Are but obscured and plaintive mirrors!"

II

L'ALBATROS

Souvent, pour s'amuser, les hommes d'équipage
Prennent des albatros, vastes oiseaux des mers,
Qui suivent, indolents compagnons de voyage,
Le navire glissant sur les gouffres amers.

À peine les ont-ils déposés sur les planches,
Que ces rois de l'azur, maladroits et honteux,
Laissent piteusement leurs grandes ailes blanches
Comme des avirons traîner à côté d'eux.

Ce voyageur ailé, comme il est gauche et veule!
Lui, naguère si beau, qu'il est comique et laid!
L'un agace son bec avec un brûle-gueule,
L'autre mime, en boitant, l'infirme qui volait!

Le Poète est semblable au prince des nuées
Qui hante la tempête et se rit de l'archer;
Exilé sur le sol au milieu des huées,
Ses ailes de géant l'empêchent de marcher.

II

THE ALBATROSS

Often, for sport, the crewmen
Capture those albatross, vast birds of the seas,
Who follow, indolent companions of the voyage,
The ship gliding over the bitter gulf.

No sooner have they laid them on the deck,
Than these kings of the azure, awkward and ashamed,
Piteously droop their great white wings
Like oars left to trail at their sides.

This wingèd voyager, how graceless and meek!
He, lately so handsome, how comic and crass!
One chafes his beak with a smoldering pipe,
Another mimes, with a limp, the cripple who flew!

The Poet is akin to the prince of the clouds
Who haunts the tempest and scoffs at the archer;
Exiled upon the soil amid hecklers,
His gigantic wings impede his stride.

ÉLÉVATION

Au-dessus des étangs, au-dessus des vallées,
Des montagnes, des bois, des nuages, des mers,
Par-delà le soleil, par-delà les éthers,
Par-delà les confins des sphères étoilées,

Mon esprit, tu te meus avec agilité,
Et, comme un bon nageur qui se pâme dans l'onde,
Tu sillonnes gaiement l'immensité profonde
Avec une indicible et mâle volupté.

Envole-toi bien loin de ces miasmes morbides;
Va te purifier dans l'air supérieur,
Et bois, comme une pure et divine liqueur,
Le feu clair qui remplit les espaces limpides.

Derrière les ennuis et les vastes chagrins
Qui chargent de leur poids l'existence brumeuse,
Heureux celui qui peut d'une aile vigoureuse
S'élancer vers les champs lumineux et sereins;

Celui dont les pensers, comme des alouettes,
Vers les cieux le matin prennent un libre essor,
— Qui plane sur la vie, et comprend sans effort
Le langage des fleurs et des choses muettes!

III

ELEVATION

Above the ponds, above the valleys,
The mountains, the woods, the clouds, the seas,
Beyond the sun, beyond the heavens,
Beyond the confines of the starry spheres,

My spirit, with agility you make your way,
And, like a skilled swimmer who glides in the deep,
You gaily plough the profound immensity
With unspeakable male sensuality.

Fly far away from these morbid miasmas;
Purify yourself in rarified air,
And drink, like a pure and divine liqueur,
The transparent fire that imbues limpid vistas.

Beyond the troubles and the vast sorrows
That lay their weight upon dim existence,
Happy is he who on vigorous wing
Soars to serene and luminous regions;

He whose thoughts, like larks,
Freely fly toward morning skies,
—Who hovers above life, and knows without strife
The language of flowers and of silent things!

IV

CORRESPONDANCES

La Nature est un temple où de vivants piliers
Laissent parfois sortir de confuses paroles;
L'homme y passe à travers des forêts de symboles
Qui l'observent avec des regards familiers.

Comme de longs échos qui de loin se confondent
Dans une ténébreuse et profonde unité,
Vaste comme la nuit et comme la clarté,
Les parfums, les couleurs et les sons se répondent.

II est des parfums frais comme des chairs d'enfants,
Doux comme les hautbois, verts comme les prairies,
— Et d'autres, corrompus, riches et triomphants,

Ayant l'expansion des choses infinies,
Comme l'ambre, le musc, le benjoin et l'encens,
Qui chantent les transports de l'esprit et des sens.

IV

CORRESPONDENCES

Nature is a temple wherein living pillars
Sometimes let slip some muddled words;
Man passes there through forests of symbols
That observe him with familiar looks.

Like long echoes that distantly enfold
In a tenebrous and profound unity,
Vast as night and as clarity,
The scents, the colors and the sounds respond.

There are scents as fresh as children's flesh,
Soft as oboes, green as meadows,
—And others, rotten, rich and triumphant,

With the expansion of infinite things,
Like amber, musk, benjamin and incense,
That sing the transports of spirit and sense.

V

J'aime le souvenir de ces époques nues,
Dont Phœbus se plaisait à dorer les statues.
Alors l'homme et la femme en leur agilité
Jouissaient sans mensonge et sans anxiété,
Et, le ciel amoureux leur caressant l'échine,
Exerçaient la santé de leur noble machine.
Cybèle alors, fertile en produits généreux,
Ne trouvait point ses fils un poids trop onéreux,
Mais, louve au cœur gonflé de tendresses communes,
Abreuvait l'univers à ses tétines brunes.
L'homme, élégant, robuste et fort, avait le droit
D'être fier des beautés qui le nommaient leur roi;
Fruits purs de tout outrage et vierges de gerçures,
Dont la chair lisse et ferme appelait les morsures!

Le Poète aujourd'hui, quand il veut concevoir
Ces natives grandeurs, aux lieux où se font voir
La nudité de l'homme et celle de la femme,
Sent un froid ténébreux envelopper son âme
Devant ce noir tableau plein d'épouvantement.
Ô monstruosités pleurant leur vêtement!
Ô ridicules troncs! torses dignes des masques!
Ô pauvres corps tordus, maigres, ventrus ou flasques,
Que le dieu de l'Utile, implacable et serein,
Enfants, emmaillota dans ses langes d'airain!
Et vous, femmes, hélas! pâles comme des cierges,
Que ronge et que nourrit la débauche, et vous, vierges,
Du vice maternel traînant l'hérédité
Et toutes les hideurs de la fécondité!

V

I love the memory of those naked epochs,
When Phoebus was pleased to gild statues with gold.
Then man and woman in their agility
Enjoyed themselves without lies and anxiety,
And, amorous sky caressing the spine,
Would exercise their noble machine.
Cybele, back then, fertile and generous,
Did not find too heavy the weight of her sons,
But, wolf with heart full of communal tenderness,
At her brown teats would water the universe.
Man, elegant, robust and strong, had the right
To be proud of the beauties who called him king;
Inviolate fruits virgin of blemish,
Whose smooth and tight flesh cried out for the teeth!

The Poet today, when he would contemplate
Those native grandeurs, wherein we see
The nudity of man and that of woman,
Feels a tenebrous cold envelop his soul
Before this frightful black tableau.
O monstrosities lamenting their clothes!
O ridiculous trunks! mask-worthy torsos!
O poor twisted bodies, weak, bloated or flabby,
Whom the god of Utility, implacable and serene,
Has wrapped like children in bronze swaddling clothes!
And you, women, alas! pale as votives,
Whom debauchery gnaws and consumes, and you, virgins,
Dragging the heredity of maternal vice
And all the horrors of fecundity!

Nous avons, il est vrai, nations corrompues,
Aux peuples anciens des beautés inconnues:
Des visages rongés par les chancres du cœur,
Et comme qui dirait des beautés de langueur;
Mais ces inventions de nos muses tardives
N'empêcheront jamais les races maladives
De rendre à la jeunesse un hommage profond,
— À la sainte jeunesse, à l'air simple, au doux front,
À l'œil limpide et clair ainsi qu'une eau courante,
Et qui va répandant sur tout, insouciante
Comme l'azur du ciel, les oiseaux et les fleurs,
Ses parfums, ses chansons et ses douces chaleurs!

We have, it is true, corrupted nations,
Some beauties the ancients did not known:
Faces gnawed by cankers of the heart,
And what they call the beauties of languor;
But these inventions of our belated muses
Will never prevent diseased descendants
From making to youth a profound homage,
—To holy youth, the simple air, the smooth brow,
The eye limpid and clear as a flowing stream,
And which pours over all, insouciant
As the azure of the sky, the birds and the flowers,
Its scents, its songs and its gentle warm breeze!

LES PHARES

Rubens, fleuve d'oubli, jardin de la paresse,
Oreiller de chair fraîche où l'on ne peut aimer,
Mais où la vie afflue et s'agite sans cesse,
Comme l'air dans le ciel et la mer dans la mer;

Léonard de Vinci, miroir profond et sombre,
Où des anges charmants, avec un doux souris
Tout chargé de mystère, apparaissent à l'ombre
Des glaciers et des pins qui ferment leur pays;

Rembrandt, triste hôpital tout rempli de murmures,
Et d'un grand crucifix décoré seulement,
Où la prière en pleurs s'exhale des ordures,
Et d'un rayon d'hiver traversé brusquement;

Michel-Ange, lieu vague où l'on voit des Hercules
Se mêler à des Christs, et se lever tout droits
Des fantômes puissants qui dans les crépuscules
Déchirent leur suaire en étirant leurs doigts;

Colères de boxeur, impudences de faune,
Toi qui sus ramasser la beauté des goujats,
Grand cœur gonflé d'orgueil, homme débile et jaune,
Puget, mélancolique empereur des forçats;

Watteau, ce carnaval où bien des cœurs illustres,
Comme des papillons, errent en flamboyant,
Décors frais et légers éclairés par des lustres
Qui versent la folie à ce bal tournoyant;

THE BEACONS

Rubens, river of oblivion, garden of indolence,
Pillow of fresh flesh where one cannot love,
But where life surges and ceaselessly tosses,
Like the air in the sky and the sea in the sea;

Leonardo de Vinci, dark and deep mirror,
Where charming angels, with a gentle smile
Charged with mystery, appear in the shadow
Of glaciers and pines that enclose their country;

Rembrandt, sad hospital full of murmurs,
And decorated only by a great crucifix,
Where the tearful prayer is exhaled from the filth,
And brusquely crossed by a winter ray;

Michelangelo, vague place where we see Hercules
Mingle with Christs, and raising themselves upright
Powerful phantoms who by twilight
Tear their shrouds by stretching their fingers;

Rage of the boxer, impudence of the faun,
You who gather the beauty of the lowest,
Great heart full of pride, man feeble and jaundiced,
Puget, melancholy emperor of convicts;

Watteau, this carnival where surfeit of illustrious hearts,
Like butterflies, wander aflame,
Décor cool and light, illuminated by chandeliers
That pour madness upon the whirling dance;

Goya, cauchemar plein de choses inconnues,
De fœtus qu'on fait cuire au milieu des sabbats,
De vieilles au miroir et d'enfants toutes nues,
Pour tenter les démons ajustant bien leurs bas;

Delacroix, lac de sang hanté des mauvais anges,
Ombragé par un bois de sapins toujours vert,
Où, sous un ciel chagrin, des fanfares étranges
Passent, comme un soupir étouffé de Weber;

Ces malédictions, ces blasphèmes, ces plaintes,
Ces extases, ces cris, ces pleurs, ces *Te Deum*,
Sont un écho redit par mille labyrinthes;
C'est pour les cœurs mortels un divin opium!

C'est un cri répété par mille sentinelles,
Un ordre renvoyé par mille porte-voix;
C'est un phare allumé sur mille citadelles,
Un appel de chasseurs perdus dans les grands bois!

Car c'est vraiment, Seigneur, le meilleur témoignage
Que nous puissions donner de notre dignité
Que cet ardent sanglot qui roule d'âge en âge
Et vient mourir au bord de votre éternité!

Goya, nightmare full of unknown things,
Fetus roasted at witches' Sabbaths,
Hags in the mirror and naked children,
Adjusting their stockings to tantalize demons;

Delacroix, lake of blood haunted by fallen angels,
Shaded by a wood of firs forever green,
Where, under a vexed sky, strange fanfares
Pass, like a suffocated sigh of Weber;

These maledictions, these blasphemies, these laments,
These ecstasies, these cries, these tears, these *Te Deum*,
Are an echo recalled by a thousand labyrinths;
A heavenly opium for mortal hearts!

A cry repeated by a thousand sentinels,
An order relayed by a thousand horns;
A beacon illuminated upon a thousand citadels,
A call of huntsmen lost in the deep woods!

For it is truly, Lord, the best testimony
We can give of our dignity
This ardent sob that rolls age upon age
To die at the threshold of your eternity!

LA MUSE MALADE

Ma pauvre muse, hélas! qu'as-tu donc ce matin?
Tes yeux creux sont peuplés de visions nocturnes,
Et je vois tour à tour réfléchis sur ton teint
La folie et l'horreur, froides et taciturnes.

Le succube verdâtre et le rose lutin
T'ont-ils versé la peur et l'amour de leurs urnes?
Le cauchemar, d'un poing despotique et mutin,
T'a-t-il noyée au fond d'un fabuleux Minturnes?

Je voudrais qu'exhalant l'odeur de la santé
Ton sein de pensers forts fût toujours fréquenté,
Et que ton sang chrétien coulât à flots rythmiques,

Comme les sons nombreux des syllabes antiques,
Où règnent tour à tour le père des chansons,
Phœbus, et le grand Pan, le seigneur des moissons.

VII

THE SICK MUSE

My poor muse, alas! what's the matter this morning?
Your hollow eyes are peopled with nocturnal visions,
And I see in turn reflected in your mien
Madness and horror, cold and taciturn.

The greenish succubus and the rosy imp
Have poured you fear and love from their urns?
The nightmare, with despotic and mutinous fist,
Has drowned you in the depths of a fabulous Minturnae?

I wish that exhaling the scent of health,
Your breast were forever inspired by great thoughts,
And that your Christian blood would flow in rhythmic waves,

Like the numbered sounds of antique syllables,
Where reign in turn the father of songs,
Phoebus, and the great Pan, lord of harvests.

VIII

LA MUSE VÉNALE

Ô muse de mon cœur, amante des palais,
Auras-tu, quand Janvier lâchera ses Borées,
Durant les noirs ennuis des neigeuses soirées,
Un tison pour chauffer tes deux pieds violets?

Ranimeras-tu donc tes épaules marbrées
Aux nocturnes rayons qui percent les volets?
Sentant ta bourse à sec autant que ton palais,
Récolteras-tu l'or des voûtes azurées?

Il te faut, pour gagner ton pain de chaque soir,
Comme un enfant de chœur, jouer de l'encensoir,
Chanter des *Te Deum* auxquels tu ne crois guère,

Ou, saltimbanque à jeun, étaler tes appas
Et ton rire trempé de pleurs qu'on ne voit pas,
Pour faire épanouir la rate du vulgaire.

VIII

THE VENAL MUSE

O my heart's muse, lover of palaces,
Will you have, when January unleashes its Boreal winds,
Through the black ennui of snowy evenings,
An ember to warm your two blue feet?

Will you reanimate your marbled shoulders
With nocturnal rays that pierce the shades?
When your purse feels as hollow as your palace,
Will you glean the gold of azure vaults?

You must, to win your bread each night,
Like a choir boy, swing the censer,
Chant some *Te Deum* you barely believe,

Or, starving acrobat, show off your charms
And your laughter soaked with tears that no one sees,
To split the sides of the vulgar.

LE MAUVAIS MOINE

Les cloîtres anciens sur leurs grandes murailles
Étalaient en tableaux la sainte Vérité,
Dont l'effet, réchauffant les pieuses entrailles,
Tempérait la froideur de leur austérité.

En ces temps où du Christ florissaient les semailles,
Plus d'un illustre moine, aujourd'hui peu cité,
Prenant pour atelier le champ des funérailles,
Glorifiait la Mort avec simplicité.

— Mon âme est un tombeau que, mauvais cénobite,
Depuis l'éternité je parcours et j'habite;
Rien n'embellit les murs de ce cloître odieux.

Ô moine fainéant! quand saurai-je donc faire
Du spectacle vivant de ma triste misère
Le travail de mes mains et l'amour de mes yeux?

THE WRETCHED MONK

Upon their vast walls the ancient cloisters
Displayed the holy Truth in tableaux,
Which by warming up the pious bowels,
Would temper their cold austerity.

In those days when the seeds of Christ were aflower,
Many an illustrious monk, seldom cited today,
Taking funeral grounds for his studio,
Would humbly glorify death.

—My soul is a tomb where, wretched cenobite,
I dwell and I pace for eternity;
Nothing embellishes the walls of this odious cloister.

O idle monk! when will I know how to make
From the living spectacle of my sad misery
The work of my hands and the love of my eyes?

L'ENNEMI

Ma jeunesse ne fut qu'un ténébreux orage,
Traversé çà et là par de brillants soleils;
Le tonnerre et la pluie ont fait un tel ravage,
Qu'il reste en mon jardin bien peu de fruits vermeils.

Voilà que j'ai touché l'automne des idées,
Et qu'il faut employer la pelle et les râteaux
Pour rassembler à neuf les terres inondées,
Où l'eau creuse des trous grands comme des tombeaux.

Et qui sait si les fleurs nouvelles que je rêve
Trouveront dans ce sol lavé comme une grève
Le mystique aliment qui ferait leur vigueur?

— Ô douleur! ô douleur! Le Temps mange la vie,
Et l'obscur Ennemi qui nous ronge le cœur
Du sang que nous perdons croît et se fortifie!

THE ENEMY

My youth was nothing but a tenebrous storm,
Crossed here and there by shafts of sun;
Thunder and rain have wreaked such ruin,
That few blushing fruits remain in my grove.

Now I have reached the autumn of ideas,
And must labor the spade and the rake
To gather afresh the flooded earth,
Where water hollows great holes like graves.

And who knows if the new flowers I dream
Will find in the soil washed like a shore
The mystical food that would fuel their force?

—O sorrow! o sorrow! Time swallows life,
And the obscure Enemy who gnaws at our heart
Swells and grows strong on the blood that we lose!

LE GUIGNON

Pour soulever un poids si lourd,
Sisyphe, il faudrait ton courage!
Bien qu'on ait du cœur à l'ouvrage,
L'Art est long et le Temps est court.

Loin des sépultures célèbres,
Vers un cimetière isolé,
Mon cœur, comme un tambour voilé,
Va battant des marches funèbres.

— Maint joyau dort enseveli
Dans les ténèbres et l'oubli,
Bien loin des pioches et des sondes;

Mainte fleur épanche à regret
Son parfum doux comme un secret
Dans les solitudes profondes.

MISFORTUNE

To lift a weight so heavy,
Sisyphus, would require your courage!
However eagerly one works,
Art is long and Time is short.

Far from renowned sepulchers,
Toward an isolated cemetery,
My heart, like a muffled drum,
Goes beating funeral marches.

—Many a gem sleeps shrouded
In shadow and oblivion,
Far from the pick and the probe;

Many a flower expends with regret
Its scent as sweet as a secret
In solitudes profound.

LA VIE ANTÉRIEURE

J'ai longtemps habité sous de vastes portiques
Que les soleils marins teignaient de mille feux,
Et que leurs grands piliers, droits et majestueux,
Rendaient pareils, le soir, aux grottes basaltiques.

Les houles, en roulant les images des cieux,
Mêlaient d'une façon solennelle et mystique
Les tout-puissants accords de leur riche musique
Aux couleurs du couchant reflété par mes yeux.

C'est là que j'ai vécu dans les voluptés calmes,
Au milieu de l'azur, des vagues, des splendeurs
Et des esclaves nus, tout imprégnés d'odeurs,

Qui me rafraîchissaient le front avec des palmes,
Et dont l'unique soin était d'approfondir
Le secret douloureux qui me faisait languir.

THE PREVIOUS LIFE

I lived a long time beneath vast porticoes
That ocean suns dyed with a thousand fires,
And whose great pillars, straight and majestic,
Made them peers, in the evening, of basalt grottos.

The swells, enfolding images of skies,
Mingled in a manner mystical and solemn
The omnipotent accords of their rich music
With the sunset colors reflected by my eyes.

There I lived a life of calm pleasures,
Amid the azure, the waves, the splendors
And the naked slaves, pregnant with perfumes,

Who refreshed my brow with palms,
And whose only care was to fathom
The dolorous secret of my languor.

BOHÉMIENS EN VOYAGE

La tribu prophétique aux prunelles ardentes
Hier s'est mise en route, emportant ses petits
Sur son dos, ou livrant à leurs fiers appétits
Le trésor toujours prêt des mamelles pendantes.

Les hommes vont à pied sous leurs armes luisantes
Le long des chariots où les leurs sont blottis,
Promenant sur le ciel des yeux appesantis
Par le morne regret des chimères absentes.

Du fond de son réduit sablonneux, le grillon,
Les regardant passer, redouble sa chanson;
Cybèle, qui les aime, augmente ses verdures,

Fait couler le rocher et fleurir le désert
Devant ces voyageurs, pour lesquels est ouvert
L'empire familier des ténèbres futures.

XIII

VOYAGING GYPSIES

The prophetic tribe with ardent eyes
Set out yesterday, bearing their babies
Upon their back, or offering to their haughty appetites
The ever-ready treasure of pendant breasts.

The men go by foot beneath gleaming weapons
Beside wagons where their kin are crouched,
Scanning the sky with eyes weighed down
By dreary longing for absent chimeras.

Deep in his sandy lair, the cricket,
Watches them pass, redoubles his song;
Cybele, who loves them, quickens her green,

Makes the rocks flow and flowers the desert
Before these voyagers, for whom unfolds
The familiar empire of tenebrous futures.

L'HOMME ET LA MER

Homme libre, toujours tu chériras la mer!
La mer est ton miroir; tu contemples ton âme
Dans le déroulement infini de sa lame,
Et ton esprit n'est pas un gouffre moins amer.

Tu te plais à plonger au sein de ton image;
Tu l'embrasses des yeux et des bras, et ton cœur
Se distrait quelquefois de sa propre rumeur
Au bruit de cette plainte indomptable et sauvage.

Vous êtes tous les deux ténébreux et discrets:
Homme, nul n'a sondé le fond de tes abîmes;
Ô mer, nul ne connaît tes richesses intimes,
Tant vous êtes jaloux de garder vos secrets!

Et cependant voilà des siècles innombrables
Que vous vous combattez sans pitié ni remords,
Tellement vous aimez le carnage et la mort,
Ô lutteurs éternels, ô frères implacables!

MAN AND SEA

Free man, you will always cherish the sea!
The sea is your mirror; you contemplate your soul
In the infinite unfolding of its swell,
And your spirit is no less bitter a gulf.

You love to plunge into the heart of your image;
You hold it in your eyes and arms, and your heart
Sometimes forgets its own murmur
At the sound of this indomitable and savage lament.

Both of you are tenebrous and discrete:
Man, no one has sounded the bottom of your abyss;
O sea, no one knows your intimate riches,
So jealously do you guard your secrets!

And yet for numberless centuries
You have fought one another without pity or remorse,
Such is your love of carnage and death,
O eternal combatants, o implacable brothers!

DON JUAN AUX ENFERS

Quand Don Juan descendit vers l'onde souterraine
Et lorsqu'il eut donné son obole à Charon,
Un sombre mendiant, l'œil fier comme Antisthène,
D'un bras vengeur et fort saisit chaque aviron.

Montrant leurs seins pendants et leurs robes ouvertes,
Des femmes se tordaient sous le noir firmament,
Et, comme un grand troupeau de victimes offertes,
Derrière lui traînaient un long mugissement.

Sganarelle en riant lui réclamait ses gages,
Tandis que Don Luis avec un doigt tremblant
Montrait à tous les morts errant sur les rivages
Le fils audacieux qui railla son front blanc.

Frissonnant sous son deuil, la chaste et maigre Elvire,
Près de l'époux perfide et qui fut son amant,
Semblait lui réclamer un suprême sourire
Où brillât la douceur de son premier serment.

Tout droit dans son armure, un grand homme de pierre
Se tenait à la barre et coupait le flot noir;
Mais le calme héros, courbé sur sa rapière,
Regardait le sillage et ne daignait rien voir.

DON JUAN IN HELL

When Don Juan went down to the underworld stream
And had paid his obol to Charon,
A somber beggar, proud-eyed as Antisthenes,
Seized each oar with strong vengeful arms.

Their open robes flaunting pendulous breasts,
Women writhed beneath the black sky,
And, like a great sacrificial herd,
Behind him there trailed a long low cry.

Laughing Sganarelle demanded his wages,
While Don Luis with a trembling finger
Showed all the dead who wandered the shores
The shameless son who had mocked his grey brow.

Shivering in mourning, chaste and thin Elvire,
Near her treacherous spouse and erstwhile lover,
Seemed to solicit a supreme smile
Where would glow the sweetness of his first vow.

Rigid in armor, a great man of stone
Stood at the helm and cut the black flood;
But the calm hero, bent on his sword,
Watched the wake and deigned to see nothing.

CHÂTIMENT DE L'ORGUEIL

En ces temps merveilleux où la Théologie
Fleurit avec le plus de sève et d'énergie,
On raconte qu'un jour un docteur des plus grands,
— Après avoir forcé les cœurs indifférents;
Les avoir remués dans leurs profondeurs noires;
Après avoir franchi vers les célestes gloires
Des chemins singuliers à lui-même inconnus,
Où les purs Esprits seuls peut-être étaient venus, —
Comme un homme monté trop haut, pris de panique,
S'écria, transporté d'un orgueil satanique:
« Jésus, petit Jésus! je t'ai poussé bien haut!
Mais, si j'avais voulu t'attaquer au défaut
De l'armure, ta honte égalerait ta gloire,
Et tu ne serais plus qu'un fœtus dérisoire! »

Immédiatement sa raison s'en alla.
L'éclat de ce soleil d'un crêpe se voila;
Tout le chaos roula dans cette intelligence,
Temple autrefois vivant, plein d'ordre et d'opulence,
Sous les plafonds duquel tant de pompe avait lui.
Le silence et la nuit s'installèrent en lui,
Comme dans un caveau dont la clef est perdue.
Dès lors il fut semblable aux bêtes de la rue,
Et, quand il s'en allait sans rien voir, à travers
Les champs, sans distinguer les étés des hivers,
Sale, inutile et laid comme une chose usée,
Il faisait des enfants la joie et la risée.

PUNISHMENT FOR PRIDE

In those marvelous times when Theology
Was fully aflower with nectar and energy,
They say that a prominent doctor one day,
—Having pried open the indifferent hearts;
Having stirred them in their deepest dark;
Having forged toward celestial glories
Certain singular paths to himself unknown,
Where only pure Spirits, perhaps, had been, —
Like a man having climbed too high, panic-stricken,
Cried out, transported by satanic pride:
"Jesus, little Jesus! I have held you high!
But, had I wished to strike at the chink
In your armor, your shame would equal your glory,
And you would be no more than a paltry fetus!"

Immediately his reason left him.
The radiance of that sun was veiled in crape;
Total chaos rolled through that intelligence,
Once a living temple, full of order and opulence,
Beneath whose vaults had glowed such pomp.
Silence and night settled into him,
As in a crypt whose key is lost.
Thenceforth he was like those brutes in the street,
And, as he went seeing nothing, across
The fields, not knowing summer from winter,
Dirty, useless and ugly as a worn out thing,
He was the joy and the laughingstock of the children.

XVII

LA BEAUTÉ

Je suis belle, ô mortels! comme un rêve de pierre,
Et mon sein, où chacun s'est meurtri tour à tour,
Est fait pour inspirer au poète un amour
Eternel et muet ainsi que la matière.

Je trône dans l'azur comme un sphinx incompris;
J'unis un cœur de neige à la blancheur des cygnes;
Je hais le mouvement qui déplace les lignes,
Et jamais je ne pleure et jamais je ne ris.

Les poètes, devant mes grandes attitudes,
Que j'ai l'air d'emprunter aux plus fiers monuments,
Consumeront leurs jours en d'austères études;

Car j'ai, pour fasciner ces dociles amants,
De purs miroirs qui font toutes choses plus belles:
Mes yeux, mes larges yeux aux clartés éternelles!

XVII

BEAUTY

I am lovely, o mortals! like a dream of stone,
And my breast, where each is bruised in turn,
Is made to inspire in the poet a love
Eternal and mute as is matter.

I reign in the azure like an inscrutable sphinx;
I unite heart of snow with whiteness of swans;
I hate the movement that unsettles the lines,
And I never laugh and I never cry.

The poets, before my lofty bearing,
Of an air transposed from proudest monuments,
Will consume their days in austere studies;

For I have, to fascinate these docile paramours,
Pure mirrors that make all things more lovely:
My eyes, my eternally lucid wide eyes!

XVIII

L'IDÉAL

Ce ne seront jamais ces beautés de vignettes,
Produits avariés, nés d'un siècle vaurien,
Ces pieds à brodequins, ces doigts à castagnettes,
Qui sauront satisfaire un cœur comme le mien.

Je laisse à Gavarni, poète des chloroses,
Son troupeau gazouillant de beautés d'hôpital,
Car je ne puis trouver parmi ces pâles roses
Une fleur qui ressemble à mon rouge idéal.

Ce qu'il faut à ce cœur profond comme un abîme,
C'est vous, Lady Macbeth, âme puissante au crime,
Rêve d'Eschyle éclos au climat des autans;

Ou bien toi, grande Nuit, fille de Michel-Ange,
Qui tors paisiblement dans une pose étrange
Tes appas façonnés aux bouches des Titans!

IDEAL

Never will these beauties in vignettes,
Debased products, born of a miscreant century,
These feet in buskins, these fingers in castanets,
Know how to satisfy a heart like mine.

I leave to Gavarni, poet of chlorosis,
His chirping flock of hospital belles,
For I cannot find among these pale roses
One flower resembling my ideal red.

Profound as an abyss, what this heart requires
Is you, Lady Macbeth, soul equal to the crime,
Dream of Aeschylus hatched in stormwinds;

Or you, great Night, Michelangelo's daughter,
Who peacefully twists in exotic pose
Your charms fashioned in the mouths of Titans!

LA GÉANTE

Du temps que la Nature en sa verve puissante
Concevait chaque jour des enfants monstrueux,
J'eusse aimé vivre auprès d'une jeune géante,
Comme aux pieds d'une reine un chat voluptueux.

J'eusse aimé voir son corps fleurir avec son âme
Et grandir librement dans ses terribles jeux;
Deviner si son cœur couve une sombre flamme
Aux humides brouillards qui nagent dans ses yeux;

Parcourir à loisir ses magnifiques formes;
Ramper sur le versant de ses genoux énormes,
Et parfois en été, quand les soleils malsains,

Lasse, la font s'étendre à travers la campagne,
Dormir nonchalamment à l'ombre de ses seins,
Comme un hameau paisible au pied d'une montagne.

THE GIANTESS

In the days when Nature with potent verve
Would conceive monstrous children every day,
I would have loved to live by a young giantess,
Like a sensuous cat at the feet of a queen.

I would have loved to see her body flourish with her soul
And grow freely amid her terrible games;
To guess if her heart keeps a somber flame
Amid the humid haze that swims in her eyes;

To roam at leisure her magnificent curves;
To crawl up the slopes of her enormous knees,
And sometimes in summer, when sickly suns,

Weary, make her stretch across the countryside,
To sleep nonchalantly in the shade of her breasts,
Like a peaceful hamlet at the foot of a mountain.

XX

LE MASQUE

Statue allégorique dans le goût de la Renaissance
À Ernest Christophe, statuaire.

Contemplons ce trésor de grâces florentines;
Dans l'ondulation de ce corps musculeux
L'Élégance et la Force abondent, sœurs divines.
Cette femme, morceau vraiment miraculeux,
Divinement robuste, adorablement mince,
Est faite pour trôner sur des lits somptueux,
Et charmer les loisirs d'un pontife ou d'un prince.

— Aussi, vois ce souris fin et voluptueux
Où la Fatuité promène son extase;
Ce long regard sournois, langoureux et moqueur;
Ce visage mignard, tout encadré de gaze,
Dont chaque trait nous dit avec un air vainqueur:
« La Volupté m'appelle et l'Amour me couronne! »
À cet être doué de tant de majesté
Vois quel charme excitant la gentillesse donne!
Approchons, et tournons autour de sa beauté.

Ô blasphème de l'art! ô surprise fatale!
La femme au corps divin, promettant le bonheur,
Par le haut se termine en monstre bicéphale!

— Mais non! ce n'est qu'un masque, un décor suborneur,
Ce visage éclairé d'une exquise grimace,
Et, regarde, voici, crispée atrocement,
La véritable tête, et la sincère face
Renversée à l'abri de la face qui ment.
Pauvre grande beauté! le magnifique fleuve

THE MASK

Allegorical Statue in the Style of the Renaissance

To Ernest Christophe, sculptor.

Let us contemplate this treasure of Florentine graces;
In the undulation of its muscular body
Elegance and Force abound, divine sisters.
This woman, truly miraculous morsel,
Divinely robust, adorably slim,
Is made for enthronement upon sumptuous beds,
And to charm the leisure of pontiff or prince.

—Again, look at this smile fine and voluptuous
Where Conceit parades its ecstasy;
This lingering sly look, languorous and mocking;
This dainty face, enframed with gauze,
Whose every feature seems to say with a conquering air:
"Lust is my calling and Love is my crown!"
To this being blessed with such majesty
See what lively charm kindness lends!
Let us draw near, and revolve around her beauty.

O blasphemy of art! o fatal surprise!
The divinely embodied woman, promising happiness,
Ends up at the top a bicephalous monster!

—But no! it's only a mask, a suborning ornament,
This face lit up by an exquisite mien,
And, look, here, atrociously contorted,
The true head, and the sincere face
Recoiling in shelter of the face that lies.
Poor noble beauty! the magnificent river

De tes pleurs aboutit dans mon cœur soucieux;
Ton mensonge m'enivre, et mon âme s'abreuve
Aux flots que la Douleur fait jaillir de tes yeux!

— Mais pourquoi pleure-t-elle? Elle, beauté parfaite
Qui mettrait à ses pieds le genre humain vaincu,
Quel mal mystérieux ronge son flanc d'athlète?

— Elle pleure, insensé, parce qu'elle a vécu!
Et parce qu'elle vit! Mais ce qu'elle déplore
Surtout, ce qui la fait frémir jusqu'aux genoux,
C'est que demain, hélas! il faudra vivre encore!
Demain, après-demain et toujours! — comme nous!

Of your tears flows within my fretful heart;
Your duplicity intoxicates me, and my soul slakes its thirst
With the floods that Sorrow pours from your eyes!

—But why does she cry? She, perfect beauty
Who could tread upon the vanquished human race,
What mysterious evil gnaws at her athletic flanks?

—She cries, fool, because she has lived!
And because she lives! But what she deplores
Above all, what makes her weak at the knees,
Is that tomorrow, alas! she must live again!
Tomorrow, the day after tomorrow and always! —like us!

XXI

HYMNE À LA BEAUTÉ

Viens-tu du ciel profond ou sors-tu de l'abîme,
Ô Beauté? ton regard, infernal et divin,
Verse confusément le bienfait et le crime,
Et l'on peut pour cela te comparer au vin.

Tu contiens dans ton œil le couchant et l'aurore;
Tu répands des parfums comme un soir orageux;
Tes baisers sont un philtre et ta bouche une amphore
Qui font le héros lâche et l'enfant courageux.

Sors-tu du gouffre noir ou descends-tu des astres?
Le Destin charmé suit tes jupons comme un chien;
Tu sèmes au hasard la joie et les désastres,
Et tu gouvernes tout et ne réponds de rien.

Tu marches sur des morts, Beauté, dont tu te moques;
De tes bijoux l'Horreur n'est pas le moins charmant,
Et le Meurtre, parmi tes plus chères breloques,
Sur ton ventre orgueilleux danse amoureusement.

L'éphémère ébloui vole vers toi, chandelle,
Crépite, flambe et dit: Bénissons ce flambeau!
L'amoureux pantelant incliné sur sa belle
A l'air d'un moribond caressant son tombeau.

Que tu viennes du ciel ou de l'enfer, qu'importe,
Ô Beauté! monstre énorme, effrayant, ingénu!
Si ton œil, ton souris, ton pied, m'ouvrent la porte
D'un Infini que j'aime et n'ai jamais connu?

HYMN TO BEAUTY

Do you fall from the heavens or rise from the abyss,
O Beauty? your gaze, infernal and divine,
Pours confusedly beneficence and crime,
And in this one may compare you to wine.

You contain in your eye the sunset and the dawn;
You spill out perfumes like a stormy evening;
Your kisses are a philter and your mouth an amphora
That make cowardly the hero and courageous the child.

Do you rise from the black chasm or descend from the stars?
Charmed Destiny trails at your petticoats like a dog;
You sow at hazard joys and disasters,
And you rule over all and answer to nothing.

You tread upon the dead, Beauty, those you mock;
Of your jewels Horror is not the least charming,
And Murder, among your most cherished trinkets,
Dances amorously on your proud paunch.

The dazzled ephemerid wings toward you, alight,
Crackling, aflame and says: Bless this beacon!
The panting lover swooned over his belle
Has the air of a moribund caressing his tomb.

That you come from heaven or from hell, who cares,
O Beauty! enormous, frightening, ingenuous monster!
If your eye, your smile, your foot, opens the door
Of an Infinite that I love and have never known?

De Satan ou de Dieu, qu'importe? Ange ou Sirène,
Qu'importe, si tu rends, — fée aux yeux de velours,
Rythme, parfum, lueur, ô mon unique reine! —
L'univers moins hideux et les instants moins lourds?

From Satan or from God, who cares? Angel or Siren,
Who cares, if you render, —velvet-eyed fairy,
Rhythm, fragrance, glimmer, o my unique queen! —
The universe less hideous and the instants less heavy?

LES BIJOUX

La très chère était nue, et, connaissant mon cœur,
Elle n'avait gardé que ses bijoux sonores,
Dont le riche attirail lui donnait l'air vainqueur
Qu'ont dans leurs jours heureux les esclaves des Mores.

Quand il jette en dansant son bruit vif et moqueur,
Ce monde rayonnant de métal et de pierre
Me ravit en extase, et j'aime à la fureur
Les choses où le son se mêle à la lumière.

Elle était donc couchée et se laissait aimer,
Et du haut du divan elle souriait d'aise
À mon amour profond et doux comme la mer,
Qui vers elle montait comme vers sa falaise.

Les yeux fixés sur moi, comme un tigre dompté,
D'un air vague et rêveur elle essayait des poses,
Et la candeur unie à la lubricité
Donnait un charme neuf à ses métamorphoses;

Et son bras et sa jambe, et sa cuisse et ses reins,
Polis comme de l'huile, onduleux comme un cygne,
Passaient devant mes yeux clairvoyants et sereins;
Et son ventre et ses seins, ces grappes de ma vigne,

S'avançaient, plus câlins que les Anges du mal,
Pour troubler le repos où mon âme était mise,
Et pour la déranger du rocher de cristal
Où, calme et solitaire, elle s'était assise.

THE JEWELS

The dearest was naked, and, knowing my heart,
She kept only her sonorous jewels,
Whose rich equipage lent her the victorious air
Of the slaves of Moors on their happy days.

When it dancingly casts its bright and mocking jangle,
This luminous world of metal and stone
Ravishes me in ecstasy, and I am furiously in love with
Things wherein sound and light mingle.

Thus she reclined and gave herself up,
And high upon the divan she smiled with pleasure
At my love deep and gentle as the sea,
Mounting toward her as toward its cliff.

Eyes fixed upon me, like a tamed tiger,
With an air vague and dreamy she tried out her poses,
And lust united with candor
Lent a novel charm to her metamorphoses;

And her arms and her legs, and her thighs and her loins,
Polished as if with oil, undulating like a swan,
Passing before my eyes clairvoyant and serene;
And her belly and breasts, grapes on my vine,

Advanced, more coaxing than malicious Angels,
To trouble the nest where my soul took rest,
And dislodge it from the crystal rock
Where, calm and alone, it had set itself.

Je croyais voir unis par un nouveau dessin
Les hanches de l'Antiope au buste d'un imberbe,
Tant sa taille faisait ressortir son bassin.
Sur ce teint fauve et brun, le fard était superbe!

— Et la lampe s'étant résignée à mourir,
Comme le foyer seul illuminait la chambre,
Chaque fois qu'il poussait un flamboyant soupir,
Il inondait de sang cette peau couleur d'ambre!

I thought I saw united by a novel tracery
The hips of Antiope with the bust of a boy,
So did her waist point up her pelvis.
On her wild brown tint, the blush was superb!

—And the lamp resigned itself to die,
As the hearth alone lit up the room,
Each time it issued a flaming sigh,
It drowned with blood this amber colored skin!

PARFUM EXOTIQUE

Quand, les deux yeux fermés, en un soir chaud d'automne,
Je respire l'odeur de ton sein chaleureux,
Je vois se dérouler des rivages heureux
Qu'éblouissent les feux d'un soleil monotone;

Une île paresseuse où la nature donne
Des arbres singuliers et des fruits savoureux;
Des hommes dont le corps est mince et vigoureux,
Et des femmes dont l'œil par sa franchise étonne.

Guidé par ton odeur vers de charmants climats,
Je vois un port rempli de voiles et de mâts
Encor tout fatigués par la vague marine,

Pendant que le parfum des verts tamariniers,
Qui circule dans l'air et m'enfle la narine,
Se mêle dans mon âme au chant des mariniers.

XXII

EXOTIC PERFUME

When, with eyes shut, on a warm autumn eve,
I breathe the scent of your balmy breast,
I see the unfolding of fortunate shores
Dazzling in the flames of a monotonous sun;

An indolent island where nature offers
Curious trees and savory fruits;
Men of slender and vigorous build,
And women with eyes of startling candor.

Guided by your scent toward pleasant climes,
I see a port replete with sails and masts
Still wearied by the tossing sea,

While the perfume of green tamarinds,
That circles in the air and swells in the nostril,
Mingles in my soul with the mariners' song.

XXIII

LA CHEVELURE

Ô toison, moutonnant jusque sur l'encolure!
Ô boucles! Ô parfum chargé de nonchaloir!
Extase! Pour peupler ce soir l'alcôve obscure
Des souvenirs dormant dans cette chevelure,
Je la veux agiter dans l'air comme un mouchoir!

La langoureuse Asie et la brûlante Afrique,
Tout un monde lointain, absent, presque défunt,
Vit dans tes profondeurs, forêt aromatique!
Comme d'autres esprits voguent sur la musique,
Le mien, ô mon amour! nage sur ton parfum.

J'irai là-bas où l'arbre et l'homme, pleins de sève,
Se pâment longuement sous l'ardeur des climats;
Fortes tresses, soyez la houle qui m'enlève!
Tu contiens, mer d'ébène, un éblouissant rêve
De voiles, de rameurs, de flammes et de mâts:

Un port retentissant où mon âme peut boire
À grands flots le parfum, le son et la couleur;
Où les vaisseaux, glissant dans l'or et dans la moire,
Ouvrent leurs vastes bras pour embrasser la gloire
D'un ciel pur où frémit l'éternelle chaleur.

Je plongerai ma tête amoureuse d'ivresse
Dans ce noir océan où l'autre est enfermé;
Et mon esprit subtil que le roulis caresse
Saura vous retrouver, ô féconde paresse,
Infinis bercements du loisir embaumé!

HAIR

O fleece, billowing at the neck!
O curls! O perfume laden with nonchalance!
Ecstasy! To people this evening the dusky alcove
With the memories dormant in this hair,
I would wave it in the air like a handkerchief!

Languorous Asia and feverish Africa,
A whole distant world, absent, nearly extinguished,
Lives in your depths, fragrant forest!
As other spirits drift upon music,
My own, o my love! swims upon your perfume.

I shall go where trees and men, brimming with sap,
Swoon at length in the atmosphere's ardor;
Powerful tresses, be the swell that carries me away!
You contain, ebony sea, a dazzling dream
Of sails, of oarsmen, of flames and of masts:

A resounding port where my soul may drink
In great waves the scent, the sound and the hue;
Where the vessels, gliding in gold and moiré,
Spread their vast arms to embrace the glory
Of a pure sky shimmering with eternal heat.

I shall plunge my head enamoured of intoxication
In this black ocean where the other is enclosed;
And my subtle spirit caressed by the swells
Will recover you, o fecund indolence,
Infinite cradlings of balmy leisure!

Cheveux bleus, pavillon de ténèbres tendues,
Vous me rendez l'azur du ciel immense et rond;
Sur les bords duvetés de vos mèches tordues
Je m'enivre ardemment des senteurs confondues
De l'huile de coco, du musc et du goudron.

Longtemps! toujours! ma main dans ta crinière lourde
Sèmera le rubis, la perle et le saphir,
Afin qu'à mon désir tu ne sois jamais sourde!
N'es-tu pas l'oasis où je rêve, et la gourde
Où je hume à longs traits le vin du souvenir?

Blue hair, pavilion of long shadows,
You bring me the azure of the immense and round sky;
Upon the downy verges of your twisted locks
I ardently intoxicate myself upon mingled fragrances
Of coconut oil, of musk and of tar.

For ages! For ever! my hand in your heavy mane
Shall sow the ruby, the pearl and the sapphire,
So that you will never be deaf to my desire!
Are you not the oasis where I dream, and the gourd
Where I drink in great draughts the wine of memory?

Je t'adore à l'égal de la voûte nocturne,
Ô vase de tristesse, ô grande taciturne,
Et t'aime d'autant plus, belle, que tu me fuis,
Et que tu me parais, ornement de mes nuits,
Plus ironiquement accumuler les lieues
Qui séparent mes bras des immensités bleues.

Je m'avance à l'attaque, et je grimpe aux assauts,
Comme après un cadavre un chœur de vermisseaux,
Et je chéris, ô bête implacable et cruelle!
Jusqu'à cette froideur par où tu m'es plus belle!

XXIV

I adore you even as the nocturnal vault,
O vase of sadness, o vast reticence,
And I love you the more, beauty, that you flee from me,
And that you seem, ornament of my nights,
More ironically to accumulate the leagues
That separate my arms from blue immensities.

I launch the attack, and I mount the assault,
Like a choir of maggots after a cadaver,
And I cherish, o beast implacable and cruel!
Even this coldness that increases your beauty!

Tu mettrais l'univers entier dans ta ruelle,
Femme impure! L'ennui rend ton âme cruelle.
Pour exercer tes dents à ce jeu singulier,
Il te faut chaque jour un cœur au râtelier.
Tes yeux, illuminés ainsi que des boutiques
Et des ifs flamboyants dans les fêtes publiques,
Usent insolemment d'un pouvoir emprunté,
Sans connaître jamais la loi de leur beauté.

Machine aveugle et sourde, en cruautés féconde!
Salutaire instrument, buveur du sang du monde,
Comment n'as-tu pas honte et comment n'as-tu pas
Devant tous les miroirs vu pâlir tes appas?
La grandeur de ce mal où tu te crois savante
Ne t'a donc jamais fait reculer d'épouvante,
Quand la nature, grande en ses desseins cachés,
De toi se sert, ô femme, ô reine des péchés,
— De toi, vil animal, — pour pétrir un génie?

Ô fangeuse grandeur! sublime ignominie!

You'd take the whole universe into your alley,
Filthy woman! Ennui makes your soul cruel.
To cut your teeth at this curious game,
You need a new heart on the rack every day.
Your eyes, lit up like the shops
And those flaming lamps at public feasts,
Burn insolently with a borrowed power,
Forever unconscious of their beauty's law.

Machine blind and deaf, fecund with cruelty!
Salutary instrument, sucking the blood of the world,
Have you no shame and have you not
Seen in the mirrors your fading charms?
Has the enormity of this evil you think you control
Never made you recoil in dread,
When nature, adept in hidden designs,
Uses you, o woman, o queen of the sins,
—you, vile animal, —to mould a genius?

O foul grandeur! sublime ignominy!

SED NON SATIATA

Bizarre déité, brune comme les nuits,
Au parfum mélangé de musc et de havane,
Œuvre de quelque obi, le Faust de la savane,
Sorcière au flanc d'ébène, enfant des noirs minuits,

Je préfère au constance, à l'opium, au nuits,
L'élixir de ta bouche où l'amour se pavane;
Quand vers toi mes désirs partent en caravane,
Tes yeux sont la citerne où boivent mes ennuis.

Par ces deux grands yeux noirs, soupiraux de ton âme,
Ô démon sans pitié! verse-moi moins de flamme;
Je ne suis pas le Styx pour t'embrasser neuf fois,

Hélas! et je ne puis, Mégère libertine,
Pour briser ton courage et te mettre aux abois,
Dans l'enfer de ton lit devenir Proserpine!

SED NON SATIATA

Bizarre deity, brown as nights,
Of perfume mixed from musk and havana,
Obeah's creation, Faust of the savanna,
Ebony sorceress, child of black midnights,

I prefer to constantia, to opium, to pinto from Nuits,
The elixir of your mouth where love pavanes;
When toward you my desires depart in caravan,
Your eyes are the cistern where drinks my ennui.

From those two great black eyes, vents of your soul,
O pitiless demon! throw a little less flame;
I am not the Styx that holds you ninefold,

And alas! I cannot, libertine Shrew,
To break your spirit and to keep you at bay,
Become Proserpine in the hell of your bed!

Avec ses vêtements ondoyants et nacrés,
Même quand elle marche on croirait qu'elle danse,
Comme ces longs serpents que les jongleurs sacrés
Au bout de leurs bâtons agitent en cadence.

Comme le sable morne et l'azur des déserts,
Insensibles tous deux à l'humaine souffrance,
Comme les longs réseaux de la houle des mers,
Elle se développe avec indifférence.

Ses yeux polis sont faits de minéraux charmants,
Et dans cette nature étrange et symbolique
Où l'ange inviolé se mêle au sphinx antique,

Où tout n'est qu'or, acier, lumière et diamants,
Resplendit à jamais, comme un astre inutile,
La froide majesté de la femme stérile.

With her wavering and pearly gowns,
Even as she walks one would think she dances,
Like those long serpents that sacred charmers
Stir in cadence at the tip of their batons.

Like the dreary sand and azure of deserts,
Both insensible to human pain,
Like the long threads of the seas' swells,
She indifferently unfurls.

Of enchanting minerals are her polished eyes,
And in this strange and symbolic nature
Where inviolate angel mingles with ancient sphinx,

Where all is gold, steel, light and diamonds,
There shines forever, like a useless star,
The cold majesty of the sterile woman.

LE SERPENT QUI DANSE

Que j'aime voir, chère indolente,
       De ton corps si beau,
Comme une étoffe vacillante,
       Miroiter la peau!

Sur ta chevelure profonde
       Aux âcres parfums,
Mer odorante et vagabonde
       Aux flots bleus et bruns,

Comme un navire qui s'éveille
       Au vent du matin,
Mon âme rêveuse appareille
       Pour un ciel lointain.

Tes yeux, où rien ne se révèle
       De doux ni d'amer,
Sont deux bijoux froids où se mêle
       L'or avec le fer.

À te voir marcher en cadence,
       Belle d'abandon,
On dirait un serpent qui danse
       Au bout d'un bâton.

Sous le fardeau de ta paresse
       Ta tête d'enfant
Se balance avec la mollesse
       D'un jeune éléphant,

THE DANCING SERPENT

How I love to see, indolent darling,
      From your beautiful body,
Like a shimmering fabric,
      The skin gleam!

Upon your fathomless hair
      With its acrid scents,
Fragrant and vagabond sea
      With its brown and blue swells,

Like a ship that lists
      In the morning wind,
My dreamy soul sets sail
      For a distant sky.

Your eyes, where nothing is revealed
      Neither sweet nor bitter,
Are two cold jewels wherein mingle
      Iron with gold.

To see you walk in cadence,
      Beautiful with abandon,
Is to see a serpent dance
      At the tip of a baton.

Beneath the burden of your indolence
      Your child's head
Balances with the droop
      Of a young elephant,

Et ton corps se penche et s'allonge
Comme un fin vaisseau
Qui roule bord sur bord et plonge
Ses vergues dans l'eau.

Comme un flot grossi par la fonte
Des glaciers grondants,
Quand l'eau de ta bouche remonte
Au bord de tes dents,

Je crois boire un vin de Bohême,
Amer et vainqueur,
Un ciel liquide qui parsème
D'étoiles mon cœur!

And your body is plied and stretched
      Like a fine ship
That rolls from side to side and plunges
      Her yards in the water.

Like a tide swelled by the melt
      Of groaning glaciers,
When the wetness of your mouth meets
      The edge of your teeth,

It seems I imbibe a Bohemian wine,
      Victorious and bitter,
A liquid sky that seeds
      My heart with stars.

UNE CHAROGNE

Rappelez-vous l'objet que nous vîmes, mon âme,
Ce beau matin d'été si doux:
Au détour d'un sentier une charogne infâme
Sur un lit semé de cailloux,

Les jambes en l'air, comme une femme lubrique,
Brûlante et suant les poisons,
Ouvrait d'une façon nonchalante et cynique
Son ventre plein d'exhalaisons.

Le soleil rayonnait sur cette pourriture,
Comme afin de la cuire à point,
Et de rendre au centuple à la grande Nature
Tout ce qu'ensemble elle avait joint;

Et le ciel regardait la carcasse superbe
Comme une fleur s'épanouir.
La puanteur était si forte, que sur l'herbe
Vous crûtes vous évanouir.

Les mouches bourdonnaient sur ce ventre putride,
D'où sortaient de noirs bataillons
De larves, qui coulaient comme un épais liquide
Le long de ces vivants haillons.

Tout cela descendait, montait comme une vague,
Ou s'élançait en pétillant;
On eût dit que le corps, enflé d'un souffle vague,
Vivait en se multipliant.

A CARRION

Recall the object we saw, my soul,
        That fine summer morning so soft:
At the bend of the path a carrion foul
        On a bed bestrewn with stones,

Legs in the air, like a woman aroused,
        Steaming and oozing poisons,
Exposing with cynical nonchalance
        Its belly full of fumes.

The sun shone upon that putrefaction,
        As if to roast it to perfection,
And restore to dame Nature a hundredfold
        All she combined in that confection;

And the sky regarded the superb carcass
        Like a flower in bloom.
The stench was so strong, that upon the grass
        You thought that you would swoon.

The flies buzzed above its putrid paunch,
        Wherefrom withdrew black battalions
Of maggots, flowing like a thick liquid
        Along those living rags.

All this was descending, rising like a wave,
        Or seething in glittering flecks;
As if the corpse, swelled with a rippling breath,
        Lived as it multiplied itself.

Et ce monde rendait une étrange musique,
  Comme l'eau courante et le vent,
Ou le grain qu'un vanneur d'un mouvement rythmique
  Agite et tourne dans son van.

Les formes s'effaçaient et n'étaient plus qu'un rêve,
  Une ébauche lente à venir,
Sur la toile oubliée, et que l'artiste achève
  Seulement par le souvenir.

Derrière les rochers une chienne inquiète
  Nous regardait d'un œil fâché,
Épiant le moment de reprendre au squelette
  Le morceau qu'elle avait lâché.

— Et pourtant vous serez semblable à cette ordure,
  À cette horrible infection,
Étoile de mes yeux, soleil de ma nature,
  Vous, mon ange et ma passion!

Oui! telle vous serez, ô la reine des grâces,
  Après les derniers sacrements,
Quand vous irez, sous l'herbe et les floraisons grasses,
  Moisir parmi les ossements.

Alors, ô ma beauté! dites à la vermine
  Qui vous mangera de baisers,
Que j'ai gardé la forme et l'essence divine
  De mes amours décomposés!

And this world issued a strange music,
        Like running water and like wind,
Or grain that a winnower with movement rhythmic
        Stirs and shakes into his bin.

These forms faded and were no more than a dream,
        A sketch slow to come,
Upon the forgotten canvas, which the artist completes
        By memory alone.

Behind the rocks a restless bitch
        Was watching us with an evil eye,
Spying the moment to pick from the bones
        The morsel she had missed.

—And yet you will come to be kin to this filth,
        To this horrible infection,
Star of my eyes, sun of my nature,
        You, my angel and my passion!

Yes! such you will be, o queen of the graces,
        After the last rites,
When you go, below grass and unctuous flowers,
        To molder among the bones.

Then, o my beauty! say to the vermin
        Who will devour you with kisses,
That I saved the form and the essence divine
        Of my lovers decomposed!

DE PROFUNDIS CLAMAVI

J'implore ta pitié, Toi, l'unique que j'aime,
Du fond du gouffre obscur où mon cœur est tombé.
C'est un univers morne à l'horizon plombé,
Où nagent dans la nuit l'horreur et le blasphème;

Un soleil sans chaleur plane au-dessus six mois,
Et les six autres mois la nuit couvre la terre;
C'est un pays plus nu que la terre polaire;
— Ni bêtes, ni ruisseaux, ni verdure, ni bois!

Or il n'est pas d'horreur au monde qui surpasse
La froide cruauté de ce soleil de glace
Et cette immense nuit semblable au vieux Chaos;

Je jalouse le sort des plus vils animaux
Qui peuvent se plonger dans un sommeil stupide,
Tant l'écheveau du temps lentement se dévide!

XXX

DE PROFUNDIS CLAMAVI

I implore your pity, You, the only one I love,
From the bottom of the obscure abyss where my heart has fallen.
It is a mournful universe of leaden horizon,
Where horror and blasphemy swim in the night;

A sun without heat hovers for six months,
And the other six months the night covers the earth;
It is a country more bare than polar regions;
—Neither beasts, nor brooks, nor green, nor woods!

For there is no horror in the world that surpasses
The cold cruelty of this sun of ice
And this immense night akin to ancient Chaos;

I envy the fate of the most vile animals
Who can plunge into a stupid slumber,
As the skein of time slowly unravels!

XXXI

LE VAMPIRE

Toi qui, comme un coup de couteau,
Dans mon cœur plaintif es entrée;
Toi qui, forte comme un troupeau
De démons, vins, folle et parée,

De mon esprit humilié
Faire ton lit et ton domaine;
— Infâme à qui je suis lié
Comme le forçat à la chaîne,

Comme au jeu le joueur têtu,
Comme à la bouteille l'ivrogne,
Comme aux vermines la charogne,
— Maudite, maudite sois-tu!

J'ai prié le glaive rapide
De conquérir ma liberté,
Et j'ai dit au poison perfide
De secourir ma lâcheté.

Hélas! le poison et le glaive
M'ont pris en dédain et m'ont dit:
« Tu n'es pas digne qu'on t'enlève
À ton esclavage maudit,

« Imbécile! — de son empire
Si nos efforts te délivraient,
Tes baisers ressusciteraient
Le cadavre de ton vampire! »

THE VAMPIRE

You, who like a knife wound,
Have come into my plaintive heart;
You, who powerful as a horde
Of demons, came, wild and armored,

To make of my humiliated spirit
Your bed and your domain;
—Infamy to whom I am bound
Like a convict to the chain,

Like the gambler to the game,
Like the drunk to the bottle,
Like the carrion to the maggots
—Accursed, be cursed!

I prayed to the swift sword
To conquer my liberty,
And I asked the perfidious poison
To relieve my cowardice.

Alas! the poison and the sword
Disdainfully said:
"You don't deserve to be relieved
Of your accursed slavery,

"Imbecile! —if from its empire
Our efforts delivered you,
Your kisses would resuscitate
The cadaver of your vampire!"

LE LÉTHÉ

Viens sur mon cœur, âme cruelle et sourde,
Tigre adoré, monstre aux airs indolents;
Je veux longtemps plonger mes doigts tremblants
Dans l'épaisseur de ta crinière lourde;

Dans tes jupons remplis de ton parfum
Ensevelir ma tête endolorie,
Et respirer, comme une fleur flétrie,
Le doux relent de mon amour défunt.

Je veux dormir! dormir plutôt que vivre!
Dans un sommeil aussi doux que la mort,
J'étalerai mes baisers sans remords
Sur ton beau corps poli comme le cuivre.

Pour engloutir mes sanglots apaisés
Rien ne me vaut l'abîme de ta couche;
L'oubli puissant habite sur ta bouche,
Et le Léthé coule dans tes baisers.

À mon destin, désormais mon délice,
J'obéirai comme un prédestiné;
Martyr docile, innocent condamné,
Dont la ferveur attise le supplice,

Je sucerai, pour noyer ma rancœur,
Le népenthès et la bonne ciguë
Aux bouts charmants de cette gorge aiguë,
Qui n'a jamais emprisonné de cœur.

LETHE

Come to my heart, cruel and deaf soul,
Adored tiger, monster with indolent airs;
Long would I plunge my trembling fingers
Into the depth of your heavy mane;

In your petticoats replete with perfume
Enshroud my aching head,
And breathe, like a withered flower,
The sweet stench of my deceased love.

I would sleep! to sleep rather than to live!
In a slumber sweet as death,
I would spread my remorseless kisses
Over your beautiful body polished as copper.

To engulf my sated sobs
Nothing compares to the abyss of your bed;
Potent oblivion inhabits your mouth,
And Lethe flows in your kisses.

My destiny, hereafter my delight,
I shall obey as a predestination;
Docile martyr, condemned innocent,
Whose fervor fuels the ordeal,

I will suck, to drown my rancor,
Nepenthe and beneficent hemlock
At the lovely tips of this pointed breast,
Which has never imprisoned a heart.

Une nuit que j'étais près d'une affreuse Juive,
Comme au long d'un cadavre un cadavre étendu,
Je me pris à songer près de ce corps vendu
A la triste beauté dont mon désir se prive.

Je me représentai sa majesté native,
Son regard de vigueur et de grâces armé,
Ses cheveux qui lui font un casque parfumé,
Et dont le souvenir pour l'amour me ravive.

Car j'eusse avec ferveur baisé ton noble corps,
Et depuis tes pieds frais jusqu'à tes noires tresses
Déroulé le trésor des profondes caresses,

Si, quelque soir, d'un pleur obtenu sans effort
Tu pouvais seulement, ô reine des cruelles!
Obscurcir la splendeur de tes froides prunelles.

One night as I lay with a frightful Jewess,
As if cadaver by cadaver stretched,
I spared a thought beside this sold body
For the sad beauty my desire denied itself.

I pictured her native majesty,
Her gaze with vigor and graces armed,
Her hair composing a perfumed casque,
The remembrance of which revives my ardor.

For fervently I'd have kissed your noble body,
And from your dear feet to your black tresses
Expended the treasure of profound caresses,

If only, one evening, with an effortless tear
You were able, o queen of the cruel!
To obscure the splendor of your cold eyes.

XXXIII

REMORDS POSTUME

Lorsque tu dormiras, ma belle ténébreuse,
Au fond d'un monument construit en marbre noir,
Et lorsque tu n'auras pour alcôve et manoir
Qu'un caveau pluvieux et qu'une fosse creuse;

Quand la pierre, opprimant ta poitrine peureuse
Et tes flancs qu'assouplit un charmant nonchaloir,
Empêchera ton cœur de battre et de vouloir,
Et tes pieds de courir leur course aventureuse,

Le tombeau, confident de mon rêve infini
(Car le tombeau toujours comprendra le poète),
Durant ces grandes nuits d'où le somme est banni,

Te dira: « Que vous sert, courtisane imparfaite,
De n'avoir pas connu ce que pleurent les morts? »
— Et le ver rongera ta peau comme un remords.

POSTHUMOUS REGRET

When you rest, my tenebrous beauty,
At the bottom of a black marble monument,
And when you have for alcove and manor
Just a rainy crypt and a hollow grave;

When the stone, oppressing your timorous breast
And your hips relaxed in lovely nonchalance,
Stops your heart from beating and yearning,
And your feet from running their intrepid race,

The tomb, confidant of my infinite dream
(For the tomb will always comprehend the poet),
Through these great nights from which sleep is banished,

Will say: "What does it profit you, imperfect courtesan,
To never have known what the dead lament?"
—And the worm will gnaw your skin like a regret.

XXXIV

LE CHAT

Viens, mon beau chat, sur mon cœur amoureux;
　　　　Retiens les griffes de ta patte,
Et laisse-moi plonger dans tes beaux yeux,
　　　　Mêlés de métal et d'agate.

Lorsque mes doigts caressent à loisir
　　　　Ta tête et ton dos élastique,
Et que ma main s'enivre du plaisir
　　　　De palper ton corps électrique,

Je vois ma femme en esprit. Son regard,
　　　　Comme le tien, aimable bête,
Profond et froid, coupe et fend comme un dard,

　　　　Et, des pieds jusques à la tête,
Un air subtil, un dangereux parfum
　　　　Nagent autour de son corps brun.

XXXIV

THE CAT

Come, my beautiful cat, to my amorous heart;
      Sheathe the claws of your paw,
And let me plunge into your beautiful eyes,
      Alloyed of metal and agate.

When my fingers caress at leisure
      Your head and your elastic spine,
And my hand is intoxicated by the pleasure
      Of stroking your electric body,

I see my woman ensouled. Her gaze,
      Like yours, loveable beast,
Profound and cold, slices and splits like a fang,

      And, from head to toe,
A subtle air, a dangerous perfume
      Swims around her brown body.

DUELLUM

Deux guerriers ont couru l'un sur l'autre; leurs armes
Ont éclaboussé l'air de lueurs et de sang.
Ces jeux, ces cliquetis du fer sont les vacarmes
D'une jeunesse en proie à l'amour vagissant.

Les glaives sont brisés! comme notre jeunesse,
Ma chère! Mais les dents, les ongles acérés,
Vengent bientôt l'épée et la dague traîtresse.
Ô fureur des cœurs mûrs par l'amour ulcérés!

Dans le ravin hanté des chats-pards et des onces
Nos héros, s'étreignant méchamment, ont roulé,
Et leur peau fleurira l'aridité des ronces.

— Ce gouffre, c'est l'enfer, de nos amis peuplé!
Roulons-y sans remords, amazone inhumaine,
Afin d'éterniser l'ardeur de notre haine!

DUELLUM

Two warriors charged one over the other; their weapons
Splattered the air with glimmers of blood.
These contests, these clashes of steel are the clamor
Of youth in the throes of sobbing love.

The blades are broken! like our youth,
My dear! But the teeth, the sharp nails,
Soon avenge the sword and the treacherous dagger.
O fury of aged hearts ulcerated by love!

Into the ravine haunted by panthers and leopards
Our heroes, spitefully embracing, have tumbled,
And their flesh will flower the arid brambles.

—This chasm, it is hell, peopled by our friends!
There let us wallow without regrets, inhuman amazon,
To render eternal the ardor of our hate!

XXXVI

LE BALCON

Mère des souvenirs, maîtresse des maîtresses,
Ô toi, tous mes plaisirs! ô toi, tous mes devoirs!
Tu te rappelleras la beauté des caresses,
La douceur du foyer et le charme des soirs,
Mère des souvenirs, maîtresse des maîtresses!

Les soirs illuminés par l'ardeur du charbon,
Et les soirs au balcon, voilés de vapeurs roses.
Que ton sein m'était doux! que ton cœur m'était bon!
Nous avons dit souvent d'impérissables choses
Les soirs illuminés par l'ardeur du charbon.

Que les soleils sont beaux dans les chaudes soirées!
Que l'espace est profond! que le cœur est puissant!
En me penchant vers toi, reine des adorées,
Je croyais respirer le parfum de ton sang.
Que les soleils sont beaux dans les chaudes soirées!

La nuit s'épaississait ainsi qu'une cloison,
Et mes yeux dans le noir devinaient tes prunelles,
Et je buvais ton souffle, ô douceur! ô poison!
Et tes pieds s'endormaient dans mes mains fraternelles.
La nuit s'épaississait ainsi qu'une cloison.

Je sais l'art d'évoquer les minutes heureuses,
Et revis mon passé blotti dans tes genoux.
Car à quoi bon chercher tes beautés langoureuses
Ailleurs qu'en ton cher corps et qu'en ton cœur si doux?
Je sais l'art d'évoquer les minutes heureuses!

THE BALCONY

Mother of memories, mistress of mistresses,
O you, all my pleasures! O you, all my bonds!
Don't forget the beauty of those caresses,
The ease of the hearth and the charm of the evenings,
Mother of memories, mistress of mistresses!

Evenings aglow with ardent coals,
And balcony evenings, veiled in vapors of rose.
How soft was your breast! how good your heart!
Often we spoke of imperishable things
Evenings aglow with ardent coals.

How beautiful the suns in sultry dusks!
How profound the space! how full the heart!
Inclining to you, queen of the adored,
I seemed to breathe the perfume of your blood.
How beautiful the suns in sultry dusks!

The night would coalesce into a screen,
And my eyes divine your pupils in the dark,
And I would drink your breath, o sweetness! o poison!
And your feet would sleep in my fraternal hands.
The night would coalesce into a screen.

I know the art of evoking happy minutes,
And reliving my past nestled in your lap.
For where to seek your languorous beauties
But in your dear body and your tender heart?
I know the art of evoking happy minutes!

Ces serments, ces parfums, ces baisers infinis,
Renaîtront-ils d'un gouffre interdit à nos sondes,
Comme montent au ciel les soleils rajeunis
Après s'être lavés au fond des mers profondes?
— Ô serments! ô parfums! ô baisers infinis!

Will these vows, these perfumes, these infinite kisses,
Be reborn from an unsoundable abyss,
Like suns growing young as they mount the heavens
Having bathed in the depths of profound seas?
—O vows! o perfumes! o infinite kisses!

LE POSSÉDÉ

Le soleil s'est couvert d'un crêpe. Comme lui,
Ô Lune de ma vie! emmitoufle-toi d'ombre;
Dors ou fume à ton gré; sois muette, sois sombre,
Et plonge tout entière au gouffre de l'Ennui;

Je t'aime ainsi! Pourtant, si tu veux aujourd'hui,
Comme un astre éclipsé qui sort de la pénombre,
Te pavaner aux lieux que la Folie encombre,
C'est bien! Charmant poignard, jaillis de ton étui!

Allume ta prunelle à la flamme des lustres!
Allume le désir dans les regards des rustres!
Tout de toi m'est plaisir, morbide ou pétulant;

Sois ce que tu voudras, nuit noire, rouge aurore;
Il n'est pas une fibre en tout mon corps tremblant
Qui ne crie : *Ô mon cher Belzébuth, je t'adore!*

THE POSSESSED

The sun is covered in crape. Like him,
O Moon of my life! wrap yourself in shadow;
Sleep or smoke as you will; be silent, be somber,
And plunge completely into the chasm of Ennui;

I love you just so! However, if today you would,
Like an eclipsed star emerging from the penumbra,
Strut around places encumbered by Madness,
That's fine! Charming dagger, spring from your sheath!

Kindle your eyes with chandelier flames!
Kindle desire in ogling boors!
Morbid or petulant, all you are is my pleasure;

Be what you will, black night, red aurora;
There is not a fiber in all my trembling body
That does not cry: *O my dear Beelzebub, it is you I adore!*

XXXVIII

UN FANTÔME

I
LES TÉNÈBRES

Dans les caveaux d'insondable tristesse
Où le Destin m'a déjà relégué;
Où jamais n'entre un rayon rose et gai;
Où, seul avec la Nuit, maussade hôtesse,

Je suis comme un peintre qu'un Dieu moqueur
Condamne à peindre, hélas! sur les ténèbres;
Où, cuisinier aux appétits funèbres,
Je fais bouillir et je mange mon cœur,

Par instants brille, et s'allonge, et s'étale
Un spectre fait de grâce et de splendeur.
À sa rêveuse allure orientale,

Quand il atteint sa totale grandeur,
Je reconnais ma belle visiteuse:
C'est Elle! noire et pourtant lumineuse.

II
LE PARFUM

Lecteur, as-tu quelquefois respiré
Avec ivresse et lente gourmandise
Ce grain d'encens qui remplit une église,
Ou d'un sachet le musc invétéré?

A PHANTOM

I
THE SHADOWS

In the crypts of unsoundable sadness
Where already I am relegated by Destiny;
Where never will enter a ray pink and gay;
Where, alone with Night, sullen hostess,

I am like a painter whom a mocking God
Condemns to paint, alas! upon shadows;
Where, like a chef with morbid appetites,
I boil and eat my own heart,

At times there shimmers, reclines, and stretches
A specter composed of grace and splendor.
In its dreamy oriental allure,

When it attains its total grandeur,
I recognize my beautiful visitor:
It is She! black and yet luminous.

II
THE PERFUME

Reader, have you sometimes inhaled
With intoxication and slow delectation
That grain of incense that suffuses a church,
Or the inveterate musk of a sachet?

Charme profond, magique, dont nous grise
Dans le présent le passé restauré!
Ainsi l'amant sur un corps adoré
Du souvenir cueille la fleur exquise.

De ses cheveux élastiques et lourds,
Vivant sachet, encensoir de l'alcôve,
Une senteur montait, sauvage et fauve,

Et des habits, mousseline ou velours,
Tout imprégnés de sa jeunesse pure,
Se dégageait un parfum de fourrure.

III
LE CADRE

Comme un beau cadre ajoute à la peinture,
Bien qu'elle soit d'un pinceau très vanté,
Je ne sais quoi d'étrange et d'enchanté
En l'isolant de l'immense nature,

Ainsi bijoux, meubles, métaux, dorure,
S'adaptaient juste à sa rare beauté;
Rien n'offusquait sa parfaite clarté,
Et tout semblait lui servir de bordure.

Même on eût dit parfois qu'elle croyait
Que tout voulait l'aimer; elle noyait
Sa nudité voluptueusement

Dans les baisers du satin et du linge,
Et, lente ou brusque, à chaque mouvement
Montrait la grâce enfantine du singe.

Profound, magical, intoxicating charm
The past in the present restored!
Thus does the lover from a body adored
Pluck the exquisite flower of remembrance.

From her hair heavy and supple,
Living sachet, the alcove's censer,
A fragrance would rise, savage and wild,

And those habits, muslin or velvet,
Pregnant with her pure youth,
Would release a scent of fur.

III
THE FRAME

As a beautiful frame adjoins to the painting,
Even from so esteemed a brush,
Some strange and enchanted quality
By isolating it from immense nature,

Thus jewels, metals, gilt, furniture,
Befitted her rare beauty;
Nothing offending her perfect clarity,
And all seemed to serve her delineation.

Sometimes it seemed as though she believed
The whole world should love her; she would drown
Her nudity voluptuously

In the kisses of satin and of lingerie,
And, slow or sudden, with every movement
Displayed the childlike grace of a monkey.

IV
LE PORTRAIT

La Maladie et la Mort font des cendres
De tout le feu qui pour nous flamboya.
De ces grands yeux si fervents et si tendres,
De cette bouche où mon cœur se noya,

De ces baisers puissants comme un dictame,
De ces transports plus vifs que des rayons,
Que reste-t-il? C'est affreux, ô mon âme!
Rien qu'un dessin fort pâle, aux trois crayons,

Qui, comme moi, meurt dans la solitude,
Et que le Temps, injurieux vieillard,
Chaque jour frotte avec son aile rude...

Noir assassin de la Vie et de l'Art,
Tu ne tueras jamais dans ma mémoire
Celle qui fut mon plaisir et ma gloire!

IV

THE PORTRAIT

Sickness and Death reduce to ashes
All the fire that flamed for us.
Of these wide eyes so fervent and tender,
Of this mouth where my heart would drown,

Of these kisses with power to cure,
Of these transports more vibrant than beams of the sun,
What remains? It is frightful, o my soul!
Nothing but a sketch so pale, in three colors,

Which, like me, perishes in solitude,
And which Time, injurious old man,
Rubs every day with his uncouth wing...

Black assassin of Life and of Art,
Never will you kill within my memory
She who was my pleasure and my glory!

Je te donne ces vers afin que si mon nom
Aborde heureusement aux époques lointaines,
Et fait rêver un soir les cervelles humaines,
Vaisseau favorisé par un grand aquilon,

Ta mémoire, pareille aux fables incertaines,
Fatigue le lecteur ainsi qu'un tympanon,
Et par un fraternel et mystique chaînon
Reste comme pendue à mes rimes hautaines;

Être maudit à qui, de l'abîme profond
Jusqu'au plus haut du ciel, rien, hors moi, ne répond!
— Ô toi qui, comme une ombre à la trace éphémère,

Foules d'un pied léger et d'un regard serein
Les stupides mortels qui t'ont jugée amère,
Statue aux yeux de jais, grand ange au front d'airain!

XXXIX

I give you these verses so that if my name
Comes happily ashore in far off times,
And brings dreams one evening to human brains,
Vessel favored by a great north wind,

Your memory, akin to dubious fables,
Like a dulcimer will weary the reader,
And by a fraternal and mystical chain
Remain as if hanged from my haughty rhymes;

Cursed being to whom, from the deep abyss
To highest heavens, nothing, beyond me, responds!
—O you whom, like a shadow's ephemeral trace,

Tread with light foot and with serene gaze
On the stupid mortals who called you bitter,
Statue with eyes of jet, great angel with brow of bronze!

SEMPER EADEM

« D'où vous vient, disiez-vous, cette tristesse étrange,
Montant comme la mer sur le roc noir et nu? »
— Quand notre cœur a fait une fois sa vendange,
Vivre est un mal. C'est un secret de tous connu,

Une douleur très simple et non mystérieuse,
Et, comme votre joie, éclatante pour tous.
Cessez donc de chercher, ô belle curieuse!
Et, bien que votre voix soit douce, taisez-vous!

Taisez-vous, ignorante! âme toujours ravie!
Bouche au rire enfantin! Plus encor que la Vie,
La Mort nous tient souvent par des liens subtils.

Laissez, laissez mon cœur s'enivrer d'un *mensonge*,
Plonger dans vos beaux yeux comme dans un beau songe,
Et sommeiller longtemps à l'ombre de vos cils!

XL

SEMPER EADEM

"From whence," you said, "this strange sadness,
  Mounting like the sea upon the rock black and bare?"
—When once our heart has plucked its grapes,
  To live is an evil. It is an open secret,

A very simple and hardly mysterious sorrow,
And, like your joy, blindingly obvious.
So call off the search, o curious beauty!
And, though your voice be sweet, shut up!

Shut up, ignoramus! ever delighted soul!
Mouth laughing like a child! More even than Life,
Death often holds us in subtle bonds.

Give leave, give leave to my heart to drink of a *lie*,
To sink into your beautiful eyes as into a beautiful dream,
And to sleep a long time in the shade of your lashes!

TOUT ENTIÈRE

Le Démon, dans ma chambre haute,
Ce matin est venu me voir,
Et, tâchant à me prendre en faute,
Me dit: « Je voudrais bien savoir,

« Parmi toutes les belles choses
Dont est fait son enchantement,
Parmi les objets noirs ou roses
Qui composent son corps charmant,

« Quel est le plus doux. » — Ô mon âme!
Tu répondis à l'Abhorré:
« Puisqu'en Elle tout est dictame,
Rien ne peut être préféré.

« Lorsque tout me ravit, j'ignore
Si quelque chose me séduit.
Elle éblouit comme l'Aurore
Et console comme la Nuit;

« Et l'harmonie est trop exquise,
Qui gouverne tout son beau corps,
Pour que l'impuissante analyse
En note les nombreux accords.

« Ô métamorphose mystique
De tous mes sens fondus en un!
Son haleine fait la musique,
Comme sa voix fait le parfum! »

XLI

ALL ENTIRE

The Demon, in my attic chamber,
Came to see me this morning,
And, trying to catch me at fault,
Said to me: "I would like to know,

"Among all the beautiful things
That comprise her enchantment,
Among those objects black or pink
That compose her charming body,

"Which is the sweetest." —O my soul!
To the Abhorrence you responded:
"Since all of Her is my balm,
Nothing may be preferred.

"When all delights, I do not know
If one thing seduces.
She blooms like Aurora
And consoles like Night;

"And too exquisite is the harmony,
Which governs her whole beautiful body,
For impotent analysis
To note the numerous chords.

"O mystical metamorphosis
Of all my senses fused in one!
Her breath makes music,
As her voice makes perfume!"

Que diras-tu ce soir, pauvre âme solitaire,
Que diras-tu, mon cœur, cœur autrefois flétri,
À la très belle, à la très bonne, à la très chère,
Dont le regard divin t'a soudain refleuri?

— Nous mettrons notre orgueil à chanter ses louanges:
Rien ne vaut la douceur de son autorité;
Sa chair spirituelle a le parfum des Anges,
Et son œil nous revêt d'un habit de clarté.

Que ce soit dans la nuit et dans la solitude,
Que ce soit dans la rue et dans la multitude,
Son fantôme dans l'air danse comme un flambeau.

Parfois il parle et dit: « Je suis belle, et j'ordonne
Que pour l'amour de moi vous n'aimiez que le Beau;
Je suis l'Ange gardien, la Muse et la Madone. »

What will you say this evening, poor solitary soul,
What will you say, my heart, once withered heart,
To her so lovely, so good, so dear,
Whose divine gaze makes you bloom once more?

—We put on our pride to sing her these praises:
Nothing matches the ease of her authority;
Her spiritual flesh has the fragrance of Angels,
And her eye arrays us in a habit of light.

Whether in the night and in solitude,
Whether in the street and the multitude,
Her phantom dances in the air like a torch.

Sometimes it speaks and says: "I am beautiful, and I ordain
That for love of me you love only Beauty;
I am guardian Angel, Madonna and Muse."

LE FLAMBEAU VIVANT

Ils marchent devant moi, ces Yeux pleins de lumières,
Qu'un Ange très savant a sans doute aimantés;
Ils marchent, ces divins frères qui sont mes frères,
Secouant dans mes yeux leurs feux diamantés.

Me sauvant de tout piège et de tout péché grave,
Ils conduisent mes pas dans la route du Beau;
Ils sont mes serviteurs et je suis leur esclave;
Tout mon être obéit à ce vivant flambeau.

Charmants Yeux, vous brillez de la clarté mystique
Qu'ont les cierges brûlant en plein jour; le soleil
Rougit, mais n'éteint pas leur flamme fantastique;

Ils célèbrent la Mort, vous chantez le Réveil;
Vous marchez en chantant le réveil de mon âme,
Astres dont nul soleil ne peut flétrir la flamme!

XLIII

THE LIVING TORCH

They go before me, these luminous Eyes,
By a cunning Angel no doubt magnetized;
They go, divine brothers who are brothers of mine,
Flashing into my eyes their fire diamantine.

They deliver me from snares and from all deadly sins,
They lead my steps down the path of Beauty;
They are my servants and I am their slave;
All I am obeys this living torch.

Lovely Eyes, with mystical clarity you shine
As votives burn in the fullness of day; the sun
Turns red, yet unfaded is your fantastic flame;

They celebrate Death, you sing the Reveil;
As you go you sing the reveil of my soul,
Stars whose flame no sun can subdue!

À CELLE QUI EST TROP GAIE

Ta tête, ton geste, ton air
Sont beaux comme un beau paysage;
Le rire joue en ton visage
Comme un vent frais dans un ciel clair.

Le passant chagrin que tu frôles
Est ébloui par la santé
Qui jaillit comme une clarté
De tes bras et de tes épaules.

Les retentissantes couleurs
Dont tu parsèmes tes toilettes
Jettent dans l'esprit des poètes
L'image d'un ballet de fleurs.

Ces robes folles sont l'emblème
De ton esprit bariolé;
Folle dont je suis affolé,
Je te hais autant que je t'aime!

Quelquefois dans un beau jardin
Où je traînais mon atonie,
J'ai senti, comme une ironie,
Le soleil déchirer mon sein;

Et le printemps et la verdure
Ont tant humilié mon cœur,
Que j'ai puni sur une fleur
L'insolence de la Nature.

TO SHE WHO IS TOO GAY

Your head, your gesture, your air
Are beautiful as a beautiful landscape;
Laughter plays in your face
Like a fresh breeze in a clear sky.

The troubled passerby you graze
Is dazzled by the health
That bursts like a ray of light
From your arms and your shoulders.

The resounding colors
With which you sprinkle your toilette
Sow in the mind of poets
The image of a ballet of flowers.

These wild dresses are the emblem
Of your motley spirit;
Madwoman who drives me crazy,
I hate you as much as I love you!

Sometimes in a beautiful garden
Where I would drag my atony,
I have felt, like an irony,
The sun rend my breast;

And the spring and the verdure
So humiliated my heart,
That I punished a flower
For the insolence of Nature.

Ainsi je voudrais, une nuit,
Quand l'heure des voluptés sonne,
Vers les trésors de ta personne,
Comme un lâche, ramper sans bruit,

Pour châtier ta chair joyeuse,
Pour meurtrir ton sein pardonné,
Et faire à ton flanc étonné
Une blessure large et creuse,

Et, vertigineuse douceur!
À travers ces lèvres nouvelles,
Plus éclatantes et plus belles,
T'infuser mon venin, ma sœur!

Thus would I, one night,
When the sensual hour sounds,
Toward the treasures of your person,
Like a coward, creep silently,

To chasten your joyous flesh,
To bruise your pardoned breast,
And to carve in your unsuspecting side
A wide and hollow wound,

And, vertiginous softness!
Through those novice lips,
More gleaming and more beautiful,
To infuse my venom, my sister!

RÉVERSIBILITÉ

Ange plein de gaieté, connaissez-vous l'angoisse,
La honte, les remords, les sanglots, les ennuis,
Et les vagues terreurs de ces affreuses nuits
Qui compriment le cœur comme un papier qu'on froisse?
Ange plein de gaieté, connaissez-vous l'angoisse?

Ange plein de bonté, connaissez-vous la haine,
Les poings crispés dans l'ombre et les larmes de fiel,
Quand la Vengeance bat son infernal rappel,
Et de nos facultés se fait le capitaine?
Ange plein de bonté, connaissez-vous la haine?

Ange plein de santé, connaissez-vous les Fièvres,
Qui, le long des grands murs de l'hospice blafard,
Comme des exilés, s'en vont d'un pied traînard,
Cherchant le soleil rare et remuant les lèvres?
Ange plein de santé, connaissez-vous les Fièvres?

Ange plein de beauté, connaissez-vous les rides,
Et la peur de vieillir, et ce hideux tourment
De lire la secrète horreur du dévouement
Dans des yeux où longtemps burent nos yeux avide?
Ange plein de beauté, connaissez-vous les rides?

Ange plein de bonheur, de joie et de lumières,
David mourant aurait demandé la santé
Aux émanations de ton corps enchanté;
Mais de toi je n'implore, ange, que tes prières,
Ange plein de bonheur, de joie et de lumières!

REVERSIBILITY

Angel of mirth, do you know anguish,
The shame, the regret, the sobs, the ennui,
And the vague terrors of those awful nights
That crush the heart like a crumpled page?
Angel of mirth, do you know anguish?

Angel of grace, do you know hate,
The fists clenched in shadow and the bitter tears,
When Vengeance beats its infernal refrain,
And captains the ship of our faculties?
Angel of grace, do you know hate?

Angel of health, do you know Fevers,
Which, along the great walls of the pallid hospice,
Like exiles, go with a dragging foot,
Seeking scarce sun and making lips quiver?
Angel of health, do you know Fevers?

Angel of beauty, do you know wrinkles,
And the fear of old age, and the hideous torment
Of reading the secret horror of devotion
In eyes where our avid eyes once drank?
Angel of beauty, do you know wrinkles?

Angel of happiness, of joy and of light,
David dying would have pleaded for health
From emanations of your enchanted body;
But I ask of you nothing, angel, but your prayers,
Angel of happiness, of joy and of light!

CONFESSION

Une fois, une seule, aimable et douce femme,
    À mon bras votre bras poli
S'appuya (sur le fond ténébreux de mon âme
    Ce souvenir n'est point pâli);

Il était tard; ainsi qu'une médaille neuve
    La pleine lune s'étalait,
Et la solennité de la nuit, comme un fleuve,
    Sur Paris dormant ruisselait.

Et le long des maisons, sous les portes cochères,
    Des chats passaient furtivement,
L'oreille au guet, ou bien, comme des ombres chères,
    Nous accompagnaient lentement.

Tout à coup, au milieu de l'intimité libre
    Éclose à la pâle clarté,
De vous, riche et sonore instrument où ne vibre
    Que la radieuse gaieté,

De vous, claire et joyeuse ainsi qu'une fanfare
    Dans le matin étincelant,
Une note plaintive, une note bizarre
    S'échappa, tout en chancelant

Comme une enfant chétive, horrible, sombre, immonde,
    Dont sa famille rougirait,
Et qu'elle aurait longtemps, pour la cacher au monde,
    Dans un caveau mise au secret.

XLV

CONFESSION

One time, once, kind and gentle woman,
      On my arm your smooth arm
Leaned (on the tenebrous ground of my soul
      This memory has not faded);

It was late; like a new medallion
      The full moon glowed,
And the solemnity of the night, like a river,
      Poured upon sleeping Paris.

And along the houses, under the carriage gates,
      The cats passed furtively,
Ears on guard, or, like cherished shadows,
      Accompanied us slowly.

Suddenly, amid the easy intimacy
      Hatched by the milky light,
From you, rich and sonorous instrument where vibrates
      Only radiant cheer,

From you, clear and joyous as a fanfare
      In the sparkling morning air,
A plaintive note, a strange note
      Escaped, faltering

Like a sickly, horrible, dark, dirty child
      Who would make her family blush,
And had long since, hidden from the world,
      Been kept in a secret cellar.

Pauvre ange, elle chantait, votre note criarde:
                « Que rien ici-bas n'est certain,
Et que toujours, avec quelque soin qu'il se farde,
                Se trahit l'égoïsme humain;

« Que c'est un dur métier que d'être belle femme,
                Et que c'est le travail banal
De la danseuse folle et froide qui se pâme
                Dans son sourire machinal;

« Que bâtir sur les cœurs est une chose sotte;
                Que tout craque, amour et beauté,
Jusqu'à ce que l'Oubli les jette dans sa hotte
                Pour les rendre à l'Éternité! »

J'ai souvent évoqué cette lune enchantée,
                Ce silence et cette langueur,
Et cette confidence horrible chuchotée
                Au confessionnal du cœur.

Poor angel, she sang, your piercing note:
      "How nothing on earth is certain,
And however carefully made up, always,
      Human egoism betrays itself;

"What hard work it is to be a beautiful woman,
      And how banal the labor
Of the cold and demented dancer who swoons
      In her machinic smile;

"How stupid it is to take things to heart;
      How things fall apart, love and beauty,
Until Oblivion throws them in his sack
      To give them back to Eternity!"

I have often recalled that enchanted moon,
      That languor and that silence,
And that horrible whispered confidence
      At the confessional of the heart.

L'AUBE SPIRITUELLE

Quand chez les débauchés l'aube blanche et vermeille
Entre en société de l'Idéal rongeur,
Par l'opération d'un mystère vengeur
Dans la brute assoupie un ange se réveille.

Des Cieux Spirituels l'inaccessible azur,
Pour l'homme terrassé qui rêve encore et souffre,
S'ouvre et s'enfonce avec l'attirance du gouffre.
Ainsi, chère Déesse, Être lucide et pur,

Sur les débris fumeux des stupides orgies
Ton souvenir plus clair, plus rose, plus charmant,
À mes yeux agrandis voltige incessamment.

Le soleil a noirci la flamme des bougies;
Ainsi, toujours vainqueur, ton fantôme est pareil,
Âme resplendissante, à l'immortel soleil!

SPIRITUAL DAWN

When among the debauchees white and vermillion dawn
Enters in league with the gnawing Ideal,
By means of some avenging mystery
In the dozing brute an angel awakes.

The inaccessible azure of those Spiritual Heavens,
For the fallen man who still dreams and suffers,
Opens and sinks with a maelstrom's tow.
Thus, dear Goddess, Being lucid and pure,

Upon the smoking debris of stupid orgies
Your memory more lovely, more rosy, more clear,
Incessantly flutters before my wide eyes.

The sun has blackened the candles' flame;
Thus, ever the victor, your shade is the same,
Resplendent soul, as the immortal sun!

HARMONIE DU SOIR

Voici venir les temps où vibrant sur sa tige
Chaque fleur s'évapore ainsi qu'un encensoir;
Les sons et les parfums tournent dans l'air du soir;
Valse mélancolique et langoureux vertige!

Chaque fleur s'évapore ainsi qu'un encensoir;
Le violon frémit comme un cœur qu'on afflige;
Valse mélancolique et langoureux vertige!
Le ciel est triste et beau comme un grand reposoir.

Le violon frémit comme un cœur qu'on afflige,
Un cœur tendre, qui hait le néant vaste et noir!
Le ciel est triste et beau comme un grand reposoir;
Le soleil s'est noyé dans son sang qui se fige.

Un cœur tendre, qui hait le néant vaste et noir,
Du passé lumineux recueille tout vestige!
Le soleil s'est noyé dans son sang qui se fige.....
Ton souvenir en moi luit comme un ostensoir!

EVENING HARMONY

Comes the time when stirring on its stem
Every flower diffuses like a censer;
Sounds and scents turn in the evening air;
Melancholy waltz and languorous vertigo!

Every flower diffuses like a censer;
The violin quivers like an afflicted heart;
Melancholy waltz and languorous vertigo!
The sky handsome and sad like a great altar.

The violin quivers like an afflicted heart,
A tender heart, which hates the vast and black nothing!
The sky handsome and sad like a great altar;
The sun has drowned in its drying blood.

A tender heart, which hates the vast and black nothing,
Recollects all vestige of luminous past!
The sun has drowned in its drying blood.....
Your memory gleams within me like a monstrance!

LE FLACON

II est de forts parfums pour qui toute matière
Est poreuse. On dirait qu'ils pénètrent le verre.
En ouvrant un coffret venu de l'Orient
Dont la serrure grince et rechigne en criant,

Ou dans une maison déserte quelque armoire
Pleine de l'âcre odeur des temps, poudreuse et noire,
Parfois on trouve un vieux flacon qui se souvient,
D'où jaillit toute vive une âme qui revient.

Mille pensers dormaient, chrysalides funèbres,
Frémissant doucement dans les lourdes ténèbres,
Qui dégagent leur aile et prennent leur essor,
Teintés d'azur, glacés de rose, lamés d'or.

Voilà le souvenir enivrant qui voltige
Dans l'air troublé; les yeux se ferment; le Vertige
Saisit l'âme vaincue et la pousse à deux mains
Vers un gouffre obscurci de miasmes humains;

II la terrasse au bord d'un gouffre séculaire,
Où, Lazare odorant déchirant son suaire,
Se meut dans son réveil le cadavre spectral
D'un vieil amour ranci, charmant et sépulcral.

Ainsi, quand je serai perdu dans la mémoire
Des hommes, dans le coin d'une sinistre armoire
Quand on m'aura jeté, vieux flacon désolé,
Décrépit, poudreux, sale, abject, visqueux, fêlé,

THE FLASK

There are powerful perfumes to which all matter
Is porous. They seem to penetrate glass.
While opening a coffer come from the Orient
Whose lock creaks and frowns in complaint,

Or some armoire in a deserted house
Full of time's acrid odor, dusty and black,
Sometimes one finds an old flask of remembrance,
From which springs quite alive a revenant soul.

A thousand sleeping thoughts, funereal chrysalides,
Rustling softly in heavy shadows,
Spread their wings and take flight,
Tints of azure, leaves of gold, glazes of rose.

Here is the intoxicating memory that flutters
In the troubled air; the eyes close; Vertigo
Grips the vanquished soul and shoves it with both hands
Toward a murky chasm of human miasmas.

He casts it to the edge of an ancient chasm,
Where, reeking Lazarus tearing his shroud,
There stirs as it wakes the spectral cadaver
Of a rancid old love, charming and sepulchral.

Just so, when I am lost in the memory
Of men, when into the corner of some sinister armoire
One has cast me, old desolate flask,
Decrepit, dusty, dirty, abject, viscous, cracked,

Je serai ton cercueil, aimable pestilence!
Le témoin de ta force et de ta virulence,
Cher poison préparé par les anges! liqueur
Qui me ronge, ô la vie et la mort de mon cœur!

I shall be your casket, loveable pestilence!
The testament of your force and your virulence,
Dear poison prepared by angels! liquor
That devours me, o the life and the death of my heart!

LE POISON

Le vin sait revêtir le plus sordide bouge
      D'un luxe miraculeux,
Et fait surgir plus d'un portique fabuleux
      Dans l'or de sa vapeur rouge,
Comme un soleil couchant dans un ciel nébuleux.

L'opium agrandit ce qui n'a pas de bornes,
      Allonge l'illimité,
Approfondit le temps, creuse la volupté,
      Et de plaisirs noirs et mornes
Remplit l'âme au-delà de sa capacité.

Tout cela ne vaut pas le poison qui découle
      De tes yeux, de tes yeux verts,
Lacs où mon âme tremble et se voit à l'envers...
      Mes songes viennent en foule
Pour se désaltérer à ces gouffres amers.

Tout cela ne vaut pas le terrible prodige
      De ta salive qui mord,
Qui plonge dans l'oubli mon âme sans remords,
      Et, charriant le vertige,
La roule défaillante aux rives de la mort!

POISON

Wine knows how to array the most sordid hovel
      In miraculous luxury,
It makes many a fabulous portico appear
      In the gold of its red haze,
Like a setting sun in a nebulous sky.

Opium enlarges that which has no bounds,
      Extends the unlimited,
Ungrounds time, hollows the voluptuous,
      And with pleasures black and bleak
Fills the soul to overflowing.

All this is not worth the poison that seeps
      From your eyes, from your green eyes,
Lakes where my soul trembles and sees its inversion...
      My dreams come crowding in
To slake their thirst on these bitter gulfs.

All this is not worth the terrible prodigy
      Of your saliva that corrodes,
That plunges my soul remorselessly into oblivion,
      And charioting vertigo,
Rolls it falteringly to the shores of death!

CIEL BROUILLÉ

On dirait ton regard d'une vapeur couvert;
Ton œil mystérieux (est-il bleu, gris ou vert?)
Alternativement tendre, rêveur, cruel,
Réfléchit l'indolence et la pâleur du ciel.

Tu rappelles ces jours blancs, tièdes et voilés,
Qui font se fondre en pleurs les cœurs ensorcelés,
Quand, agités d'un mal inconnu qui les tord,
Les nerfs trop éveillés raillent l'esprit qui dort.

Tu ressembles parfois à ces beaux horizons
Qu'allument les soleils des brumeuses saisons.....
Comme tu resplendis, paysage mouillé
Qu'enflamment les rayons tombant d'un ciel brouillé!

Ô femme dangereuse, ô séduisants climats!
Adorerai-je aussi ta neige et vos frimas,
Et saurai-je tirer de l'implacable hiver
Des plaisirs plus aigus que la glace et le fer?

HAZY SKY

Your gaze as if overcast with mist;
Your mysterious eye (blue, grey or green?)
Alternately tender, dreamy, cruel,
Reflects the indolence and the pallor of the sky.

You recall those colorless days, tepid and veiled,
That melt ensorcelled hearts to tears,
When, troubled and twisted by an unknown evil,
The wakeful nerves mock the spirit that sleeps.

Sometimes you resemble those beautiful horizons
That the sun sets alight in foggy seasons.....
Resplendent like you, lachrymose landscape
Aflame with falling rays from a hazy sky!

O dangerous woman, o seductive climes!
Will I adore as well your snow and your frost,
And will I know how to draw from implacable winter
Those pleasures more piercing than iron or ice?

LE CHAT

I

Dans ma cervelle se promène,
Ainsi qu'en son appartement,
Un beau chat, fort, doux et charmant.
Quand il miaule, on l'entend à peine,

Tant son timbre est tendre et discret;
Mais que sa voix s'apaise ou gronde,
Elle est toujours riche et profonde.
C'est là son charme et son secret.

Cette voix, qui perle et qui filtre
Dans mon fonds le plus ténébreux,
Me remplit comme un vers nombreux
Et me réjouit comme un philtre.

Elle endort les plus cruels maux
Et contient toutes les extases;
Pour dire les plus longues phrases,
Elle n'a pas besoin de mots.

Non, il n'est pas d'archet qui morde
Sur mon cœur, parfait instrument,
Et fasse plus royalement
Chanter sa plus vibrante corde,

Que ta voix, chat mystérieux,
Chat séraphique, chat étrange,
En qui tout est, comme en un ange,
Aussi subtil qu'harmonieux!

LI

THE CAT

I

In my brain there strolls,
As if in his apartment,
A beautiful cat, strong, soft and charming.
When he meows, one hardly hears,

His timbre is so tender and discrete;
But whether his voice would soothe or scold,
It is always rich and profound.
Therein lies his charm and his secret.

This voice, that purls and filters
Into my most tenebrous depths,
Fulfills me like a measured verse
And revives me like a philter.

It allays the cruelest illnesses
And it contains all ecstasies;
To say the longest sentences,
It has no need of words.

No, there is no bow that bites
My heart, perfect instrument,
And makes more royally
Sing its most vibrant string,

Than your voice, mysterious cat,
Seraphic cat, strange cat,
In whom everything is, like an angel,
As harmonious as subtle!

II

De sa fourrure blonde et brune
Sort un parfum si doux, qu'un soir
J'en fus embaumé, pour l'avoir
Caressée une fois, rien qu'une.

C'est l'esprit familier du lieu;
Il juge, il préside, il inspire
Toutes choses dans son empire;
Peut-être est-il fée, est-il dieu?

Quand mes yeux, vers ce chat que j'aime
Tirés comme par un aimant,
Se retournent docilement
Et que je regarde en moi-même,

Je vois avec étonnement
Le feu de ses prunelles pâles,
Clairs fanaux, vivantes opales,
Qui me contemplent fixement.

II

From his blond and brown fur
Comes a scent so soft, that one evening
I was embalmed, by
One caress, just one.

He is the familiar spirit of this place;
He judges, he presides, he inspires
All things are within his empire;
Perhaps he is a fairy, is he a god?

When my eyes, turned to this cat I love
As if by a lover drawn,
With docility turn back
So that I look into myself,

I see with astonishment
The fire of his pellucid eyes,
Clear lamps, living opals,
That fix me in contemplation.

LE BEAU NAVIRE

Je veux te raconter, ô molle enchanteresse!
Les diverses beautés qui parent ta jeunesse;
     Je veux te peindre ta beauté,
Où l'enfance s'allie à la maturité.

Quand tu vas balayant l'air de ta jupe large,
Tu fais l'effet d'un beau vaisseau qui prend le large,
     Chargé de toile, et va roulant
Suivant un rythme doux, et paresseux, et lent.

Sur ton cou large et rond, sur tes épaules grasses,
Ta tête se pavane avec d'étranges grâces;
     D'un air placide et triomphant
Tu passes ton chemin, majestueuse enfant.

Je veux te raconter, ô molle enchanteresse!
Les diverses beautés qui parent ta jeunesse;
     Je veux te peindre ta beauté,
Où l'enfance s'allie à la maturité.

Ta gorge qui s'avance et qui pousse la moire,
Ta gorge triomphante est une belle armoire
     Dont les panneaux bombés et clairs
Comme les boucliers accrochent des éclairs;

Boucliers provoquants, armés de pointes roses!
Armoire à doux secrets, pleine de bonnes choses,
     De vins, de parfums, de liqueurs
Qui feraient délirer les cerveaux et les cœurs!

THE BEAUTIFUL SHIP

I would recite to you, o soft enchantress!
The diverse beauties that attend your youth;
  I would paint for you your beauty,
Where childhood joins maturity.

When you sweep through the air with your open skirt,
You seem like a ship that sets to sea,
  With billowed sail, and swaying along
In a rhythm mild, and lazy, and slow.

On your ample round neck, on your shoulders plump,
Your head pavanes with a curious grace;
  With a placid and triumphant air
You make your way, majestic child.

I would recite to you, o soft enchantress!
The diverse beauties that attend your youth;
  I would paint for you your beauty,
Where childhood joins maturity.

Your bosom that rises and presses the moire,
Your triumphant bosom is a gorgeous armoire
  Of panels curved and clear
Like shields that catch the light;

Provocative shields armed with pink points!
Armoire of sweet secrets, full of fine things,
  Of wine, of perfumes, of liqueurs
That would intoxicate both brains and hearts!

Quand tu vas balayant l'air de ta jupe large,
Tu fais l'effet d'un beau vaisseau qui prend le large,
   Chargé de toile, et va roulant
Suivant un rythme doux, et paresseux, et lent.

Tes nobles jambes, sous les volants qu'elles chassent,
Tourmentent les désirs obscurs et les agacent,
   Comme deux sorcières qui font
Tourner un philtre noir dans un vase profond.

Tes bras, qui se joueraient des précoces hercules,
Sont des boas luisants les solides émules,
   Faits pour serrer obstinément,
Comme pour l'imprimer dans ton cœur, ton amant.

Sur ton cou large et rond, sur tes épaules grasses,
Ta tête se pavane avec d'étranges grâces;
   D'un air placide et triomphant
Tu passes ton chemin, majestueuse enfant.

When you sweep through the air with your open skirt,
You seem like a ship that sets to sea,
　　　　With billowed sail, and swaying along
In a rhythm mild, and lazy, and slow.

Your noble legs, under flounces they chase,
Torment and tease obscure desires,
　　　　Like two witches who
Stir a black philter in a deep vase.

Your arms, which could play a precocious Hercules,
Are worthy rivals of glistening boas,
　　　　Made for clinging obstinately,
As if to stamp in your heart, your lover.

On your ample round neck, on your shoulders plump,
Your head pavanes with a curious grace;
　　　　With a placid and triumphant air
You make your way, majestic child.

L'INVITATION AU VOYAGE

Mon enfant, ma sœur,
Songe à la douceur
D'aller là-bas vivre ensemble!
Aimer à loisir,
Aimer et mourir
Au pays qui te ressemble!
Les soleils mouillés
De ces ciels brouillés
Pour mon esprit ont les charmes
Si mystérieux
De tes traîtres yeux,
Brillant à travers leurs larmes.

Là, tout n'est qu'ordre et beauté,
Luxe, calme et volupté.

Des meubles luisants,
Polis par les ans,
Décoreraient notre chambre;
Les plus rares fleurs
Mêlant leurs odeurs
Aux vagues senteurs de l'ambre,
Les riches plafonds,
Les miroirs profonds,
La splendeur orientale,
Tout y parlerait
À l'âme en secret
Sa douce langue natale.

Là, tout n'est qu'ordre et beauté,
Luxe, calme et volupté.

INVITATION TO THE VOYAGE

My child, my sister
Imagine the sweetness
Of going there to live together!
To love at leisure,
To love and to die
In a land resembling yourself!
The misty suns
Of those hazy skies
Have for me the charms
So mysterious
Of your dissembling eyes,
Shining through your tears.

There, all is order and beauty,
Pleasure, calm and luxury.

Gleaming furnishings,
Polished by the years,
Would decorate our chamber;
The rarest flowers
Mingling their scents
With the faint fragrance of amber,
The lavish ceilings,
The fathomless mirrors,
The oriental splendor,
All would speak
To the soul in secret
Its soothing native tongue.

There, all is order and beauty,
Pleasure, calm and luxury.

Vois sur ces canaux
Dormir ces vaisseaux
Dont l'humeur est vagabonde;
C'est pour assouvir
Ton moindre désir
Qu'ils viennent du bout du monde.
— Les soleils couchants
Revêtent les champs,
Les canaux, la ville entière,
D'hyacinthe et d'or;
Le monde s'endort
Dans une chaude lumière.

Là, tout n'est qu'ordre et beauté,
Luxe, calme et volupté.

See on these canals
These ships asleep
Whose humor is to wander;
It's to satisfy
Your least desire
That they come from the ends of the earth.
—The setting suns
Adorn the fields
The canals, the city entire,
With hyacinth and gold;
The world drifts off
Amid warm illumination.

There, all is order and beauty,
Pleasure, calm and luxury.

L'IRRÉPARABLE

Pouvons-nous étouffer le vieux, le long Remords,
       Qui vit, s'agite et se tortille,
Et se nourrit de nous comme le ver des morts,
       Comme du chêne la chenille?
Pouvons-nous étouffer l'implacable Remords?

Dans quel philtre, dans quel vin, dans quelle tisane,
       Noierons-nous ce vieil ennemi,
Destructeur et gourmand comme la courtisane,
       Patient comme la fourmi?
Dans quel philtre? — dans quel vin? — dans quelle tisane?

Dis-le, belle sorcière, oh! dis, si tu le sais,
       À cet esprit comblé d'angoisse
Et pareil au mourant qu'écrasent les blessés,
       Que le sabot du cheval froisse,
Dis-le, belle sorcière, oh! dis, si tu le sais,

À cet agonisant que le loup déjà flaire
       Et que surveille le corbeau,
À ce soldat brisé! s'il faut qu'il désespère
       D'avoir sa croix et son tombeau;
Ce pauvre agonisant que déjà le loup flaire!

Peut-on illuminer un ciel bourbeux et noir?
       Peut-on déchirer des ténèbres
Plus denses que la poix, sans matin et sans soir,
       Sans astres, sans éclairs funèbres?
Peut-on illuminer un ciel bourbeux et noir?

THE IRREPARABLE

Can we stifle the old, the long Remorse,
　　　Which lives, writhing and twisting,
And feeds upon us like the worm upon the dead,
　　　Like the canker upon the oak?
Can we stifle the implacable Remorse?

In what philter, what wine, in what tisane,
　　　Shall we drown this ancient enemy,
Destructive and gluttonous as the courtesan,
　　　Patient as the ant?
In what philter? —in what wine? —in what tisane?

Say, lovely witch, oh! say, if you know,
　　　To this spirit wracked with anguish
Like a dying man whom the wounded crush,
　　　Trampled by the horse's hoof,
Say, lovely witch, oh! say, if you know,

To this dying man whom the wolf has sniffed
　　　And the raven now surveys,
To this broken soldier! if he must despair
　　　Of having his cross and his tomb;
To this dying man whom the wolf has sniffed!

May we light up a black and muddy sky?
　　　May we pierce the darkness
More dense than pitch, without dawn and without dusk,
　　　Without stars, without funereal flashes?
May we light up a black and muddy sky?

L'Espérance qui brille aux carreaux de l'Auberge
  Est soufflée, est morte à jamais!
Sans lune et sans rayons, trouver où l'on héberge
  Les martyrs d'un chemin mauvais!
Le Diable a tout éteint aux carreaux de l'Auberge!

Adorable sorcière, aimes-tu les damnés?
  Dis, connais-tu l'irrémissible?
Connais-tu le Remords, aux traits empoisonnés,
  À qui notre cœur sert de cible?
Adorable sorcière, aimes-tu les damnés?

L'Irréparable ronge avec sa dent maudite
  Notre âme, piteux monument,
Et souvent il attaque ainsi que le termite,
  Par la base le bâtiment.
L'Irréparable ronge avec sa dent maudite!

— J'ai vu parfois, au fond d'un théâtre banal
  Qu'enflammait l'orchestre sonore,
Une fée allumer dans un ciel infernal
  Une miraculeuse aurore;
J'ai vu parfois au fond d'un théâtre banal

Un être, qui n'était que lumière, or et gaze,
  Terrasser l'énorme Satan;
Mais mon cœur, que jamais ne visite l'extase,
  Est un théâtre où l'on attend
Toujours, toujours en vain, l'Être aux ailes de gaze!

The Hope that shines in the panes of the Inn
            Is snuffed, is forever dead!
No moon and no beams, to show us shelter
            Martyrs of a twisted path!
The Devil has darkened the panes of the Inn!

Adorable witch, do you love the damned?
            Say, do you know the irremissible?
Do you know the Regrets, with poisoned tips,
            For which our hearts are targets?
Adorable witch, do you love the damned?

The Irreparable gnaws with its damnable teeth
            Our soul, this piteous monument,
And it often attacks as a termite does,
            The building through its base.
The Irreparable gnaws with its damnable teeth!

—I have sometimes seen, back a common stage
            Enflamed by the orchestra's din,
A fairy light up a hellish sky
            A miraculous aurora;
I have sometimes seen back a common stage

A being, of nothing but light, gold or gauze,
            Overthrow enormous Satan;
But my heart, which ecstasy never visits,
            Is a theater where one awaits
Always, always in vain, the Being with wings of gauze!

CAUSERIE

Vous êtes un beau ciel d'automne, clair et rose!
Mais la tristesse en moi monte comme la mer,
Et laisse, en refluant, sur ma lèvre morose
Le souvenir cuisant de son limon amer.

— Ta main se glisse en vain sur mon sein qui se pâme;
Ce qu'elle cherche, amie, est un lieu saccagé
Par la griffe et la dent féroce de la femme.
Ne cherchez plus mon cœur; les bêtes l'ont mangé.

Mon cœur est un palais flétri par la cohue;
On s'y soûle, on s'y tue, on s'y prend aux cheveux!
— Un parfum nage autour de votre gorge nue!...

Ô Beauté, dur fléau des âmes, tu le veux!
Avec tes yeux de feu, brillants comme des fêtes,
Calcine ces lambeaux qu'ont épargnés les bêtes!

CHIT-CHAT

You are a beautiful autumn sky, clear and pink!
But sadness rises in me like the sea,
And leaves, receding, on my morose lip
The burning memory of its bitter silt.

—Your hand glides in vain on my swooning breast;
What it seeks, my love, is a place laid waste
By woman's ferocious tooth and claw.
Look no more for my heart; it was eaten by beasts.

My heart is a palace debased by the rabble;
Where they booze, and they kill, and they tear out hair!
—A scent swims round your throat laid bare!...

O Beauty, hard scourge of souls, have your will!
With your eyes of fire, dazzling as feasts,
Calcine these scraps that were spared by the beasts!

CHANT D'AUTUMNE

I

Bientôt nous plongerons dans les froides ténèbres;
Adieu, vive clarté de nos étés trop courts!
J'entends déjà tomber avec des chocs funèbres
Le bois retentissant sur le pavé des cours.

Tout l'hiver va rentrer dans mon être: colère,
Haine, frissons, horreur, labeur dur et forcé,
Et, comme le soleil dans son enfer polaire,
Mon cœur ne sera plus qu'un bloc rouge et glacé.

J'écoute en frémissant chaque bûche qui tombe;
L'échafaud qu'on bâtit n'a pas d'écho plus sourd.
Mon esprit est pareil à la tour qui succombe
Sous les coups du bélier infatigable et lourd.

Il me semble, bercé par ce choc monotone,
Qu'on cloue en grande hâte un cercueil quelque part.
Pour qui? — C'était hier l'été; voici l'automne!
Ce bruit mystérieux sonne comme un départ.

II

J'aime de vos longs yeux la lumière verdâtre,
Douce beauté, mais tout aujourd'hui m'est amer,
Et rien, ni votre amour, ni le boudoir, ni l'âtre,
Ne me vaut le soleil rayonnant sur la mer.

SONG OF AUTUMN

I

Soon we will plunge into frigid shadows;
Farewell, living light of our too brief summers!
Already I hear fall with deadening thuds
The wood resounding on courtyard cobbles.

The whole of winter will enter my being: wrath,
Hatred, shivers, horror, forced and hard labor,
And, like the sun in its polar hell,
My heart will be naught but a frozen red block.

I hear with a shudder each log that falls;
No echo more muffled from the scaffold we build.
My spirit is akin to the tower that succumbs
To the tireless blows of the battering ram.

It seems to me, lulled by this monotone thud,
That a coffin is being nailed in great haste.
For whom? —Yesterday it was summer; autumn is here!
Like the ring of departure this mysterious sound.

II

I love the greenish light of your almond eyes,
Gentle beauty, but today all seems bitter,
And nothing, not your love, nor our bed, nor the hearth,
Could I cherish as the sun shining upon the sea.

Et pourtant aimez-moi, tendre cœur! soyez mère,
Même pour un ingrat, même pour un méchant;
Amante ou sœur, soyez la douceur éphémère
D'un glorieux automne ou d'un soleil couchant.

Courte tâche! La tombe attend; elle est avide!
Ah! laissez-moi, mon front posé sur vos genoux,
Goûter, en regrettant l'été blanc et torride,
De l'arrière-saison le rayon jaune et doux!

Yet love me, tender heart! be my mother,
Even for an ingrate, even for a brat;
Lover or sister, be the ephemeral sweetness
Of a glorious autumn or a setting sun.

Brief task! The tomb waits; it is hungry!
Ah! give me leave, my brow pressed on your knees,
To taste, while missing the pale torrid summer,
The soft yellow light of the latest season.

À UNE MADONE

Ex-Voto dans le goût Espagnol

Je veux bâtir pour toi, Madone, ma maîtresse,
Un autel souterrain au fond de ma détresse,
Et creuser dans le coin le plus noir de mon cœur,
Loin du désir mondain et du regard moqueur,
Une niche, d'azur et d'or tout émaillée,
Où tu te dresseras, Statue émerveillée.
Avec mes Vers polis, treillis d'un pur métal
Savamment constellé de rimes de cristal,
Je ferai pour ta tête une énorme Couronne;
Et dans ma Jalousie, ô mortelle Madone,
Je saurai te tailler un Manteau, de façon
Barbare, roide et lourd, et doublé de soupçon,
Qui, comme une guérite, enfermera tes charmes;
Non de Perles brodé, mais de toutes mes Larmes!
Ta Robe, ce sera mon Désir, frémissant,
Onduleux, mon Désir qui monte et qui descend,
Aux pointes se balance, aux vallons se repose,
Et revêt d'un baiser tout ton corps blanc et rose.
Je te ferai de mon Respect de beaux Souliers
De satin, par tes pieds divins humiliés,
Qui, les emprisonnant dans une molle étreinte,
Comme un moule fidèle en garderont l'empreinte.
Si je ne puis, malgré tout mon art diligent,
Pour Marchepied tailler une Lune d'argent,
Je mettrai le Serpent qui me mord les entrailles
Sous tes talons, afin que tu foules et railles,
Reine victorieuse et féconde en rachats,
Ce monstre tout gonflé de haine et de crachats.
Tu verras mes Pensers, rangés comme les Cierges

TO A MADONNA

Ex-Voto in the Spanish Style

I would build for you, Madonna, my mistress,
An underground altar deep within my distress,
And dig into the blackest corner of my heart,
Far from mocking looks and from mundane desire
A niche, enameled in gold and azure,
Wherein you shall stand, enchanted Statue.
With my polished Verse, pure metal trellis
Skillfully constellated with crystal rhymes,
I'll compose for your head an enormous Crown;
And in my Jealousy, o mortal Madonna,
I'll divine to tailor a Mantle, of barbaric design
Stiff and heavy, with suspicion lined,
Which, like a sentry box, would lock up your charms;
Not embroidered with Pearls, but rather my Tears!
Your Gown, it will be my Desire, trembling,
Swelling, my Desire that rises and falls,
That perches on peaks, that settles in valleys,
And adorns with a kiss your pink and white body.
Of my Respect I'll make you beautiful Slippers
Of satin, put to shame by your divine feet,
Imprisoning those in a soft embrace, they
Would hold their shape like a faithful mold.
Should I fail, despite my diligent art,
To carve for a Footrest a silver Moon,
I would place the Serpent that gnaws my entrails
Beneath your heels, for you to crush and deride,
Queen victorious and fecund with pardons,
This monster bloated with hatred and bile.
You will see my Thoughts, like Candles arrayed

Devant l'autel fleuri de la Reine des Vierges,
Étoilant de reflets le plafond peint en bleu,
Te regarder toujours avec des yeux de feu;
Et comme tout en moi te chérit et t'admire,
Tout se fera Benjoin, Encens, Oliban, Myrrhe,
Et sans cesse vers toi, sommet blanc et neigeux,
En Vapeurs montera mon Esprit orageux.

Enfin, pour compléter ton rôle de Marie,
Et pour mêler l'amour avec la barbarie,
Volupté noire! des sept Péchés capitaux,
Bourreau plein de remords, je ferai sept Couteaux
Bien affilés, et comme un jongleur insensible,
Prenant le plus profond de ton amour pour cible,
Je les planterai tous dans ton Cœur pantelant,
Dans ton Cœur sanglotant, dans ton Cœur ruisselant!

At the enflowered altar of the Queen of the Virgins,
Starring with sparkles the ceiling of blue,
Watching you always with eyes of fire;
And as all within me cherishes and admires you,
All becomes Benjamin, Incense, Olibanum, and Myrrh,
And ever toward you, summit snowy and white,
In Vapors my stormy Spirit will rise.

At last, to flesh out your role as Mary,
And to mingle love with barbarity
Black Pleasure! from the seven deadly Sins,
Remorseful executioner, I would forge seven Knives
Well honed, and like an insensible juggler,
Targeting the deepest depth of your love,
I would plant them all in your panting Heart,
In your sobbing Heart, in your weeping Heart!

LVIII

CHANSON D'APRÈS MIDI

Quoique tes sourcils méchants
Te donnent un air étrange
Qui n'est pas celui d'un ange,
Sorcière aux yeux alléchants,

Je t'adore, ô ma frivole,
Ma terrible passion!
Avec la dévotion
Du prêtre pour son idole.

Le désert et la forêt
Embaument tes tresses rudes,
Ta tête a les attitudes
De l'énigme et du secret.

Sur ta chair le parfum rôde
Comme autour d'un encensoir;
Tu charmes comme le soir,
Nymphe ténébreuse et chaude.

Ah! les philtres les plus forts
Ne valent pas ta paresse,
Et tu connais la caresse
Qui fait revivre les morts!

Tes hanches sont amoureuses
De ton dos et de tes seins,
Et tu ravis les coussins
Par tes poses langoureuses.

SONG OF THE AFTERNOON

Though your mischievous brows
Lend you a strange air
Hardly that of an angel,
Sorceress with alluring eyes,

I adore you, o my trifle,
My terrible passion!
With the devotion
Of a priest for his idol.

The desert and the forest
Embalm your rough braids,
Your head has the bearing
Of enigma and secret.

Perfume prowls upon your flesh
As around a censer;
You charm like the evening,
Ardent and tenebrous nymph.

Ah! the strongest philters
Are no match for your indolence,
And you know the caress
That could raise the dead!

Your hips are in love
With your back and your breasts,
And you ravish the cushions
With your languorous poses.

Quelquefois, pour apaiser
Ta rage mystérieuse,
Tu prodigues, sérieuse,
La morsure et le baiser;

Tu me déchires, ma brune,
Avec un rire moqueur,
Et puis tu mets sur mon cœur
Ton œil doux comme la lune.

Sous tes souliers de satin,
Sous tes charmants pieds de soie,
Moi, je mets ma grande joie,
Mon génie et mon destin,

Mon âme par toi guérie,
Par toi, lumière et couleur!
Explosion de chaleur
Dans ma noire Sibérie!

Sometimes, to appease
Your mysterious rage,
You lavish, gravely,
The bite and the kiss;

You rend me, my dark one,
With a mocking laughter,
And then you lay upon my heart
Your eye as gentle as the moon.

Beneath your satin slippers,
Beneath your lovely feet of silk,
I lay down all my happiness,
My destiny and my genius,

My soul by you restored,
By you, light and color!
Explosion of heat
In my black Siberia!

LIX

SISINA

Imaginez Diane en galant équipage,
Parcourant les forêts ou battant les halliers,
Cheveux et gorge au vent, s'enivrant de tapage,
Superbe et défiant les meilleurs cavaliers!

Avez-vous vu Théroigne, amante du carnage,
Excitant à l'assaut un peuple sans souliers,
La joue et l'œil en feu, jouant son personnage,
Et montant, sabre au poing, les royaux escaliers?

Telle la Sisina! Mais la douce guerrière
A l'âme charitable autant que meurtrière;
Son courage, affolé de poudre et de tambours,

Devant les suppliants sait mettre bas les armes,
Et son cœur, ravagé par la flamme, a toujours,
Pour qui s'en montre digne, un réservoir de larmes.

SISINA

Imagine Diana with gallant equipage,
Charging through forests and beating the brush,
Hair and breast to the wind, drunk on the din,
Superb and flouting the finest cavaliers!

Have you seen Théroigne, lover of carnage,
Rousing the unshod masses to battle,
Cheek and eye aflame, playing her part,
And mounting, saber in fist, the royal stairs?

Such is Sisina! But the gentle warrior
In her soul is as charitable as murderous;
Her courage, stirred by powder and drums,

Knows to lay down arms before suppliants,
And her heart, ravaged by flame, has always,
For those who deserve them, a reservoir of tears.

FRANCISCÆ MEÆ LAUDES

Novis te cantabo chordis,
O novelletum quod ludis
In solitudine cordis.

Esto sertis implicata,
O femina delicata
Per quam solvuntur peccata!

Sicut beneficum Lethe,
Hauriam oscula de te,
Quæ imbuta es magnete.

Quum vitiorum tempestas
Turbabat omnes semitas,
Apparuisti, Deitas,

Velut stella salutaris
In naufragiis amaris.....
Suspendam cor tuis aris!

Piscina plena virtutis,
Fons æternæ juventutis,
Labris vocem redde mutis!

Quod erat spurcum, cremasti;
Quod rudius, exæquasti;
Quod debile, confirmasti.

FRANCISCAE MEAE LAUDES

On new strings shall I sing you,
O sapling who plays
In heart's solitude.

In garlands be implicate,
O delicate woman
Absolver of sins!

As beneficent Lethe,
I shall draw your kisses,
Of magnet imbued.

When tempest of vices,
Troubled all paths,
Goddess, you appeared

As salvation's star
Above bitter shipwreck.....
At your altars shall I hang my heart!

Pool full of virtue,
Fount of eternal youth,
Lend voice to mute lips!

What was filthy, you burned;
What was rough, you refined;
What enfeebled, you fortified.

In fame mea taberna,
In nocte mea lucerna,
Recte me semper guberna.

Adde nunc vires viribus,
Dulce balneum suavibus
Unguentatum odoribus!

Meos circa lumbos mica,
O castitatis lorica,
Aqua tincta seraphica;

Patera gemmis corusca,
Panis salsus, mollis esca,
Divinum vinum, Francisca!

In hunger my tavern,
In night my lantern,
Guide me always to the good.

Now add strength to the strong,
Sweet bath gently
Scented with perfume!

Limn my loins with light,
O chastity's corslet,
Dipped in seraphic waters;

Jewel encrusted chalice,
Salted bread, soft morsel,
Divine wine, Francisca!

À UNE DAME CRÉOLE

Au pays parfumé que le soleil caresse,
J'ai connu, sous un dais d'arbres tout empourprés
Et de palmiers d'où pleut sur les yeux la paresse,
Une dame créole aux charmes ignorés.

Son teint est pâle et chaud; la brune enchanteresse
A dans le cou des airs noblement maniérés;
Grande et svelte en marchant comme une chasseresse,
Son sourire est tranquille et ses yeux assurés.

Si vous alliez, Madame, au vrai pays de gloire,
Sur les bords de la Seine ou de la verte Loire,
Belle digne d'orner les antiques manoirs,

Vous feriez, à l'abri des ombreuses retraites,
Germer mille sonnets dans le cœur des poètes,
Que vos grands yeux rendraient plus soumis que vos noirs.

TO A CREOLE LADY

In a perfumed land caressed by the sun,
I knew, beneath a canopy of crimson trees
And palms that rain idleness upon the eyes,
A creole lady of unrecognized charms.

Her hue is pale and warm; brown enchantress
Whose neck bears noble manners;
Tall and svelte in stride like a huntress,
Her smile is tranquil and her eyes assured.

Should you go, Madame, to the true land of glory,
Upon the banks of the Seine or the verdant Loire,
Beauty fit to ornament venerable manors,

You would, within an arbor of reclusive shadows,
Germinate a thousand sonnets in the heart of the poets,
Whom your wide eyes would make more submissive than your blacks.

LXII

MŒSTA ET ERRABUNDA

Dis-moi ton cœur parfois s'envole-t-il, Agathe,
Loin du noir océan de l'immonde cité,
Vers un autre océan où la splendeur éclate,
Bleu, clair, profond, ainsi que la virginité?
Dis-moi, ton cœur parfois s'envole-t-il, Agathe?

La mer, la vaste mer, console nos labeurs!
Quel démon a doté la mer, rauque chanteuse
Qu'accompagne l'immense orgue des vents grondeurs,
De cette fonction sublime de berceuse?
La mer, la vaste mer, console nos labeurs!

Emporte-moi, wagon! enlève-moi, frégate!
Loin! loin! ici la boue est faite de nos pleurs!
— Est-il vrai que parfois le triste cœur d'Agathe
Dise: Loin des remords, des crimes, des douleurs,
Emporte-moi, wagon, enlève-moi, frégate?

Comme vous êtes loin, paradis parfumé,
Où sous un clair azur tout n'est qu'amour et joie,
Où tout ce que l'on aime est digne d'être aimé,
Où dans la volupté pure le cœur se noie!
Comme vous êtes loin, paradis parfumé!

Mais le vert paradis des amours enfantines,
Les courses, les chansons, les baisers, les bouquets,
Les violons vibrant derrière les collines,
Avec les brocs de vin, le soir, dans les bosquets,
— Mais le vert paradis des amours enfantines,

MOESTA ET ERRABUNDA

Tell me, Agathe, does your heart sometimes soar,
Far from the black ocean of the foul city,
Toward another ocean where splendor flares,
Blue, clear, profound, as virginity?
Tell me, Agathe, does your heart sometimes soar?

The sea, the vast sea, assuages our toils!
What demon has granted the sea, hoarse songstress
Accompanied by the immense organ of growling winds,
The sublime office of singing lullabies?
The sea, the vast sea, assuages our toils!

Carry me wagon! Abscond with me, frigate!
Far! far away! here the mire is made of our tears!
—Is it true that sometimes the sad heart of Agathe
Pleads: Far from regrets, from crimes, from pains,
Carry me, wagon, abscond with me, frigate?

How distant you are, perfumed paradise,
Where all is love and joy below clear azure,
Where all that we love is worthy of love,
Where the heart is drowned in pure pleasure!
How distant you are, perfumed paradise!

But the green paradise of childhood loves,
The races, the songs, the kisses, the bouquets,
The violins humming behind the hills,
With the jugs of wine, in the evening, in groves,
—But the green paradise of childhood loves,

L'innocent paradis, plein de plaisirs furtifs,
Est-il déjà plus loin que l'Inde et que la Chine?
Peut-on le rappeler avec des cris plaintifs,
Et l'animer encor d'une voix argentine,
L'innocent paradis plein de plaisirs furtifs?

The innocent paradise, full of furtive pleasures,
Is it already further than India or China?
Can we call it back with plaintive cries?
And with silvery voice make it live once more,
The innocent paradise full of furtive pleasures?

LE REVENANT

Comme les anges à l'œil fauve,
Je reviendrai dans ton alcôve
Et vers toi glisserai sans bruit
Avec les ombres de la nuit;

Et je te donnerai, ma brune,
Des baisers froids comme la lune
Et des caresses de serpent
Autour d'une fosse rampant.

Quand viendra le matin livide,
Tu trouveras ma place vide,
Où jusqu'au soir il fera froid.

Comme d'autres par la tendresse,
Sur ta vie et sur ta jeunesse,
Moi, je veux régner par l'effroi.

THE REVENANT

Like wild-eyed angels,
I will return to your alcove
And glide silently toward you
With the shadows of night;

And I will give you, my dark one,
Kisses cold as the moon
And caresses of serpents
That writhe in a pit.

When livid morning returns,
You will find my void place,
Chilled until evening.

As others by tenderness,
Over your life and your youth,
Me, I would reign by terror.

SONNET D'AUTOMNE

Ils me disent, tes yeux, clairs comme le cristal:
« Pour toi, bizarre amant, quel est donc mon mérite? »
— Sois charmante et tais-toi! Mon cœur, que tout irrite,
Excepté la candeur de l'antique animal,

Ne veut pas te montrer son secret infernal,
Berceuse dont la main aux longs sommeils m'invite,
Ni sa noire légende avec la flamme écrite.
Je hais la passion et l'esprit me fait mal!

Aimons-nous doucement. L'Amour dans sa guérite,
Ténébreux, embusqué, bande son arc fatal.
Je connais les engins de son vieil arsenal:

Crime, horreur et folie! — Ô pâle marguerite!
Comme moi n'es-tu pas un soleil automnal,
Ô ma si blanche, ô ma si froide Marguerite?

AUTUMN SONNET

They ask, your eyes, clear as crystal:
"To you, strange lover, what makes me worthwhile?"
—Be charming and shut up! My heart, which all irritates,
Except the candor of the ancient animal,

Would rather not disclose its infernal secret,
Nurse whose hand lulls me to sleep,
Nor its black legend written in flame.
I hate passion and wit makes me sick!

Let us love mildly. Love in his watchtower,
Tenebrous, in ambush, bends his fatal bow.
I know the implements in his old arsenal:

Crime, horror and madness! —O pale marguerite!
Are you not like me an autumn sun,
O my Marguerite, so white, so cold?

TRISTESSES DE LA LUNE

Ce soir, la lune rêve avec plus de paresse;
Ainsi qu'une beauté, sur de nombreux coussins,
Qui d'une main distraite et légère caresse
Avant de s'endormir le contour de ses seins,

Sur le dos satiné des molles avalanches,
Mourante, elle se livre aux longues pâmoisons,
Et promène ses yeux sur les visions blanches
Qui montent dans l'azur comme des floraisons.

Quand parfois sur ce globe, en sa langueur oisive,
Elle laisse filer une larme furtive,
Un poète pieux, ennemi du sommeil,

Dans le creux de sa main prend cette larme pâle,
Aux reflets irisés comme un fragment d'opale,
Et la met dans son cœur loin des yeux du soleil.

SORROWS OF THE MOON

Tonight, the moon dreams more lazily;
As if some beauty, upon heaps of cushions,
Caresses with a light and distracted hand
The curve of her breasts before she sleeps,

Upon the satiny back of soft avalanches,
Dying, she surrenders to long swoons,
And drifts her eyes over white visions
That rise like blossoms in the azure.

When sometimes on this globe, in her idle languor,
She lets fall a furtive tear,
A pious poet, enemy of sleep,

Takes in the hollow of his hand this pale tear,
Iridescent like a fragment of opal,
And sets it in his heart far from the eyes of the sun.

LXVI

LES CHATS

Les amoureux fervents et les savants austères
Aiment également, dans leur mûre saison,
Les chats puissants et doux, orgueil de la maison,
Qui comme eux sont frileux et comme eux sédentaires.

Amis de la science et de la volupté,
Ils cherchent le silence et l'horreur des ténèbres;
L'Érèbe les eût pris pour ses coursiers funèbres,
S'ils pouvaient au servage incliner leur fierté.

Ils prennent en songeant les nobles attitudes
Des grands sphinx allongés au fond des solitudes,
Qui semblent s'endormir dans un rêve sans fin;

Leurs reins féconds sont pleins d'étincelles magiques,
Et des parcelles d'or, ainsi qu'un sable fin,
Étoilent vaguement leurs prunelles mystiques.

LXVI

CATS

Fervent lovers and the austere sage
Love equally, in ripe old age,
Their strong and gentle cats, pride of the home,
Sensitive and sedentary like them.

Friends of science and sensuality,
They seek the silence and the horror of shadows;
Erebus would take them as funereal envoys,
If to service their pride would incline.

In contemplation they take the noble postures
Of great sphinxes stretched in depths of solitude,
Who seem to sleep in endless dream;

Their fecund loins are charged with magic sparks,
And specks of gold, like a fine sand,
Faintly star their mystical eyes.

LES HIBOUX

Sous les ifs noirs qui les abritent,
Les hiboux se tiennent rangés,
Ainsi que des dieux étrangers,
Dardant leur œil rouge. Ils méditent.

Sans remuer ils se tiendront
Jusqu'à l'heure mélancolique
Où, poussant le soleil oblique,
Les ténèbres s'établiront.

Leur attitude au sage enseigne
Qu'il faut en ce monde qu'il craigne
Le tumulte et le mouvement;

L'homme ivre d'une ombre qui passe
Porte toujours le châtiment
D'avoir voulu changer de place.

OWLS

Under the shelter of black yews,
The owls perch in file,
Like alien gods,
Darting their red eye. They meditate.

Unmoving they will remain
Until the melancholic hour
When, pressing the oblique sun,
The shadows settle in.

Their attitude instructs the sage
That in this world one must fear
Tumult and movement;

The man drunk on passing shadows
Bears always the punishment
Of having wanted to trade places.

LA PIPE

Je suis la pipe d'un auteur;
On voit, à contempler ma mine
D'Abyssinienne ou de Cafrine,
Que mon maître est un grand fumeur.

Quand il est comblé de douleur,
Je fume comme la chaumine
Où se prépare la cuisine
Pour le retour du laboureur.

J'enlace et je berce son âme
Dans le réseau mobile et bleu
Qui monte de ma bouche en feu,

Et je roule un puissant dictame
Qui charme son cœur et guérit
De ses fatigues son esprit.

LXVIII

THE PIPE

I am the pipe of an author;
One sees, contemplating
My Abyssinian or Kaffir complexion,
That my master is a heavy smoker.

When he is laden with sorrow,
I smoke like the cottage
Where one cooks
For the plowman's return.

I entwine and I cradle his soul
In a blue and mobile mesh
That mounts from my fiery mouth,

And I whorl a powerful balm
That charms his heart and heals
His weary spirit.

LA MUSIQUE

La musique souvent me prend comme une mer!
Vers ma pâle étoile,
Sous un plafond de brume ou dans un vaste éther,
Je mets à la voile;

La poitrine en avant et les poumons gonflés
Comme de la toile,
J'escalade le dos des flots amoncelés
Que la nuit me voile;

Je sens vibrer en moi toutes les passions
D'un vaisseau qui souffre;
Le bon vent, la tempête et ses convulsions

Sur l'immense gouffre
Me bercent. D'autres fois, calme plat, grand miroir
De mon désespoir!

MUSIC

Music often sweeps me away like a sea!
        Toward my pale star,
Beneath a ceiling of mist or within a vast ether,
        I set sail;

Chest thrust forth and lungs swelled
        Like the cloth,
I ride the back of mounting waves
        Veiled by night;

I feel stir within me all the passions
        Of a tossing ship;
The strong wind, the tempest and its convulsions

        Over the immense gulf
Rock me. At other times, dull calm, great mirror
        Of my despair!

LXX

SÉPULTURE

Si par une nuit lourde et sombre
Un bon chrétien, par charité,
Derrière quelque vieux décombre
Enterre votre corps vanté,

À l'heure où les chastes étoiles
Ferment leurs yeux appesantis,
L'araignée y fera ses toiles,
Et la vipère ses petits;

Vous entendrez toute l'année
Sur votre tête condamnée
Les cris lamentables des loups

Et des sorcières faméliques,
Les ébats des vieillards lubriques
Et les complots des noirs filous.

LXX

SEPULCHER

If upon a somber and heavy night
A good Christian, out of charity,
Behind some old ruin
Buries your vaunted corpse,

At the hour when the chaste stars
Close their heavy eyes,
There shall the spider make her webs,
And the viper her brood;

You shall hear all through the year
Upon your damned head
The doleful howls of the wolves

And of scrawny witches,
The frolics of dirty old men
And the plots of shady thieves.

UNE GRAVURE FANTASTIQUE

Ce spectre singulier n'a pour toute toilette,
Grotesquement campé sur son front de squelette,
Qu'un diadème affreux sentant le carnaval.
Sans éperons, sans fouet, il essouffle un cheval,
Fantôme comme lui, rosse apocalyptique,
Qui bave des naseaux comme un épileptique.
Au travers de l'espace ils s'enfoncent tous deux,
Et foulent l'infini d'un sabot hasardeux.
Le cavalier promène un sabre qui flamboie
Sur les foules sans nom que sa monture broie,
Et parcourt, comme un prince inspectant sa maison,
Le cimetière immense et froid, sans horizon,
Où gisent, aux lueurs d'un soleil blanc et terne,
Les peuples de l'histoire ancienne et moderne.

A FANTASTIC ENGRAVING

This singular specter has nothing to wear but,
Grotesquely set on his skeletal brow,
A ghastly diadem reeking of carnival.
Without spurs, without whip, he wearies a horse,
A phantom like him, apocalyptic nag,
Whose nostrils foam like an epileptic.
The two of them sink as they pass through space,
And trample the infinite with hazardous hoof.
The cavalier flaunts a saber aflame
Over nameless hordes trodden down by his mount,
And surveys, like a prince inspecting his home,
The horizonless cemetery, cold and immense,
Where lie, amid dull and white glimmers of sun,
The people of ancient and modern history.

LE MORT JOYEUX

Dans une terre grasse et pleine d'escargots
Je veux creuser moi-même une fosse profonde,
Où je puisse à loisir étaler mes vieux os
Et dormir dans l'oubli comme un requin dans l'onde.

Je hais les testaments et je hais les tombeaux;
Plutôt que d'implorer une larme du monde,
Vivant, j'aimerais mieux inviter les corbeaux
À saigner tous les bouts de ma carcasse immonde.

Ô vers! noirs compagnons sans oreille et sans yeux,
Voyez venir à vous un mort libre et joyeux;
Philosophes viveurs, fils de la pourriture,

À travers ma ruine allez donc sans remords,
Et dites-moi s'il est encor quelque torture
Pour ce vieux corps sans âme et mort parmi les morts!

THE HAPPY CORPSE

In a soil rich and full of snails
I would dig myself a deep grave,
Where at leisure I can stretch out my elderly bones
And sleep in oblivion like a shark in the wave.

I hate testaments and I hate tombs;
Instead of begging a tear from the world,
While alive, I'd rather invite the ravens
To bleed every scrap of my foul carcass.

O worms! black companions without ears and eyes,
Behold the arrival of a free and happy corpse;
Bon vivant philosophers, scions of decay,

Remorselessly make your way through my ruins,
And let me know if some torture remains
For this old body without soul and dead among the dead!

LE TONNEAU DE LA HAINE

La Haine est le tonneau des pâles Danaïdes;
La Vengeance éperdue aux bras rouges et forts
A beau précipiter dans ses ténèbres vides
De grands seaux pleins du sang et des larmes des morts,

Le Démon fait des trous secrets à ces abîmes,
Par où fuiraient mille ans de sueurs et d'efforts,
Quand même elle saurait ranimer ses victimes,
Et pour les pressurer ressusciter leurs corps.

La Haine est un ivrogne au fond d'une taverne,
Qui sent toujours la soif naître de la liqueur
Et se multiplier comme l'hydre de Lerne.

— Mais les buveurs heureux connaissent leur vainqueur,
Et la Haine est vouée à ce sort lamentable
De ne pouvoir jamais s'endormir sous la table.

THE CASK OF HATE

Hate is the cask of the pale Danaïdes;
Frantic Vengeance with strong and red arms
Blithely hurls into its empty darkness
Great buckets of blood and of tears of the dead,

The Demon drills secret holes in these depths,
Draining thousands of years of toil and sweat,
Even so she would still revive her victims,
And breathe life in their bodies to press them again.

Hate is a drunk at end the bar,
Whose thirst for liquor is always newborn
And self-multiplies like the Lernaean hydra.

—But merry drinkers know their conqueror,
And Hate is pledged to the lamentable fate
Of never being able to sleep under the table.

LA CLOCHE FÊLÉE

Il est amer et doux, pendant les nuits d'hiver,
D'écouter, près du feu qui palpite et qui fume,
Les souvenirs lointains lentement s'élever
Au bruit des carillons qui chantent dans la brume.

Bienheureuse la cloche au gosier vigoureux
Qui, malgré sa vieillesse, alerte et bien portante,
Jette fidèlement son cri religieux,
Ainsi qu'un vieux soldat qui veille sous la tente!

Moi, mon âme est fêlée, et lorsqu'en ses ennuis
Elle veut de ses chants peupler l'air froid des nuits,
Il arrive souvent que sa voix affaiblie

Semble le râle épais d'un blessé qu'on oublie
Au bord d'un lac de sang, sous un grand tas de morts,
Et qui meurt, sans bouger, dans d'immenses efforts.

THE CRACKED BELL

It is bitter sweet, during winter nights,
To hear, by the fire that flickers and smokes,
The distant memories slowly ascend
At the sound of the chimes that sing in the fog.

Blessed is the full-throated bell
Which, despite its old age, alert and upright,
Faithfully flings its pious cry,
Like an old soldier keeping watch from his tent!

As for me, my soul is cracked, and in her ennui
When she would people the cold night air with songs,
It often happens that her enfeebled voice

Resembles the thick rattle of one wounded and forgotten
At the edge of a lake of blood, under a heap of corpses,
And who dies, unmoving, with great pains.

SPLEEN

Pluviôse, irrité contre la ville entière,
De son urne à grands flots verse un froid ténébreux
Aux pâles habitants du voisin cimetière
Et la mortalité sur les faubourgs brumeux.

Mon chat sur le carreau cherchant une litière
Agite sans repos son corps maigre et galeux;
L'âme d'un vieux poète erre dans la gouttière
Avec la triste voix d'un fantôme frileux.

Le bourdon se lamente, et la bûche enfumée
Accompagne en fausset la pendule enrhumée,
Cependant qu'en un jeu plein de sales parfums,

Héritage fatal d'une vieille hydropique,
Le beau valet de cœur et la dame de pique
Causent sinistrement de leurs amours défunts.

SPLEEN

Pluvius, irritated with the city entire,
From his urn in great waves pours a tenebrous cold
Upon the pale occupants of the bordering cemetery
And mortality upon the foggy neighborhoods.

Treading the tiles in search of a nest my cat
Restlessly shifts his meager and mangy frame;
The soul of an old poet strays in the gutter
With the sad voice of a shivering phantom.

The great bell laments, and the smoking log
Accompanies falsetto the wheezing clock,
While in a deck full of filthy scents,

The fatal heritage of a dropsical hag,
The fine Jack of Hearts and the Queen of Spades
Chatter sinisterly of their dead lovers.

SPLEEN

J'ai plus de souvenirs que si j'avais mille ans.

Un gros meuble à tiroirs encombré de bilans,
De vers, de billets doux, de procès, de romances,
Avec de lourds cheveux roulés dans des quittances,
Cache moins de secrets que mon triste cerveau.
C'est une pyramide, un immense caveau,
Qui contient plus de morts que la fosse commune.
— Je suis un cimetière abhorré de la lune,
Où comme des remords se traînent de longs vers
Qui s'acharnent toujours sur mes morts les plus chers.
Je suis un vieux boudoir plein de roses fanées,
Où gît tout un fouillis de modes surannées,
Où les pastels plaintifs et les pâles Boucher,
Seuls, respirent l'odeur d'un flacon débouché.

Rien n'égale en longueur les boiteuses journées,
Quand sous les lourds flocons des neigeuses années
L'ennui, fruit de la morne incuriosité,
Prend les proportions de l'immortalité.
— Désormais tu n'es plus, ô matière vivante!
Qu'un granit entouré d'une vague épouvante,
Assoupi dans le fond d'un Sahara brumeux;
Un vieux sphinx ignoré du monde insoucieux,
Oublié sur la carte, et dont l'humeur farouche
Ne chante qu'aux rayons du soleil qui se couche.

SPLEEN

I have more memories than if I'd lived a thousand years.

A huge chest of drawers encumbered with accounts,
With verse, love letters, lawsuits, romances,
Heavy locks of hair rolled up in receipts,
Hides fewer secrets than my mournful brain.
It is a pyramid, an immense mausoleum,
Containing more dead than a common grave.
—I am a cemetery abhorred by the moon,
Where long worms crawl like old regrets
Forever tormenting my dearest dead.
I am an old boudoir full of withered roses,
Where lies a whole tangle of outdated fashions,
Where plaintive pastels and pale Bouchers,
Alone, breathe the scent of an uncorked flask.

Nothing equals the length of limping days,
When beneath heavy flakes of snowy years
Ennui, fruit of bleak incuriosity,
Takes on the proportions of immortality.
—Then you are no more, o living matter!
Than a stone attended by a vague terror,
Sunk in the depths of a hazy Sahara;
An old sphinx ignored by insouciant society,
Overlooked on the map, and whose fierce humor
Sings only to rays of the setting sun.

LXXVII

SPLEEN

Je suis comme le roi d'un pays pluvieux,
Riche, mais impuissant, jeune et pourtant très vieux,
Qui, de ses précepteurs méprisant les courbettes,
S'ennuie avec ses chiens comme avec d'autres bêtes.
Rien ne peut l'égayer, ni gibier, ni faucon,
Ni son peuple mourant en face du balcon.
Du bouffon favori la grotesque ballade
Ne distrait plus le front de ce cruel malade;
Son lit fleurdelisé se transforme en tombeau,
Et les dames d'atour, pour qui tout prince est beau,
Ne savent plus trouver d'impudique toilette
Pour tirer un souris de ce jeune squelette.
Le savant qui lui fait de l'or n'a jamais pu
De son être extirper l'élément corrompu,
Et dans ces bains de sang qui des Romains nous viennent,
Et dont sur leurs vieux jours les puissants se souviennent,
Il n'a su réchauffer ce cadavre hébété
Où coule au lieu de sang l'eau verte du Léthé.

LXXVII

SPLEEN

I am like the king of a rainy country,
Rich, but impotent, young yet so old,
Who, scorning his tutor's scraping bows,
Is as bored with his dogs as with other beasts.
Nothing amuses, neither hunt, nor falconry,
Nor his people dying in front of the balcony.
The grotesque ballad of his beloved jester
Cannot ease the brow of this cruel sickly soul;
His fleur-de-lys couch becomes a tomb,
And the ladies in waiting, who find any prince handsome,
Can find nothing amid their shameless toilette,
To pull a smile from this young skeleton.
The sage who gleans gold has never been able
To draw from his being corrupt inclusions,
And in baths of blood which the Romans bequeathed,
Recalled by the mighty in declining days,
He cannot warm over this dull cadaver
Where in place of blood flow green waters of Lethe.

SPLEEN

Quand le ciel bas et lourd pèse comme un couvercle
Sur l'esprit gémissant en proie aux longs ennuis,
Et que de l'horizon embrassant tout le cercle
Il nous verse un jour noir plus triste que les nuits;

Quand la terre est changée en un cachot humide,
Où l'Espérance, comme une chauve-souris,
S'en va battant les murs de son aile timide
Et se cognant la tête à des plafonds pourris;

Quand la pluie étalant ses immenses traînées
D'une vaste prison imite les barreaux,
Et qu'un peuple muet d'infâmes araignées
Vient tendre ses filets au fond de nos cerveaux,

Des cloches tout à coup sautent avec furie
Et lancent vers le ciel un affreux hurlement,
Ainsi que des esprits errants et sans patrie
Qui se mettent à geindre opiniâtrement.

— Et de longs corbillards, sans tambours ni musique,
Défilent lentement dans mon âme; l'Espoir,
Vaincu, pleure, et l'Angoisse atroce, despotique,
Sur mon crâne incliné plante son drapeau noir.

SPLEEN

When the sky low and heavy weighs like a lid
On the groaning mind prey to endless ennui,
And circles entire the horizon's ring
It pours a black day more sad than the nights.

When the earth becomes a humid cell,
Where Hope, like a bat,
Bangs the walls with its timid wings
And bumps its head on the crumbling vaults;

When the rain sparkling its immense trails
Mimes the bars of a vast prison,
And a mute nation of infamous spiders
Tighten their webs at the bottom of our brains,

The bells suddenly sound with fury
And launch at the sky a ghastly roar,
Like wandering spirits without a country
Who air their tedious gripes like a bore.

—And the long cortège, without drums or music,
Files slowly within my soul; Hope,
Vanquished, weeps, and atrocious Anguish, despotic,
Plants his black flag on my bowed skull.

OBSESSION

Grands bois, vous m'effrayez comme des cathédrales;
Vous hurlez comme l'orgue; et dans nos cœurs maudits,
Chambres d'éternel deuil où vibrent de vieux râles,
Répondent les échos de vos *De profundis*.

Je te hais, Océan! tes bonds et tes tumultes,
Mon esprit les retrouve en lui; ce rire amer
De l'homme vaincu, plein de sanglots et d'insultes,
Je l'entends dans le rire énorme de la mer.

Comme tu me plairais, ô nuit! sans ces étoiles
Dont la lumière parle un langage connu!
Car je cherche le vide, et le noir, et le nu!

Mais les ténèbres sont elles-mêmes des toiles
Où vivent, jaillissant de mon œil par milliers,
Des êtres disparus aux regards familiers.

OBSESSION

Deep woods, you frighten me like cathedrals;
You howl like the organ; and in our damned hearts,
Chambers of eternal mourning where old death rattles vibrate,
Respond the echoes of your *De profundis.*

I hate you, Ocean! your swells and your tumults,
My mind finds them in itself; this bitter laughter
Of the vanquished man, full of sobs and insults,
I hear in the enormous laughter of the sea.

How you would please me, o night! without these stars
Whose light speaks a language we know!
For I seek the void, and the black, and the bare!

But the shadows are themselves canvases
Where live, bursting from my eye by thousands,
Those vanished beings with familiar gazes.

LXXX

LE GOÛT DU NÉANT

Morne esprit, autrefois amoureux de la lutte,
L'Espoir, dont l'éperon attisait ton ardeur,
Ne veut plus t'enfourcher! Couche-toi sans pudeur,
Vieux cheval dont le pied à chaque obstacle bute.

Résigne-toi, mon cœur; dors ton sommeil de brute.

Esprit vaincu, fourbu! Pour toi, vieux maraudeur,
L'amour n'a plus de goût, non plus que la dispute;
Adieu donc, chants du cuivre et soupirs de la flûte!
Plaisirs, ne tentez plus un cœur sombre et boudeur!

Le Printemps adorable a perdu son odeur!

Et le Temps m'engloutit minute par minute,
Comme la neige immense un corps pris de roideur;
— Je contemple d'en haut le globe en sa rondeur
Et je n'y cherche plus l'abri d'une cahute.

Avalanche, veux-tu m'emporter dans ta chute?

THE TASTE FOR NOTHINGNESS

Dreary spirit, once enamored of struggle,
Hope, whose spur pricked your ardor,
Will no longer mount you! Sleep shamelessly,
Old horse whose hoof strikes every obstacle.

Resign yourself, my heart; sleep your bestial sleep.

Vanquished spirit, exhausted! For you, old marauder,
Love has lost its savor, as has strife;
Farewell then, songs of brass and sighs of the flute!
Pleasures, tempt no more a somber and sulking heart!

Adorable Spring has lost its scent!

And Time engulfs me minute by minute,
Like the immense snow a stiffened body;
—I gaze from on high at the globe in its round
And I no longer look for a sheltering hut.

Avalanche, will you carry me off in your fall?

ALCHIMIE DE LA DOULEUR

L'un t'éclaire avec son ardeur,
L'autre en toi met son deuil, Nature!
Ce qui dit à l'un: Sépulture!
Dit à l'autre: Vie et splendeur!

Hermès inconnu qui m'assistes
Et qui toujours m'intimidas,
Tu me rends l'égal de Midas,
Le plus triste des alchimistes;

Par toi je change l'or en fer
Et le paradis en enfer;
Dans le suaire des nuages

Je découvre un cadavre cher,
Et sur les célestes rivages
Je bâtis de grands sarcophages.

ALCHEMY OF SORROW

The one sets you alight with his ardor,
The other sets within you his grief, Nature!
That which says to one: Sepulcher!
Says to the other: Life and splendor!

Occult Hermes who helps me
And who always overawes,
You make me the equal of Midas,
Saddest of all alchemists;

Through you I turn gold to iron
And heaven to hell;
In the shroud of the clouds

I uncover a treasured cadaver,
And upon celestial shores
I build great sarcophagi.

LXXXII

HORREUR SYMPATHETIQUE

De ce ciel bizarre et livide,
Tourmenté comme ton destin,
Quels pensers dans ton âme vide
Descendent? réponds, libertin.

— Insatiablement avide
De l'obscur et de l'incertain,
Je ne geindrai pas comme Ovide
Chassé du paradis latin.

Cieux déchirés comme des grèves,
En vous se mire mon orgueil;
Vos vastes nuages en deuil

Sont les corbillards de mes rêves,
Et vos lueurs sont le reflet
De l'Enfer où mon cœur se plaît.

LXXXII

SYMPATHETIC HORROR

From this strange and livid sky,
Tormented like your destiny,
What thoughts into your void soul
Descend? answer, libertine.

—Insatiably hungry
For the obscure and uncertain,
I would not whine like Ovid
Chased from Latin paradise.

Skies torn like shores,
In you my pride is mirrored;
Your vast clouds in mourning

Are the hearses of my dreams,
And your glimmers the reflection
Of Hell where my heart is happy.

L'HÉAUTONTIMOROUMÉNOS

À J.G.F.

Je te frapperai sans colère
Et sans haine, comme un boucher,
Comme Moïse le rocher!
Et je ferai de ta paupière,

Pour abreuver mon Sahara,
Jaillir les eaux de la souffrance.
Mon désir gonflé d'espérance
Sur tes pleurs salés nagera

Comme un vaisseau qui prend le large,
Et dans mon cœur qu'ils soûleront
Tes chers sanglots retentiront
Comme un tambour qui bat la charge!

Ne suis-je pas un faux accord
Dans la divine symphonie,
Grâce à la vorace Ironie
Qui me secoue et qui me mord?

Elle est dans ma voix, la criarde!
C'est tout mon sang, ce poison noir!
Je suis le sinistre miroir
Où la mégère se regarde.

Je suis la plaie et le couteau!
Je suis le soufflet et la joue!
Je suis les membres et la roue,
Et la victime et le bourreau!

LXXXIII

HEAUTON TIMORUMENOS

To J.G.F.

I would strike you without anger
And without hatred, like a butcher,
Like Moses the rock!
And from your eyelids I would make,

To quench my Sahara,
The waters of suffering flow.
Swelled with hope my desire
Will swim upon your salty tears

Like a ship that sets to sea,
And within my drunken heart
Your dear sobs will resound
Like a drum that leads the charge!

Am I not a false chord
In the divine symphony,
Thanks to the voracious Irony
That shakes me and sinks in its teeth?

She inhabits my voice, the shrieker!
It is my blood, this black poison!
I am the sinister mirror
Wherein the shrew sees herself.

I am the wound and the knife!
I am the slap and the cheek!
I am the limbs and the rack,
And the victim and the torturer!

Je suis de mon cœur le vampire,
— Un de ces grands abandonnés
Au rire éternel condamnés,
Et qui ne peuvent plus sourire!

I am the vampire of my heart,
—One of those abandoned greats
Condemned to eternal laughter,
And to smile no more!

LXXXIV

L'IRRÉMÉDIABLE

I

Une Idée, une Forme, un Être
Parti de l'azur et tombé
Dans un Styx bourbeux et plombé
Où nul œil du Ciel ne pénètre;

Un Ange, imprudent voyageur
Qu'a tenté l'amour du difforme,
Au fond d'un cauchemar énorme
Se débattant comme un nageur,

Et luttant, angoisses funèbres!
Contre un gigantesque remous
Qui va chantant comme les fous
Et pirouettant dans les ténèbres;

Un malheureux ensorcelé
Dans ses tâtonnements futiles,
Pour fuir d'un lieu plein de reptiles,
Cherchant la lumière et la clé;

Un damné descendant sans lampe,
Au bord d'un gouffre dont l'odeur
Trahit l'humide profondeur,
D'éternels escaliers sans rampe,

Où veillent des monstres visqueux
Dont les larges yeux de phosphore
Font une nuit plus noire encore
Et ne rendent visibles qu'eux;

THE IRREMEDIABLE

I

An Idea, a Form, a Being
Parted the azure and fell
In a murky and leaden Styx
Where no eye of Heaven penetrates;

An Angel, imprudent voyager
Lured by love of disform,
To the depth of an enormous nightmare
Floundering like a swimmer,

And struggling, funereal anguish!
Against a gigantic vortex
That sings like the insane
And pirouettes in the shadows;

A wretch ensorcelled
Amid futile efforts,
To flee a viper's nest,
Seeking candle and key;

One damned descending without a lamp,
At the edge of a gulf whose stench
Betrays the dank depth,
Of eternal stairs without a rail,

Where viscous monsters keep watch
Whose wide eyes of phosphorous
Blacken even the night
And make visible only themselves;

Un navire pris dans le pôle,
Comme en un piège de cristal,
Cherchant par quel détroit fatal
Il est tombé dans cette geôle;

— Emblèmes nets, tableau parfait
D'une fortune irrémédiable,
Qui donne à penser que le Diable
Fait toujours bien tout ce qu'il fait!

II

Tête-à-tête sombre et limpide
Qu'un cœur devenu son miroir!
Puits de Vérité, clair et noir,
Où tremble une étoile livide,

Un phare ironique, infernal,
Flambeau des grâces sataniques,
Soulagement et gloire uniques,
— La conscience dans le Mal!

A ship caught in the pole,
Like a crystal snare,
Seeking to discover by what fatal strait
He has fallen into this gaol;

—Spotless emblems, perfect tableaux
Of an irremediable fortune,
Which goes to show that the Devil
Is good at whatever he does!

II

Somber and limpid tête-à-tête
Of a heart become its own mirror!
Well of Truth, clear and black,
Where trembles a livid star,

Ironic beacon, infernal,
Torch of satanic graces,
Singular glory and solace,
—The conscience within Evil!

L'HORLOGE

Horloge! dieu sinistre, effrayant, impassible,
Dont le doigt nous menace et nous dit: « *Souviens-toi!*
Les vibrantes Douleurs dans ton cœur plein d'effroi
Se planteront bientôt comme dans une cible;

« Le Plaisir vaporeux fuira vers l'horizon
Ainsi qu'une sylphide au fond de la coulisse;
Chaque instant te dévore un morceau du délice
À chaque homme accordé pour toute sa saison.

« Trois mille six cents fois par heure, la Seconde
Chuchote: *Souviens-toi!* — Rapide, avec sa voix
D'insecte, Maintenant dit: Je suis Autrefois,
Et j'ai pompé ta vie avec ma trompe immonde!

« *Remember! Souviens-toi!* prodigue! *Esto memor!*
(Mon gosier de métal parle toutes les langues.)
Les minutes, mortel folâtre, sont des gangues
Qu'il ne faut pas lâcher sans en extraire l'or!

« *Souviens-toi* que le Temps est un joueur avide
Qui gagne sans tricher, à tout coup! c'est la loi.
Le jour décroît; la nuit augmente; *souviens-toi!*
Le gouffre a toujours soif; la clepsydre se vide.

« Tantôt sonnera l'heure où le divin Hasard,
Où l'auguste Vertu, ton épouse encor vierge,
Où le Repentir même (oh! la dernière auberge!),
Où tout te dira: Meurs, vieux lâche! il est trop tard! »

THE CLOCK

Clock! sinister god, frightening, impassive,
By whose menacing hands we are told: "*Remember!*
The throbbing Pains of your fearful heart
Soon plant themselves as if into a target;

Vaporous Pleasure will flee toward the horizon
Like a sylph into the wings;
Every instant you devour a piece of the delight
Accorded every man for his season."

Three thousand six hundred times an hour, the Second
Whispers: "*Remember!*" —Quickly, with the voice
Of an insect, Now says: "I am Once Upon a Time,
And I have sucked out your life with my filthy snout!

"*Souviens-toi! Remember!* prodigal! *Esto memor!*
(My metal throat speaks all tongues.)
The minutes, silly mortal, are the dross
Which one must never cede without extracting gold!

"*Remember* that Time is an avid gambler
Who wins without cheating, every time! such is the law.
The day declines; the night gathers; *Remember!*
The abyss is always thirsty; the hourglass empties.

"Soon the hour sounds when divine Hazard,
When august Virtue, your still virgin spouse,
When even Repentance (oh! last refuge!),
When all will say: Die, old coward! it's too late!"

TABLEAUX PARISIENS

PARISIAN TABLEAUX

LXXXVI

PAYSAGE

Je veux, pour composer chastement mes églogues,
Coucher auprès du ciel, comme les astrologues,
Et, voisin des clochers, écouter en rêvant
Leurs hymnes solennels emportés par le vent.
Les deux mains au menton, du haut de ma mansarde,
Je verrai l'atelier qui chante et qui bavarde;
Les tuyaux, les clochers, ces mâts de la cité,
Et les grands ciels qui font rêver d'éternité.

Il est doux, à travers les brumes, de voir naître
L'étoile dans l'azur, la lampe à la fenêtre,
Les fleuves de charbon monter au firmament
Et la lune verser son pâle enchantement.
Je verrai les printemps, les étés, les automnes;
Et quand viendra l'hiver aux neiges monotones,
Je fermerai partout portières et volets
Pour bâtir dans la nuit mes féeriques palais.
Alors je rêverai des horizons bleuâtres,
Des jardins, des jets d'eau pleurant dans les albâtres,
Des baisers, des oiseaux chantant soir et matin,
Et tout ce que l'Idylle a de plus enfantin.
L'Émeute, tempêtant vainement à ma vitre,
Ne fera pas lever mon front de mon pupitre;
Car je serai plongé dans cette volupté
D'évoquer le Printemps avec ma volonté,
De tirer un soleil de mon cœur, et de faire
De mes pensers brûlants une tiède atmosphère.

LANDSCAPE

I would like, the more chastely to compose my eclogues,
To sleep near the sky, like astrologers,
And, beside the belfries, listen dreamily
To their solemn hymns carried by the wind.
Chin in my hands, from the height of my garret,
I'll watch the workshop that gossips and sings;
The chimneys, the belfries, those masts of the city,
And the vast skies that turn dreams to eternity.

It is sweet, through the mist, to see born
The star in the heavens, the lamp in the window,
The rivers of coal ascending the firmament
And the moon pouring her pale enchantment.
I'll watch the spring, the summer, the autumn;
And when winter arrives with monotonous snow,
I'll close all the doors and the shutters
So as to build my fairy castles in the night.
Thus will I dream of bluish horizons,
Of gardens, of jets of water weeping in alabaster,
Of kisses, of birds that sing evening and morning,
And every childish thing the Idyll can include.
The Riot, vainly haranguing my windowpane,
Will not raise my brow from my desk;
For I will be plunged in the pleasure
Of conjuring Springtime at will,
Of coaxing a sun from my heart, and of making
From my burning thoughts a mild atmosphere.

LE SOLEIL

Le long du vieux faubourg, où pendent aux masures
Les persiennes, abri des secrètes luxures,
Quand le soleil cruel frappe à traits redoublés
Sur la ville et les champs, sur les toits et les blés,
Je vais m'exercer seul à ma fantasque escrime,
Flairant dans tous les coins les hasards de la rime,
Trébuchant sur les mots comme sur les pavés,
Heurtant parfois des vers depuis longtemps rêvés.

Ce père nourricier, ennemi des chloroses,
Éveille dans les champs les vers comme les roses;
Il fait s'évaporer les soucis vers le ciel,
Et remplit les cerveaux et les ruches de miel.
C'est lui qui rajeunit les porteurs de béquilles
Et les rend gais et doux comme des jeunes filles,
Et commande aux moissons de croître et de mûrir
Dans le cœur immortel qui toujours veut fleurir!

Quand, ainsi qu'un poète, il descend dans les villes,
Il ennoblit le sort des choses les plus viles,
Et s'introduit en roi, sans bruit et sans valets,
Dans tous les hôpitaux et dans tous les palais.

THE SUN

Along the old neighborhood, where the shacks are hung
With Persian blinds, concealing secret lecheries,
When the cruel sun strikes with sharpening shafts
The city and the fields, the roofs and the wheat,
I practice my fantastic fencing as I go,
Sniffing every corner for the chance of rhyme,
Stumbling over words like paving stones,
Bumping into lines dreamed long ago.

This benevolent father, enemy of chlorosis,
In the fields awakens verses like roses;
He evaporates worries up into the sky,
And he fills both brains and hives with honey.
It is he who rejuvenates those with crutches
And makes them gay and sweet as young girls,
And bids the crops to grow and ripen
In the ever-flourishing immortal heart!

When, like the poet, he descends into cities,
He ennobles the lot of things most vile,
And kingly he comes, without fanfare or servants,
Into all the hospitals and all the palaces.

À UNE MENDIANTE ROUSSE

Blanche fille aux cheveux roux,
Dont la robe par ses trous
Laisse voir la pauvreté
    Et la beauté,

Pour moi, poète chétif,
Ton jeune corps maladif,
Plein de taches de rousseur,
    A sa douceur.

Tu portes plus galamment
Qu'une reine de roman
Ses cothurnes de velours
    Tes sabots lourds.

Au lieu d'un haillon trop court,
Qu'un superbe habit de cour
Traîne à plis bruyants et longs
    Sur tes talons;

En place de bas troués,
Que pour les yeux des roués
Sur ta jambe un poignard d'or
    Reluise encor;

Que des nœuds mal attachés
Dévoilent pour nos péchés
Tes deux beaux seins, radieux
    Comme des yeux;

LXXXVIII

TO A REDHEADED BEGGAR

White girl with red hair,
The holes of whose dress
Expose poverty
      And beauty,

For me, penniless poet,
Your sickly young body,
Covered in freckles,
      Has its charms.

You wear more gallantly
Than a queen of some romance
Her sandals of velvet
      Your heavy clogs.

Rather than a skimpy rag,
Let a superb courtly gown
Trail in long and rustling folds
      Over your heels;

Instead of torn stockings,
To catch the eyes of the rakes
May a dagger of gold from your garter
      Gleam again;

May poorly tied knots
Release for our sins
Your two beautiful breasts, radiant
      As your eyes;

Que pour te déshabiller
Tes bras se fassent prier
Et chassent à coups mutins
    Les doigts lutins,

Perles de la plus belle eau,
Sonnets de maître Belleau
Par tes galants mis aux fers
    Sans cesse offerts,

Valetaille de rimeurs
Te dédiant leurs primeurs
Et contemplant ton soulier
    Sous l'escalier,

Maint page épris du hasard,
Maint seigneur et maint Ronsard
Épieraient pour le déduit
    Ton frais réduit!

Tu compterais dans tes lits
Plus de baisers que de lis
Et rangerais sous tes lois
    Plus d'un Valois!

— Cependant tu vas gueusant
Quelque vieux débris gisant
Au seuil de quelque Véfour
    De carrefour;

Tu vas lorgnant en dessous
Des bijoux de vingt-neuf sous
Dont je ne puis, oh! pardon!
    Te faire don.

To be stripped bare
May your arms coax a prayer
And mischievously parry
        The impish fingers,

Pearls of the finest waters,
Sonnets by masterful Belleau
By suitors in shackles
        Endlessly offered,

A rabble of rimesters
Dedicate their first fruits
And contemplate your shoe
        From beneath the stairs,

Many a page smitten with hazard,
Many a lord and many a Ronsard
Would spy to locate
        Your drafty keep!

You would count in your beds
More kisses than lilies
And would subject to your laws
        More than one Valois!

—Yet you go on begging
For any old scrap lying
At the threshold of some
        Cut-rate Véfour;

You go on suggestively eyeing
Those jewels at twenty-nine sous
Which I cannot, oh! forgive me!
        Make you a gift.

Va donc, sans autre ornement,
Parfum, perles, diamant,
Que ta maigre nudité,
　　Ô ma beauté!

Go then, with no other ornament,
Perfume, pearls, diamonds,
Than your meager nudity,
     O my beauty!

LXXXIX

LE CYGNE

À *Victor Hugo*.

I

Andromaque, je pense à vous! Ce petit fleuve,
Pauvre et triste miroir où jadis resplendit
L'immense majesté de vos douleurs de veuve,
Ce Simoïs menteur qui par vos pleurs grandit,

A fécondé soudain ma mémoire fertile,
Comme je traversais le nouveau Carrousel.
Le vieux Paris n'est plus (la forme d'une ville
Change plus vite, hélas! que le cœur d'un mortel);

Je ne vois qu'en esprit tout ce camp de baraques,
Ces tas de chapiteaux ébauchés et de fûts,
Les herbes, les gros blocs verdis par l'eau des flaques,
Et, brillant aux carreaux, le bric-à-brac confus.

Là s'étalait jadis une ménagerie;
Là je vis, un matin, à l'heure où sous les cieux
Froids et clairs le Travail s'éveille, où la voirie
Pousse un sombre ouragan dans l'air silencieux,

Un cygne qui s'était évadé de sa cage,
Et, de ses pieds palmés frottant le pavé sec,
Sur le sol raboteux traînait son blanc plumage.
Près d'un ruisseau sans eau la bête ouvrant le bec

THE SWAN

To Victor Hugo.

I

Andromache, I think of you! This little stream,
Poor and sad mirror where once reflected
The immense majesty of your widow's grief,
This duplicitous Simois swelled by your tears,

Suddenly made fecund my fertile memory,
As I was crossing the new Carrousel.
The Paris of old is no more (the form of a city
Changes more swiftly, alas! than a mortal heart);

I see only in the mind's eye this camp of stalls,
These heaps of rough-hewn capitals and shafts,
The weeds, the great blocks greened by the water of puddles,
And, sparkling in shop windows, the confused bric-a-brac.

There long ago a menagerie unfurled;
There I saw, one morning, at the hour when under the sky
Cold and clear Work awakens, when the street cleaners
Drive a somber storm in the silent air,

A swan that had escaped its cage,
And, webbed feet scraping dry stones,
Dragged his white plumage upon uneven ground.
Near a waterless gutter the beast with gaping beak

Baignait nerveusement ses ailes dans la poudre,
Et disait, le cœur plein de son beau lac natal:
« Eau, quand donc pleuvras-tu? quand tonneras-tu, foudre? »
Je vois ce malheureux, mythe étrange et fatal,

Vers le ciel quelquefois, comme l'homme d'Ovide,
Vers le ciel ironique et cruellement bleu,
Sur son cou convulsif tendant sa tête avide,
Comme s'il adressait des reproches à Dieu!

II

Paris change! mais rien dans ma mélancolie
N'a bougé! palais neufs, échafaudages, blocs,
Vieux faubourgs, tout pour moi devient allégorie,
Et mes chers souvenirs sont plus lourds que des rocs.

Aussi devant ce Louvre une image m'opprime:
Je pense à mon grand cygne, avec ses gestes fous,
Comme les exilés, ridicule et sublime,
Et rongé d'un désir sans trêve! et puis à vous,

Andromaque, des bras d'un grand époux tombée,
Vil bétail, sous la main du superbe Pyrrhus,
Auprès d'un tombeau vide en extase courbée;
Veuve d'Hector, hélas! et femme d'Hélénus!

Je pense à la négresse, amaigrie et phtisique,
Piétinant dans la boue, et cherchant, l'œil hagard,
Les cocotiers absents de la superbe Afrique
Derrière la muraille immense du brouillard;

Nervously bathed its wings in the dust,
And said, heart full with the beautiful lake of his birth:
"Water, when will you rain? thunder, when will you boom?"
I see this malcontent, myth strange and fatal,

Toward the sky sometimes, like man in Ovid,
Toward the sky ironic and cruelly blue,
On his convulsive neck stretch his avid head,
As if addressing reproaches to God!

II

Paris changes! but nothing in my melancholy
Has stirred! new palaces, scaffoldings, blocks,
Old neighborhoods, for me everything becomes allegory,
And my cherished memories more weighty than rocks.

And so before the Louvre I am oppressed by an image:
I think of my great swan, with his mad gestures,
Like exiles, ridiculous and sublime,
And gnawed by an insatiable desire! and then of you,

Andromache, fallen from the arms of a mighty husband,
Lowly chattel, under the sway of haughty Pyrrhus,
Bowed in a trance beside an empty tomb;
Widow of Hector, alas! and wife of Helenus!

I think of the negress, gaunt and consumptive,
Trudging in sludge, and seeking, eyes haggard,
The absent palms of splendid Africa
Behind the immense barrier of fog;

À quiconque a perdu ce qui ne se retrouve
Jamais, jamais! à ceux qui s'abreuvent de pleurs
Et tètent la Douleur comme une bonne louve!
Aux maigres orphelins séchant comme des fleurs!

Ainsi dans la forêt où mon esprit s'exile
Un vieux Souvenir sonne à plein souffle du cor!
Je pense aux matelots oubliés dans une île,
Aux captifs, aux vaincus!... à bien d'autres encor!

Of whoever has lost what cannot be found
Never, never! of those who drink their own tears
And suckle Sorrow like a gracious she-wolf!
Of starving orphans parched as flowers!

Thus in the forest of my mind's exile
An ancient Memory sounds a full-throated horn!
I think of sailors forgotten upon an isle,
Of the captives, of the vanquished!... and of many more!

LES SEPT VIEILLARDS

À Victor Hugo.

Fourmillante cité, cité pleine de rêves,
Où le spectre en plein jour raccroche le passant!
Les mystères partout coulent comme des sèves
Dans les canaux étroits du colosse puissant.

Un matin, cependant que dans la triste rue
Les maisons, dont la brume allongeait la hauteur,
Simulaient les deux quais d'une rivière accrue,
Et que, décor semblable à l'âme de l'acteur,

Un brouillard sale et jaune inondait tout l'espace,
Je suivais, roidissant mes nerfs comme un héros
Et discutant avec mon âme déjà lasse,
Le faubourg secoué par les lourds tombereaux.

Tout à coup, un vieillard dont les guenilles jaunes
Imitaient la couleur de ce ciel pluvieux,
Et dont l'aspect aurait fait pleuvoir les aumônes,
Sans la méchanceté qui luisait dans ses yeux,

M'apparut. On eût dit sa prunelle trempée
Dans le fiel; son regard aiguisait les frimas,
Et sa barbe à longs poils, roide comme une épée,
Se projetait, pareille à celle de Judas.

Il n'était pas voûté, mais cassé, son échine
Faisant avec sa jambe un parfait angle droit,
Si bien que son bâton, parachevant sa mine,
Lui donnait la tournure et le pas maladroit

THE SEVEN OLD MEN

To Victor Hugo.

Swarming city, city full of dreams,
Where the specter in broad daylight seizes the passerby!
Mysteries seep everywhere like sap
Through the pinched arteries of the mighty colossus.

One morning, while in the dismal street
The houses, stretched high by the haze,
Were simulating two quays of a swollen river,
And while, scenery akin to an actor's soul,

A filthy yellow fog flooded all round,
I traced, steeling my nerves like a hero
And bickering with my long-suffering soul,
The neighborhood shaken by carts loaded down.

Suddenly, an old man whose yellow rags
Mimicked the color of the rainy sky,
And whose aspect would have drawn showers of alms,
Were it not for the malice that gleamed in his eyes,

Appeared. It was as if his eye was soaked
In bile; his gaze would have whet hoarfrost,
And his long beard, stiff as a sword,
Jutted out, like that of Judas.

He was not bent, but broken, his spine
Forming a perfect right angle with his leg,
So that his cane, the finishing touch,
Gave him the shape and the faltering step

D'un quadrupède infirme ou d'un juif à trois pattes.
Dans la neige et la boue il allait s'empêtrant,
Comme s'il écrasait des morts sous ses savates,
Hostile à l'univers plutôt qu'indifférent.

Son pareil le suivait: barbe, œil, dos, bâton, loques,
Nul trait ne distinguait, du même enfer venu,
Ce jumeau centenaire, et ces spectres baroques
Marchaient du même pas vers un but inconnu.

À quel complot infâme étais-je donc en butte,
Ou quel méchant hasard ainsi m'humiliait?
Car je comptai sept fois, de minute en minute,
Ce sinistre vieillard qui se multipliait!

Que celui-là qui rit de mon inquiétude,
Et qui n'est pas saisi d'un frisson fraternel,
Songe bien que malgré tant de décrépitude
Ces sept monstres hideux avaient l'air éternel!

Aurais-je, sans mourir, contemplé le huitième,
Sosie inexorable, ironique et fatal,
Dégoûtant Phénix, fils et père de lui-même?
— Mais je tournai le dos au cortège infernal.

Exaspéré comme un ivrogne qui voit double,
Je rentrai, je fermai ma porte, épouvanté,
Malade et morfondu, l'esprit fiévreux et trouble,
Blessé par le mystère et par l'absurdité!

Of an infirm quadruped or a three-legged Jew.
In snow and sludge he scuffled along,
As if crushing the dead beneath worn out shoes,
More hostile than indifferent to the universe.

His double followed him: beard, eye, back, cane, rags,
No trait distinguished them, come from the same hell,
This centenarian twin, and these baroque specters
Marched in step to an unknown end.

Of what infamous conspiracy was I the dupe,
Or what spiteful fortune would humiliate me thus?
For I counted seven times, minute by minute,
This sinister old man who multiplied himself!

Whoever laughs at my disquiet,
And is not seized by a fraternal shiver,
Note well that despite such decrepitude
These seven hideous monsters had an eternal air!

Could I, without dying, have contemplated the eighth,
Inexorable copy, ironic and fatal,
Disgusting Phoenix, self-same father and son?
—But I turned my back on the infernal procession.

Exasperated like a drunk who sees double,
I went home, I locked my door, terrified,
Sick and despondent, mind feverish and troubled,
Wounded by the mystery and absurdity!

Vainement ma raison voulait prendre la barre;
La tempête en jouant déroutait ses efforts,
Et mon âme dansait, dansait, vieille gabarre
Sans mâts, sur une mer monstrueuse et sans bords!

Vainly my reason tried to take the helm;
The beguiling tempest baffled its efforts,
And my soul danced, danced, old barge
Without sails, upon a monstrous and unbounded sea!

LES PETITES VIEILLES

À Victor Hugo.

I

Dans les plis sinueux des vieilles capitales,
Où tout, même l'horreur, tourne aux enchantements,
Je guette, obéissant à mes humeurs fatales,
Des êtres singuliers, décrépits et charmants.

Ces monstres disloqués furent jadis des femmes,
Éponine ou Laïs! Monstres brisés, bossus
Ou tordus, aimons-les! ce sont encor des âmes.
Sous des jupons troués et sous de froids tissus

Ils rampent, flagellés par les bises iniques,
Frémissant au fracas roulant des omnibus,
Et serrant sur leur flanc, ainsi que des reliques,
Un petit sac brodé de fleurs ou de rébus;

Ils trottent, tout pareils à des marionnettes;
Se traînent, comme font les animaux blessés,
Ou dansent, sans vouloir danser, pauvres sonnettes
Où se pend un Démon sans pitié! Tout cassés

Qu'ils sont, ils ont des yeux perçants comme une vrille,
Luisants comme ces trous où l'eau dort dans la nuit;
Ils ont les yeux divins de la petite fille
Qui s'étonne et qui rit à tout ce qui reluit.

THE LITTLE OLD LADIES

To Victor Hugo.

I

In the sinuous folds of old capitals,
Where all, even horror, turns to enchantment,
I spy, obeying my fatal humors,
Certain singular beings, decrepit and charming.

These disjointed monsters who once were women,
Éponine or Laïs! Broken monsters, hunchbacked
Or twisted, let us love them! they are still ensouled.
Under tattered skirts and flimsy fabrics

They creep, whipped by iniquitous winds,
Trembling amid the omnibus clatter,
And clutching to their hip, as if some relic,
A purse embroidered with flowers or rebus;

They trot, as if they were marionettes;
Limp along, as wounded animals do,
Or dance, without meaning to dance, poor bells
From which dangles some pitiless Demon! Cracked

Though they are, their eyes pierce like a drill,
Gleaming like those holes where water sleeps at night;
Divine eyes like those of the little girl
Who startles and laughs at all that shines.

— Avez-vous observé que maints cercueils de vieilles
Sont presque aussi petits que celui d'un enfant?
La Mort savante met dans ces bières pareilles
Un symbole d'un goût bizarre et captivant,

Et lorsque j'entrevois un fantôme débile
Traversant de Paris le fourmillant tableau,
Il me semble toujours que cet être fragile
S'en va tout doucement vers un nouveau berceau;

À moins que, méditant sur la géométrie,
Je ne cherche, à l'aspect de ces membres discords,
Combien de fois il faut que l'ouvrier varie
La forme de la boîte où l'on met tous ces corps.

— Ces yeux sont des puits faits d'un million de larmes,
Des creusets qu'un métal refroidi pailleta...
Ces yeux mystérieux ont d'invincibles charmes
Pour celui que l'austère Infortune allaita!

II

De Frascati défunt Vestale enamourée;
Prêtresse de Thalie, hélas! dont le souffleur
Enterré sait le nom; célèbre évaporée
Que Tivoli jadis ombragea dans sa fleur,

Toutes m'enivrent; mais parmi ces êtres frêles
Il en est qui, faisant de la douleur un miel,
Ont dit au Dévouement qui leur prêtait ses ailes:
Hippogriffe puissant, mène-moi jusqu'au ciel!

—Have you noticed how many coffins of old ladies
Are nearly as small as that of a child?
Learnèd Death posits in these caskets akin
A symbol at once bizarre and beguiling,

And when I glimpse an enfeebled phantom
Traversing the swarming tableau of Paris,
It seems always as if this fragile being
Gently carries herself toward a new cradle;

Unless, meditating upon geometry,
I think only, at the sight of discordant limbs,
Of how many times the worker must vary
The form of the box where we put every corpse.

—These eyes are wells made of a million tears,
Crucibles spangled by cooling metal...
These mysterious eyes have invincible charms
For one suckled by austere Misfortune!

II

Vestal beloved of defunct Frascati;
Priestess of Thalia, alas! the buried prompter
Knows the name; evaporated fame
Once shaded by Tivoli in full flower,

All intoxicate; yet among these frail beings
Are those who, turning sadness to honey,
Have said to Devotion who lends them his wings:
Powerful Hippogriff, carry me to heaven!

L'une, par sa patrie au malheur exercée,
L'autre, que son époux surchargea de douleurs,
L'autre, par son enfant Madone transpercée,
Toutes auraient pu faire un fleuve avec leurs pleurs!

III

Ah! que j'en ai suivi de ces petites vieilles!
Une, entre autres, à l'heure où le soleil tombant
Ensanglante le ciel de blessures vermeilles,
Pensive, s'asseyait à l'écart sur un banc,

Pour entendre un de ces concerts, riches de cuivre,
Dont les soldats parfois inondent nos jardins,
Et qui, dans ces soirs d'or où l'on se sent revivre,
Versent quelque héroïsme au cœur des citadins.

Celle-là, droite encor, fière et sentant la règle,
Humait avidement ce chant vif et guerrier;
Son œil parfois s'ouvrait comme l'œil d'un vieil aigle;
Son front de marbre avait l'air fait pour le laurier!

IV

Telles vous cheminez, stoïques et sans plaintes,
À travers le chaos des vivantes cités,
Mères au cœur saignant, courtisanes ou saintes,
Dont autrefois les noms par tous étaient cités.

Vous qui fûtes la grâce ou qui fûtes la gloire,
Nul ne vous reconnaît! un ivrogne incivil
Vous insulte en passant d'un amour dérisoire;
Sur vos talons gambade un enfant lâche et vil.

One, by her country schooled in hardship,
Another, whom her husband has surcharged with sorrow,
Another, by child made transpierced Madonna,
All could have poured out a river of tears!

III

Ah! how many of these little old ladies I have followed!
One, among others, when the falling sun
Bloodies the sky with vermillion wounds,
Pensive, would sit apart upon a bench,

To listen to one of those concerts, rich with brass,
With which soldiers sometimes drown our gardens,
And which, in those evenings of gold when we feel reborn,
Pour some heroism into the heart of city dwellers.

This one, still upright, proud and on guard,
Taking avid draughts of the bright warlike song;
Her eye would sometimes open like an old eagle's;
Her brow of marble as if made for the laurel!

IV

Such are your paths, stoic and uncomplaining,
Across the chaos of teeming cities,
Mothers of the bleeding heart, courtesans or saints,
Whose names were once noted by all.

You who were grace or you who were glory,
Now known to none! an uncivil drunk
Insults you in passing with mock propositions;
A despicable child gambols at your heels.

Honteuses d'exister, ombres ratatinées,
Peureuses, le dos bas, vous côtoyez les murs;
Et nul ne vous salue, étranges destinées!
Débris d'humanité pour l'éternité mûrs!

Mais moi, moi qui de loin tendrement vous surveille,
L'œil inquiet, fixé sur vos pas incertains,
Tout comme si j'étais votre père, ô merveille!
Je goûte à votre insu des plaisirs clandestins:

Je vois s'épanouir vos passions novices;
Sombres ou lumineux, je vis vos jours perdus;
Mon cœur multiplié jouit de tous vos vices!
Mon âme resplendit de toutes vos vertus!

Ruines! ma famille! ô cerveaux congénères!
Je vous fais chaque soir un solennel adieu!
Où serez-vous demain, Èves octogénaires,
Sur qui pèse la griffe effroyable de Dieu?

Ashamed to exist, shriveled shadows,
Timorous, backs bent, you cling to the walls;
And no one salutes you, estranged destinies!
Debris of humanity ripe for eternity!

But I, I who tenderly surveil you from afar,
Restless eye, fixed upon your uncertain steps,
As though I were your father, o marvel!
Unknown to you I taste clandestine pleasures:

I see the flowering of your novice passions;
Somber or luminous, I live your lost days;
My multiplied heart enjoys all your vices!
My soul is resplendent with all your virtues!

Ruins! my family! o congenerous brains!
I bid you each evening a solemn adieu!
Where will you be tomorrow, octogenarian Eves,
Upon whom presses God's fearsome claw?

LES AVEUGLES

Contemple-les, mon âme; ils sont vraiment affreux!
Pareils aux mannequins; vaguement ridicules;
Terribles, singuliers comme les somnambules;
Dardant on ne sait où leurs globes ténébreux.

Leurs yeux, d'où la divine étincelle est partie,
Comme s'ils regardaient au loin, restent levés
Au ciel; on ne les voit jamais vers les pavés
Pencher rêveusement leur tête appesantie.

Ils traversent ainsi le noir illimité,
Ce frère du silence éternel. Ô cité!
Pendant qu'autour de nous tu chantes, ris et beugles,

Éprise du plaisir jusqu'à l'atrocité,
Vois! je me traîne aussi! mais, plus qu'eux hébété,
Je dis: Que cherchent-ils au Ciel, tous ces aveugles?

XCII

THE BLIND

Consider them, my soul; they are truly ghastly!
Like mannequins; vaguely ridiculous;
Terrible, singular as somnambulists;
Darting their tenebrous globes who knows where.

Their eyes, from which the divine spark has departed,
As though watching the distance, remain raised
To the sky; toward the street one never sees them
Dreamily bow their heavy head.

Thus they traverse the unlimited black,
That brother of eternal silence. O city!
While all around us you sing, laugh and bellow,

Taken with pleasure to the point of atrocity,
See! I also drag myself along! but, more dazed than them,
I ask: What do they look for in Heaven, the blind?

À UNE PASSANTE

La rue assourdissante autour de moi hurlait.
Longue, mince, en grand deuil, douleur majestueuse,
Une femme passa, d'une main fastueuse
Soulevant, balançant le feston et l'ourlet;

Agile et noble, avec sa jambe de statue.
Moi, je buvais, crispé comme un extravagant,
Dans son œil, ciel livide où germe l'ouragan,
La douceur qui fascine et le plaisir qui tue.

Un éclair... puis la nuit! — Fugitive beauté
Dont le regard m'a fait soudainement renaître,
Ne te verrai-je plus que dans l'éternité?

Ailleurs, bien loin d'ici! trop tard! *jamais* peut-être!
Car j'ignore où tu fuis, tu ne sais où je vais,
Ô toi que j'eusse aimée, ô toi qui le savais!

TO A PASSERBY

The deafening street howled around me.
Tall, slender, in full mourning, sadness majestic,
A woman passed, with an ostentatious hand
Lifting, swaying the festoon and the hem;

Agile and noble, of statuesque leg.
Me, I drank, trembling like an extravagant,
In her eye, livid sky where brews the storm,
The sweetness that fascinates and the pleasure that kills.

A flash... then the night! —Fugitive beauty
In whose gaze I am suddenly reborn,
Shall I see you no more till eternity?

Elsewhere, far away! too late! *never* perhaps!
For I know not where you flee, you know not where I go,
O you whom I could have loved, o you who understood!

LE SQUELETTE LABOUREUR

I

Dans les planches d'anatomie
Qui traînent sur ces quais poudreux
Où maint livre cadavéreux
Dort comme une antique momie,

Dessins auxquels la gravité
Et le savoir d'un vieil artiste,
Bien que le sujet en soit triste,
Ont communiqué la Beauté,

On voit, ce qui rend plus complètes
Ces mystérieuses horreurs,
Bêchant comme des laboureurs,
Des Écorchés et des Squelettes.

II

De ce terrain que vous fouillez,
Manants résignés et funèbres,
De tout l'effort de vos vertèbres,
Ou de vos muscles dépouillés,

Dites, quelle moisson étrange,
Forçats arrachés au charnier,
Tirez-vous, et de quel fermier
Avez-vous à remplir la grange?

THE SKELETON LABORER

I

In anatomical plates
That lie around the dusty quays
Where many a cadaverous book
Sleeps like an ancient mummy,

Drawings wherein the gravitas
And the sagacity of a seasoned artist,
Notwithstanding their sad subject,
Have communicated Beauty,

One sees, the finishing touch
On these mysterious horrors,
Digging like laborers,
The Skinned and the Skeletons.

II

From this ground that you excavate,
Resigned and funereal churls,
With what's left of your backbone,
Or your muscles flayed bare,

Tell us, what strange harvest,
Slaves snatched from the charnel,
Do you reap, and for what farmer
Must you fill the barn?

Voulez-vous (d'un destin trop dur
Épouvantable et clair emblème!)
Montrer que dans la fosse même
Le sommeil promis n'est pas sûr;

Qu'envers nous le Néant est traître;
Que tout, même la Mort, nous ment,
Et que sempiternellement,
Hélas! il nous faudra peut-être

Dans quelque pays inconnu
Écorcher la terre revêche
Et pousser une lourde bêche
Sous notre pied sanglant et nu?

Do you want (of too dour a fate
Emblem ghastly and clear!)
To demonstrate that even in the grave
Our promised sleep is uncertain;

That Nothingness would betray us;
That all, even Death, deceives us,
And that sempiternally,
Alas! we may be made

In some unknown country
To flay the bitter earth
And to shove a heavy spade
Beneath our bare and bloody feet?

LE CRÉPUSCULE DU SOIR

Voici le soir charmant, ami du criminel;
Il vient comme un complice, à pas de loup; le ciel
Se ferme lentement comme une grande alcôve,
Et l'homme impatient se change en bête fauve.

Ô soir, aimable soir, désiré par celui
Dont les bras, sans mentir, peuvent dire: Aujourd'hui
Nous avons travaillé! — C'est le soir qui soulage
Les esprits que dévore une douleur sauvage,
Le savant obstiné dont le front s'alourdit,
Et l'ouvrier courbé qui regagne son lit.
Cependant des démons malsains dans l'atmosphère
S'éveillent lourdement, comme des gens d'affaire,
Et cognent en volant les volets et l'auvent.
À travers les lueurs que tourmente le vent
La Prostitution s'allume dans les rues;
Comme une fourmilière elle ouvre ses issues;
Partout elle se fraye un occulte chemin,
Ainsi que l'ennemi qui tente un coup de main;
Elle remue au sein de la cité de fange
Comme un ver qui dérobe à l'Homme ce qu'il mange.
On entend çà et là les cuisines siffler,
Les théâtres glapir, les orchestres ronfler;
Les tables d'hôte, dont le jeu fait les délices,
S'emplissent de catins et d'escrocs, leurs complices,
Et les voleurs, qui n'ont ni trêve ni merci,
Vont bientôt commencer leur travail, eux aussi,
Et forcer doucement les portes et les caisses
Pour vivre quelques jours et vêtir leurs maîtresses.

XCV

EVENING TWILIGHT

Here is the charming evening, friend of the criminal;
He comes like an accomplice, discretely; the sky
Closes slowly like a great alcove,
And impatient man becomes a wild beast.

O evening, lovely evening, desired by he
Whose arms, without lying, can say: Today
We have worked! —It is the evening who soothes
Those spirits devoured by an untamed sorrow,
The stubborn scholar whose brow weighs heavy,
And the slumped worker who regains his bed.
Meanwhile unwholesome demons in the atmosphere
Wake heavily, like business men,
And bump in flight the shutters and the eves.
Traversing the glimmers tormented by the wind
Prostitution alights in the streets;
Like an anthill she opens her exits;
Everywhere spawning an occult path,
As an enemy launches a surprise attack;
She writhes in the heart of the city of mud
Like a worm that steals from Man what he eats.
The sound here and there of the wheezing kitchens,
The squalling theaters, the snoring orchestras;
The public tables, spread with gambling's delicacies,
Fill up with whores and swindlers, accomplices,
And thieves, who know neither truce nor mercy,
Soon set about their work, they as well,
Gently coercing doors and coffers
To live a few days and adorn their mistresses.

Recueille-toi, mon âme, en ce grave moment,
Et ferme ton oreille à ce rugissement.
C'est l'heure où les douleurs des malades s'aigrissent!
La sombre Nuit les prend à la gorge; ils finissent
Leur destinée et vont vers le gouffre commun;
L'hôpital se remplit de leurs soupirs. — Plus d'un
Ne viendra plus chercher la soupe parfumée,
Au coin du feu, le soir, auprès d'une âme aimée.

Encore la plupart n'ont-ils jamais connu
La douceur du foyer et n'ont jamais vécu!

Recollect yourself, my soul, in this grave moment,
And close your ears to this clamor.
It is the hour that sharpens the pains of the sick!
The somber Night takes them by the throat; they fulfill
Their destiny and sink into the common chasm;
The hospital replete with their sighs. —More than one
Will come no longer for the fragrant soup,
At fireside, in the evening, close to a beloved soul.

Yet most have never known
The sweetness of the hearth and have never lived at all!

LE JEU

Dans des fauteuils fanés des courtisanes vieilles,
Pâles, le sourcil peint, l'œil câlin et fatal,
Minaudant, et faisant de leurs maigres oreilles
Tomber un cliquetis de pierre et de métal;

Autour des verts tapis des visages sans lèvre,
Des lèvres sans couleur, des mâchoires sans dent,
Et des doigts convulsés d'une infernale fièvre,
Fouillant la poche vide ou le sein palpitant;

Sous de sales plafonds un rang de pâles lustres
Et d'énormes quinquets projetant leurs lueurs
Sur des fronts ténébreux de poètes illustres
Qui viennent gaspiller leurs sanglantes sueurs;

Voilà le noir tableau qu'en un rêve nocturne
Je vis se dérouler sous mon œil clairvoyant.
Moi-même, dans un coin de l'antre taciturne,
Je me vis accoudé, froid, muet, enviant,

Enviant de ces gens la passion tenace,
De ces vieilles putains la funèbre gaieté,
Et tous gaillardement trafiquant à ma face,
L'un de son vieil honneur, l'autre de sa beauté!

Et mon cœur s'effraya d'envier maint pauvre homme
Courant avec ferveur à l'abîme béant,
Et qui, soûl de son sang, préférerait en somme
La douleur à la mort et l'enfer au néant!

GAMBLING

In faded armchairs some old courtesans,
Pale, painted brows, eyes alluring and fatal,
Mincing, and toying with their meager ears
That droop with jangling stone and metal;

Around the green felt some lipless faces,
Bloodless lips, toothless jaws,
And fingers convulsed with infernal fever,
Rifling through empty pockets or quivering breasts;

Pale chandeliers under soiled ceilings
And enormous lamps projecting their glimmers
On the tenebrous brows of illustrious poets
Who come here to squander their sanguine sweat;

Such the black tableau of a nocturnal dream
I saw unwind under my clairvoyant eye.
Myself, in a corner of the taciturn den,
I saw propped, cold, silent, envious,

Envious of these people's tenacious passion,
Of the funereal cheer of the aging whores,
And all of them trafficking right in my face,
One his hoary honor, the other her beauty!

And my heart was horrified to envy such wretches
Running fervently into the gaping abyss,
And who, drunk on their blood, would prefer after all
Agony to death and hell to nothingness!

DANSE MACABRE

À *Ernest Christophe*.

Fière, autant qu'un vivant, de sa noble stature,
Avec son gros bouquet, son mouchoir et ses gants,
Elle a la nonchalance et la désinvolture
D'une coquette maigre aux airs extravagants.

Vit-on jamais au bal une taille plus mince?
Sa robe exagérée, en sa royale ampleur,
S'écroule abondamment sur un pied sec que pince
Un soulier pomponné, joli comme une fleur.

La ruche qui se joue au bord des clavicules,
Comme un ruisseau lascif qui se frotte au rocher,
Défend pudiquement des lazzi ridicules
Les funèbres appas qu'elle tient à cacher.

Ses yeux profonds sont faits de vide et de ténèbres,
Et son crâne, de fleurs artistement coiffé,
Oscille mollement sur ses frêles vertèbres.
Ô charme d'un néant follement attifé!

Aucuns t'appelleront une caricature,
Qui ne comprennent pas, amants ivres de chair,
L'élégance sans nom de l'humaine armature.
Tu réponds, grand squelette, à mon goût le plus cher!

XCVII

DANSE MACABRE

To Ernest Christophe.

Proud, as any among the living, of noble stature,
With her great bouquet, her handkerchief and gloves,
She has the nonchalance and the flippancy
Of a skinny coquette with extravagant airs.

Was there ever so slender a waist at the ball?
Her exorbitant gown, in its regal plenitude,
Drapes abundantly over a dry foot pinched
In a pompomed slipper, pretty as a flower.

The frill that plays at the edge of the clavicles,
Like a lascivious stream that rubs on the rocks,
Primly defends from ridiculous gibes
The funereal charms she keeps close to her chest.

Her deep eyes are made of void and of shadow,
And her skull, with flowers artistically coiffed,
Wobbles gently upon her frail vertebrae.
O the charm of a nothingness dressed to the nines!

A caricature they'll call you,
Those who don't grasp, lovers drunken with flesh,
The nameless elegance of human armature.
You answer, grand skeleton, my most cherished inclination!

Viens-tu troubler, avec ta puissante grimace,
La fête de la Vie? ou quelque vieux désir,
Éperonnant encor ta vivante carcasse,
Te pousse-t-il, crédule, au sabbat du Plaisir?

Au chant des violons, aux flammes des bougies,
Espères-tu chasser ton cauchemar moqueur,
Et viens-tu demander au torrent des orgies
De rafraîchir l'enfer allumé dans ton cœur?

Inépuisable puits de sottise et de fautes!
De l'antique douleur éternel alambic!
À travers le treillis recourbé de tes côtes
Je vois, errant encor, l'insatiable aspic.

Pour dire vrai, je crains que ta coquetterie
Ne trouve pas un prix digne de ses efforts;
Qui, de ces cœurs mortels, entend la raillerie?
Les charmes de l'horreur n'enivrent que les forts!

Le gouffre de tes yeux, plein d'horribles pensées,
Exhale le vertige, et les danseurs prudents
Ne contempleront pas sans d'amères nausées
Le sourire éternel de tes trente-deux dents.

Pourtant, qui n'a serré dans ses bras un squelette,
Et qui ne s'est nourri des choses du tombeau?
Qu'importe le parfum, l'habit ou la toilette?
Qui fait le dégoûté montre qu'il se croit beau.

Bayadère sans nez, irrésistible gouge,
Dis donc à ces danseurs qui font les offusqués:
« Fiers mignons, malgré l'art des poudres et du rouge
Vous sentez tous la mort! Ô squelettes musqués,

Have you come to trouble, with your mighty grimace,
The party of Life? or does some old desire,
Still spurring your living carcass,
Drive you, credulous, toward the sabbath of Pleasure?

With the song of violins, with the flames of candles,
Do you hope to dispel your mocking nightmare,
And have you come to ask this torrent of orgies
To cool the hell that burns in your heart?

Inexhaustible well of folly and error!
Eternal alembic of ancient sorrow!
Through the curved trellis of your ribs
I see, wending still, the insatiable aspic.

To be honest, I fear that your coquetry
May not fetch a price worth your pains;
Who, among these mortal hearts, gets the joke?
Horror's charms intoxicate only the strong!

The abyss of your eyes, full of horrible thoughts,
Exhales vertigo, and the prudent dancers
Cannot behold without bitter nausea
The eternal smile of your thirty-two teeth.

Yet, who has not clutched a skeleton in his arms,
And who has not fed upon things of the grave?
What matter the perfume, the clothes or the toilette?
He who feigns disgust shows he thinks himself handsome.

Bayadère without nose, irresistible gouge,
Say then to the dancers who take such offense:
"Proud darlings, despite the art of powders and rouge
You all smell of death! O musky skeletons,

« Antinoüs flétris, dandys à face glabre,
Cadavres vernissés, lovelaces chenus,
Le branle universel de la danse macabre
Vous entraîne en des lieux qui ne sont pas connus!

« Des quais froids de la Seine aux bords brûlants du Gange,
Le troupeau mortel saute et se pâme, sans voir
Dans un trou du plafond la trompette de l'Ange
Sinistrement béante ainsi qu'un tromblon noir.

« En tout climat, sous tout soleil, la Mort t'admire
En tes contorsions, risible Humanité,
Et souvent, comme toi, se parfumant de myrrhe,
Mêle son ironie à ton insanité! »

"Withered Antinoi, dandies with glabrous faces,
Varnished cadavers, hoary lovelaces,
The universal jerk of the danse macabre
Sweeps you off to unknown places!

"From cold quays of the Seine to burning shores of the Ganges,
The mortal herd skips and swoons, not seeing
The Angel's horn in a hole in the ceiling
Gaping sinisterly like a black blunderbuss.

"In every clime, under every sun, Death admires you
In your contortions, risible Humanity,
And often, like you, scents herself with myrrh,
Mingling her irony with your insanity!"

XCVIII

L'AMOUR DU MENSONGE

Quand je te vois passer, ô ma chère indolente,
Au chant des instruments qui se brise au plafond
Suspendant ton allure harmonieuse et lente,
Et promenant l'ennui de ton regard profond;

Quand je contemple, aux feux du gaz qui le colore,
Ton front pâle, embelli par un morbide attrait,
Où les torches du soir allument une aurore,
Et tes yeux attirants comme ceux d'un portrait,

Je me dis: Qu'elle est belle! et bizarrement fraîche!
Le souvenir massif, royale et lourde tour,
La couronne, et son cœur, meurtri comme une pêche,
Est mûr, comme son corps, pour le savant amour.

Es-tu le fruit d'automne aux saveurs souveraines?
Es-tu vase funèbre attendant quelques pleurs,
Parfum qui fait rêver aux oasis lointaines,
Oreiller caressant, ou corbeille de fleurs?

Je sais qu'il est des yeux, des plus mélancoliques,
Qui ne recèlent point de secrets précieux;
Beaux écrins sans joyaux, médaillons sans reliques,
Plus vides, plus profonds que vous-mêmes, ô Cieux!

Mais ne suffit-il pas que tu sois l'apparence,
Pour réjouir un cœur qui fuit la vérité?
Qu'importe ta bêtise ou ton indifférence?
Masque ou décor, salut! J'adore ta beauté.

LOVE OF THE LIE

When I see you pass by, my dear indolent one,
To the instruments' song that breaks on the ceiling
Suspending your slow and harmonious allure,
And parading the ennui of your fathomless gaze;

When I contemplate, colored by gaslight,
Your pale brow, embellished by a morbid attraction,
Where evening torches light an aurora,
And your come-hither eyes like those of a portrait,

I say to myself: How beautiful she is! and strangely fresh!
Massive memory, regal and heavy tower,
Crowns her, and her heart, bruised like a peach,
Is ripe, like her body, for knowledge of love.

Are you autumn fruit with its sovereign savor?
Are you funerary vase awaiting some tears,
Perfume breeding dreams of distant oases,
Caressing pillow, or basket of flowers?

I know there are eyes, most melancholic,
That conceal no precious secrets;
Beautiful cases without jewels, medallions without relics,
More empty, more profound than yourself, o Heavens!

But suffices it not that you be semblance,
To rejoice a heart that flees from the truth?
What matter your stupidity or indifference?
Mask or decor, there you are! I adore your beauty.

Je n'ai pas oublié, voisine de la ville,
Notre blanche maison, petite mais tranquille;
Sa Pomone de plâtre et sa vieille Vénus
Dans un bosquet chétif cachant leurs membres nus,
Et le soleil, le soir, ruisselant et superbe,
Qui, derrière la vitre où se brisait sa gerbe,
Semblait, grand œil ouvert dans le ciel curieux,
Contempler nos dîners longs et silencieux,
Répandant largement ses beaux reflets de cierge
Sur la nappe frugale et les rideaux de serge.

I have not forgotten, next to the city,
Our white house, little but tranquil;
Its plaster Pomona and its elderly Venus
In a meager copse hiding their naked members,
And the sun, in the evening, streaming down and superb,
Which, behind the pane where its sheaf would shatter,
Seemed, great open eye in the curious sky,
To contemplate our long and silent dinners,
Spreading widely its beautiful candle reflections
Upon the frugal cloth and the serge curtains.

La servante au grand cœur dont vous étiez jalouse,
Et qui dort son sommeil sous une humble pelouse,
Nous devrions pourtant lui porter quelques fleurs.
Les morts, les pauvres morts, ont de grandes douleurs,
Et quand Octobre souffle, émondeur des vieux arbres,
Son vent mélancolique à l'entour de leurs marbres,
Certe, ils doivent trouver les vivants bien ingrats,
À dormir, comme ils font, chaudement dans leurs draps,
Tandis que, dévorés de noires songeries,
Sans compagnon de lit, sans bonnes causeries,
Vieux squelettes gelés travaillés par le ver,
Ils sentent s'égoutter les neiges de l'hiver
Et le siècle couler, sans qu'amis ni famille
Remplacent les lambeaux qui pendent à leur grille.

Lorsque la bûche siffle et chante, si le soir,
Calme, dans le fauteuil je la voyais s'asseoir,
Si, par une nuit bleue et froide de décembre,
Je la trouvais tapie en un coin de ma chambre,
Grave, et venant du fond de son lit éternel
Couver l'enfant grandi de son œil maternel,
Que pourrais-je répondre à cette âme pieuse,
Voyant tomber des pleurs de sa paupière creuse?

C

The big-hearted servant of whom you were jealous,
And who sleeps her slumber below a humble lawn,
We really should take her some flowers.
The dead, the poor dead, they suffer great pains,
And when October blows, pruner of old trees,
His melancholy wind around their marbles,
Surely, they find the living ungrateful,
To sleep, as they do, warm in their sheets,
Whereas, devoured by dark reveries,
Without bedfellow, without pillow talk,
Old frozen skeletons polished by the worm,
They feel the snows of winter seep in
And the century aflow, without friend or family
To replace the tatters that hang on their rail.

When the log hisses and sings, if one evening,
Calm, in the chair where I would watch her sit,
If, on a blue and cold December night,
I should find her crouched in a corner of my room,
Grave, and come from the depth of her eternal bed
To brood on the grown child with her motherly gaze,
How could I answer this pious soul,
Seeing tears fall from her weathered lids?

BRUMES ET PLUIES

Ô fins d'automne, hivers, printemps trempés de boue
Endormeuses saisons! je vous aime et vous loue
D'envelopper ainsi mon cœur et mon cerveau
D'un linceul vaporeux et d'un vague tombeau.

Dans cette grande plaine où l'autan froid se joue,
Où par les longues nuits la girouette s'enroue,
Mon âme mieux qu'au temps du tiède renouveau
Ouvrira largement ses ailes de corbeau.

Rien n'est plus doux au cœur plein de choses funèbres,
Et sur qui dès longtemps descendent les frimas,
Ô blafardes saisons, reines de nos climats,

Que l'aspect permanent de vos pâles ténèbres,
— Si ce n'est, par un soir sans lune, deux à deux,
D'endormir la douleur sur un lit hasardeux.

MISTS AND RAINS

O ends of autumn, winters, springs drenched in mud
Drowsy seasons! I love you and praise you
For enveloping my heart and my brain
Within a vaporous shroud and a hazy tomb.

In this great plain where frolics the cold south wind,
Where the weathervane croaks through long nights,
More widely than in times of tepid renewal my soul
Will spread its raven wings.

Nothing is sweeter to the heart full of funereal things,
And upon which the frost has long since settled,
O pallid seasons, queens of our climes,

Than the permanent aspect of your pale shadows,
—If not, on a moonless night, side by side,
To lay sorrow to sleep on a reckless bed.

CII

RÊVE PARISIEN
À *Constantin Guys.*

I

De ce terrible paysage,
Tel que jamais mortel n'en vit,
Ce matin encore l'image,
Vague et lointaine, me ravit.

Le sommeil est plein de miracles!
Par un caprice singulier,
J'avais banni de ces spectacles
Le végétal irrégulier,

Et, peintre fier de mon génie,
Je savourais dans mon tableau
L'enivrante monotonie
Du métal, du marbre et de l'eau.

Babel d'escaliers et d'arcades,
C'était un palais infini,
Plein de bassins et de cascades
Tombant dans l'or mat ou bruni;

Et des cataractes pesantes,
Comme des rideaux de cristal,
Se suspendaient, éblouissantes,
À des murailles de métal.

CII

PARISIAN DREAM

To Constantin Guys.

I

This terrible landscape,
Such as never a mortal has seen,
Still this morning its image,
Vague and distant, ravishes me.

Sleep is full of miracles!
By a singular caprice,
I banished from these spectacles
The irregular vegetal,

And, painter proud of my genius,
I savored within my tableau
The intoxicating monotony
Of metal, marble and water.

Babel of stairs and arcades,
It was an infinite palace,
Full of fountains and cascades
Falling in matte or burnished gold;

And of weighty cataracts,
Like curtains of crystal,
Suspended, gleaming,
Along walls of metal.

Non d'arbres, mais de colonnades
Les étangs dormants s'entouraient,
Où de gigantesques naïades,
Comme des femmes, se miraient.

Des nappes d'eau s'épanchaient, bleues,
Entre des quais roses et verts,
Pendant des millions de lieues,
Vers les confins de l'univers;

C'étaient des pierres inouïes
Et des flots magiques; c'étaient
D'immenses glaces éblouies
Par tout ce qu'elles reflétaient!

Insouciants et taciturnes,
Des Ganges, dans le firmament,
Versaient le trésor de leurs urnes
Dans des gouffres de diamant.

Architecte de mes féeries,
Je faisais, à ma volonté,
Sous un tunnel de pierreries
Passer un océan dompté;

Et tout, même la couleur noire,
Semblait fourbi, clair, irisé;
Le liquide enchâssait sa gloire
Dans le rayon cristallisé.

Nul astre d'ailleurs, nuls vestiges
De soleil, même au bas du ciel,
Pour illuminer ces prodiges,
Qui brillaient d'un feu personnel!

No trees, but colonnades
Encircled the sleeping ponds,
Where gigantic Naiads,
Like women, were mirrored.

Sheets of water poured, blue,
Between the green and pink quays,
Stretching for millions of leagues,
Toward the borders of the universe;

There were unheard of stones
And magic waves; there were
Immense mirrors dazzled
By all they reflected!

Insouciant and taciturn,
Some Ganges, in the sky,
Poured the treasure of their urns
Into chasms of diamond.

Architect of my enchantments,
I made, at will,
Through a tunnel of precious stones
A tamed ocean pass;

And everything, even the color black,
Seemed polished, clear, iridescent;
Liquid set its glory
In crystalized ray.

Not so much as a star, no vestige
Of sun, even low in the sky,
To illuminate these prodigies,
That sparkled with intrinsic fire!

Et sur ces mouvantes merveilles
Planait (terrible nouveauté!
Tout pour l'œil, rien pour les oreilles!)
Un silence d'éternité.

II

En rouvrant mes yeux pleins de flamme
J'ai vu l'horreur de mon taudis,
Et senti, rentrant dans mon âme,
La pointe des soucis maudits;

La pendule aux accents funèbres
Sonnait brutalement midi,
Et le ciel versait des ténèbres
Sur le triste monde engourdi.

And over these marvelous movements
Hovered (terrible novelty!
All for the eye, nothing for the ears!)
An eternal silence.

II

Opening again my eyes full of flame
I saw the horror of my hovel,
And felt, re-entering my soul,
The barb of accursed cares;

In funereal accents the clock
Brutally sounded noon,
And the sky poured shadows
Upon the sad numbed world.

LE CRÉPUSCULE DU MATIN

La diane chantait dans les cours des casernes,
Et le vent du matin soufflait sur les lanternes.

C'était l'heure où l'essaim des rêves malfaisants
Tord sur leurs oreillers les bruns adolescents;
Où, comme un œil sanglant qui palpite et qui bouge,
La lampe sur le jour fait une tache rouge;
Où l'âme, sous le poids du corps revêche et lourd,
Imite les combats de la lampe et du jour.
Comme un visage en pleurs que les brises essuient,
L'air est plein du frisson des choses qui s'enfuient,
Et l'homme est las d'écrire et la femme d'aimer.

Les maisons çà et là commençaient à fumer.
Les femmes de plaisir, la paupière livide,
Bouche ouverte, dormaient de leur sommeil stupide;
Les pauvresses, traînant leurs seins maigres et froids,
Soufflaient sur leurs tisons et soufflaient sur leurs doigts.
C'était l'heure où parmi le froid et la lésine
S'aggravent les douleurs des femmes en gésine;
Comme un sanglot coupé par un sang écumeux
Le chant du coq au loin déchirait l'air brumeux;
Une mer de brouillards baignait les édifices,
Et les agonisants dans le fond des hospices
Poussaient leur dernier râle en hoquets inégaux.
Les débauchés rentraient, brisés par leurs travaux.

MORNING TWILIGHT

The clarion sang through the barracks,
And the morning wind fluttered over the lanterns.

It was the hour in which the swarm of evil dreams
Twists swarthy adolescents upon their pillows;
In which, like a bleeding eye that throbs and darts,
The lamp daubs a red stain upon the day.
In which the soul, under the weight of sullen body,
Mimics the combat of the lamp and the day.
Like a tearful face dried by the wind,
The air shivers with fleeting things,
And man wearies of writing and woman of love.

The houses here and there began to smoke.
The ladies of pleasure, eyelids livid,
Mouths gaping, were dozing their stupid sleep;
Beggar-women, dragging cold and meager breasts,
Blew on their embers and blew on their fingers.
It was the hour in which cold and thrift
Aggravate the pains of women in labor;
Like a sob cut short by a bubble of blood
The distant cock's cry tore the misty air;
A sea of fog bathed the buildings,
And in the depths of hospices the dying
Forced their last gasp in ragged hiccups.
The debauchees retreated, broken by their exertions.

L'aurore grelottante en robe rose et verte
S'avançait lentement sur la Seine déserte,
Et le sombre Paris, en se frottant les yeux,
Empoignait ses outils, vieillard laborieux.

Shivering dawn in pink and green gown
Slowly advanced on the deserted Seine,
And somber Paris, rubbing his eyes,
Took up his tools, laborious old man.

LE VIN

WINE

CIV

L'ÂME DU VIN

Un soir, l'âme du vin chantait dans les bouteilles:
« Homme, vers toi je pousse, ô cher déshérité,
Sous ma prison de verre et mes cires vermeilles,
Un chant plein de lumière et de fraternité!

« Je sais combien il faut, sur la colline en flamme,
De peine, de sueur et de soleil cuisant
Pour engendrer ma vie et pour me donner l'âme;
Mais je ne serai point ingrat ni malfaisant,

« Car j'éprouve une joie immense quand je tombe
Dans le gosier d'un homme usé par ses travaux,
Et sa chaude poitrine est une douce tombe
Où je me plais bien mieux que dans mes froids caveaux.

« Entends-tu retentir les refrains des dimanches
Et l'espoir qui gazouille en mon sein palpitant?
Les coudes sur la table et retroussant tes manches,
Tu me glorifieras et tu seras content;

« J'allumerai les yeux de ta femme ravie;
À ton fils je rendrai sa force et ses couleurs
Et serai pour ce frêle athlète de la vie
L'huile qui raffermit les muscles des lutteurs.

« En toi je tomberai, végétale ambroisie,
Grain précieux jeté par l'éternel Semeur,
Pour que de notre amour naisse la poésie
Qui jaillira vers Dieu comme une rare fleur! »

CIV

THE SOUL OF WINE

One evening, the soul of wine sang in the bottles:
"Man, I press toward you, o dear disinherited,
Behind my prison of glass and my vermillion seals,
A song full of light and fraternity!

"I know how much it takes, upon the blazing hills,
Of toil, of sweat and of scorching sun
To engender my life and endow me with soul;
Nor would I ever be ungrateful or malicious,

"Since I feel immense joy when I fall
Down the throat of a man worn by work,
And his warm breast is a soft tomb
Which I much prefer to my cold cellars.

"Can you hear the Sunday refrains resound
And the hope that warbles in my fluttering breast?
Elbows on table and sleeves rolled up,
You will glorify me and you will be content;

"I will kindle the eyes of your enraptured wife;
To your son restore his strength and color
And will be for this frail wrestler in the ring of life
The oil that firms the muscles.

"Into you I will fall, vegetal ambrosia,
Precious grain cast by the eternal Sower,
So that poetry born of our love
Will burst toward God like a rare flower!"

LE VIN DES CHIFFONNIERS

Souvent, à la clarté rouge d'un réverbère
Dont le vent bat la flamme et tourmente le verre,
Au cœur d'un vieux faubourg, labyrinthe fangeux
Où l'humanité grouille en ferments orageux,

On voit un chiffonnier qui vient, hochant la tête,
Butant, et se cognant aux murs comme un poète,
Et, sans prendre souci des mouchards, ses sujets,
Épanche tout son cœur en glorieux projets.

Il prête des serments, dicte des lois sublimes,
Terrasse les méchants, relève les victimes,
Et sous le firmament comme un dais suspendu
S'enivre des splendeurs de sa propre vertu.

Oui, ces gens harcelés de chagrins de ménage,
Moulus par le travail et tourmentés par l'âge,
Éreintés et pliant sous un tas de débris,
Vomissement confus de l'énorme Paris,

Reviennent, parfumés d'une odeur de futailles,
Suivis de compagnons, blanchis dans les batailles,
Dont la moustache pend comme les vieux drapeaux.
Les bannières, les fleurs et les arcs triomphaux

Se dressent devant eux, solennelle magie!
Et dans l'étourdissante et lumineuse orgie
Des clairons, du soleil, des cris et du tambour,
Ils apportent la gloire au peuple ivre d'amour!

THE WINE OF RAGPICKERS

Often, in the red light of a street lamp
As wind flickers the flame and rattles the glass,
In the heart of an old neighborhood, muddy labyrinth
Where humanity swarms in stormy ferment,

One sees a ragpicker approach, bobbing his head,
Stumbling, and bumping the walls like a poet,
And, caring nothing for snitches, his subjects,
Pours his whole heart into glorious projects.

He swears oaths, dictates sublime laws,
Casts down the wicked, lifts up the weak,
And under the firmament suspended like a canopy
Gets drunk upon the splendors of his virtue.

Yes, these men harassed by domestic griefs,
Ground down by work and tormented by age,
Exhausted and bent beneath a heap of debris,
The muddled vomit of enormous Paris,

Return, perfumed by an odor of casks,
Followed by companions, bleached by battles,
Mustache drooping like old flags.
The banners, the garlands and triumphal arches

Rise up before them, solemn magic!
And in the deafening and luminous orgy
Of clarions, of sun, of cries and of drums,
They bring glory to the people drunk with love!

C'est ainsi qu'à travers l'Humanité frivole
Le vin roule de l'or, éblouissant Pactole;
Par le gosier de l'homme il chante ses exploits
Et règne par ses dons ainsi que les vrais rois.

Pour noyer la rancœur et bercer l'indolence
De tous ces vieux maudits qui meurent en silence,
Dieu, touché de remords, avait fait le sommeil;
L'Homme ajouta le Vin, fils sacré du Soleil!

So it is that through frivolous Humanity
Wine flows with gold, dazzling Pactolus;
Through the throat of man it sings its exploits
And reigns through its gifts as true kings do.

To drown the rancor and soothe the indolence
Of all these damned old men who die in silence,
God, touched by remorse, made sleep;
Man added Wine, sacred son of the Sun!

CVI

LE VIN DE L'ASSASSIN

Ma femme est morte, je suis libre!
Je puis donc boire tout mon soûl.
Lorsque je rentrais sans un sou,
Ses cris me déchiraient la fibre.

Autant qu'un roi je suis heureux;
L'air est pur, le ciel admirable...
Nous avions un été semblable
Lorsque j'en devins amoureux!

L'horrible soif qui me déchire
Aurait besoin pour s'assouvir
D'autant de vin qu'en peut tenir
Son tombeau; — ce n'est pas peu dire:

Je l'ai jetée au fond d'un puits,
Et j'ai même poussé sur elle
Tous les pavés de la margelle.
— Je l'oublierai si je le puis!

Au nom des serments de tendresse,
Dont rien ne peut nous délier,
Et pour nous réconcilier
Comme au beau temps de notre ivresse,

J'implorai d'elle un rendez-vous,
Le soir, sur une route obscure.
Elle y vint! — folle créature!
Nous sommes tous plus ou moins fous!

CVI

THE WINE OF THE MURDERER

My wife is dead, I'm free!
I can drink to my heart's content.
When I would come home without a cent,
Her cries tore my very fiber.

I'm happy as a king;
Fresh air, fine sky...
We had a similar summer
When I fell in love with her!

The horrible thirst that tears me apart
Could only be quenched
By enough wine to fill
Her tomb; —that's not nothing:

I threw her down a well,
And cast upon her
All the stones of its rim.
—I'll forget her if I can!

In the name of vows of tenderness,
From which nothing unbinds us,
And to reconcile us
As in fairweather infatuation,

I implored her to meet,
At night, in a dark alley.
She showed up! —crazy creature!
We're all more or less crazy!

Elle était encore jolie,
Quoique bien fatiguée! et moi,
Je l'aimais trop! voilà pourquoi
Je lui dis: Sors de cette vie!

Nul ne peut me comprendre. Un seul
Parmi ces ivrognes stupides
Songea-t-il dans ses nuits morbides
À faire du vin un linceul?

Cette crapule invulnérable
Comme les machines de fer
Jamais, ni l'été ni l'hiver,
N'a connu l'amour véritable,

Avec ses noirs enchantements,
Son cortège infernal d'alarmes,
Ses fioles de poison, ses larmes,
Ses bruits de chaîne et d'ossements!

— Me voilà libre et solitaire!
Je serai ce soir ivre mort;
Alors, sans peur et sans remords,
Je me coucherai sur la terre,

Et je dormirai comme un chien!
Le chariot aux lourdes roues
Chargé de pierres et de boues,
Le wagon enragé peut bien

Écraser ma tête coupable
Ou me couper par le milieu,
Je m'en moque comme de Dieu,
Du Diable ou de la Sainte Table!

She still looked pretty good,
Though quite weary! and me,
I loved her too much! which is why
I told her: Leave this life!

Nobody understands me. Has one
Among these stupid drunks
Ever thought amid his morbid nights
To make of wine a shroud?

This invulnerable rabble
Like iron machines
Has never, neither summer nor winter,
Known true love,

With its black enchantments,
Its infernal procession of panics,
Its vials of poison, its tears,
Its rattles of chains and of bones!

—Here I am free and clear!
Tonight I'll drink myself dead;
Then, without fear or regrets,
I'll sleep on the ground,

And I'll sleep like a dog!
The cart with massive wheels
Loaded with stones and sludge,
The furious wagon may well

Crush my guilty head
Or cut me in half,
I sneer as I do at God,
The Devil or the Holy Table!

LE VIN DU SOLITAIRE

Le regard singulier d'une femme galante
Qui se glisse vers nous comme le rayon blanc
Que la lune onduleuse envoie au lac tremblant,
Quand elle y veut baigner sa beauté nonchalante;

Le dernier sac d'écus dans les doigts d'un joueur;
Un baiser libertin de la maigre Adeline;
Les sons d'une musique énervante et câline,
Semblable au cri lointain de l'humaine douleur,

Tout cela ne vaut pas, ô bouteille profonde,
Les baumes pénétrants que ta panse féconde
Garde au cœur altéré du poète pieux;

Tu lui verses l'espoir, la jeunesse et la vie,
— Et l'orgueil, ce trésor de toute gueuserie,
Qui nous rend triomphants et semblables aux Dieux!

THE WINE OF THE HERMIT

The singular gaze of a licentious woman
That glides toward us like a white beam
Sent by the sinuous moon to the trembling lake,
When she would bathe her nonchalant beauty;

The last bag of crowns in a gambler's fingers;
A libertine kiss from the slim Adeline;
The sounds of an irksome and coaxing music,
Like some distant cry of human pain,

All this is not worth, o profound bottle,
The penetrating balm that your fecund paunch
Holds for the thirsty heart of the pious poet;

For him you pour hope, youth and life,
—And pride, that treasure of all beggary,
Which makes us triumphant and akin to the Gods!

CVIII

LE VIN DES AMANTS

Aujourd'hui l'espace est splendide!
Sans mors, sans éperons, sans bride,
Partons à cheval sur le vin
Pour un ciel féerique et divin!

Comme deux anges que torture
Une implacable calenture,
Dans le bleu cristal du matin
Suivons le mirage lointain!

Mollement balancés sur l'aile
Du tourbillon intelligent,
Dans un délire parallèle,

Ma sœur, côte à côte nageant,
Nous fuirons sans repos ni trêves
Vers le paradis de mes rêves!

CVIII

THE WINE OF LOVERS

How splendid the atmosphere today!
No bit, no spurs, no bridle,
Let's ride upon wine
Toward a fairy sky divine.

Like two angels goaded
By implacable calenture,
In the crystalline blue of morning
Let's keep pace with the far-off mirage!

Gently swaying on the wing
Of the mindful whirlwind,
In parallel delirium,

My sister, swimming side by side,
We'll flee with neither rest nor respite
Toward the paradise of my dreams!

FLEURS DU MAL

FLOWERS OF EVIL

LA DESTRUCTION

Sans cesse à mes côtés s'agite le Démon;
Il nage autour de moi comme un air impalpable;
Je l'avale et le sens qui brûle mon poumon
Et l'emplit d'un désir éternel et coupable.

Parfois il prend, sachant mon grand amour de l'Art,
La forme de la plus séduisante des femmes,
Et, sous de spécieux prétextes de cafard,
Accoutume ma lèvre à des philtres infâmes.

Il me conduit ainsi, loin du regard de Dieu,
Haletant et brisé de fatigue, au milieu
Des plaines de l'Ennui, profondes et désertes,

Et jette dans mes yeux pleins de confusion
Des vêtements souillés, des blessures ouvertes,
Et l'appareil sanglant de la Destruction!

DESTRUCTION

Ceaselessly the Demon flickers at my side;
He swims around me as impalpable air;
I breathe him in and feel him burn my lungs
And suffuse them with eternal and guilty desire.

Sometimes he takes, knowing my great love of Art,
The form of the most seductive woman,
And, under specious pretext of malaise,
Accustoms my lip to infamous philters.

He leads me thus, far from the gaze of God,
Panting and broken with fatigue, amid
The plains of Ennui, deep and deserted,

And casts before my eyes full of confusion
Soiled garments, open wounds,
And the bloody weapons of Destruction!

UNE MARTYRE

Dessin d'un Maître inconnu.

Au milieu des flacons, des étoffes lamées
      Et des meubles voluptueux,
Des marbres, des tableaux, des robes parfumées
      Qui traînent à plis somptueux,

Dans une chambre tiède où, comme en une serre,
      L'air est dangereux et fatal,
Où des bouquets mourants dans leurs cercueils de verre
      Exhalent leur soupir final,

Un cadavre sans tête épanche, comme un fleuve,
      Sur l'oreiller désaltéré
Un sang rouge et vivant, dont la toile s'abreuve
      Avec l'avidité d'un pré.

Semblable aux visions pâles qu'enfante l'ombre
      Et qui nous enchaînent les yeux,
La tête, avec l'amas de sa crinière sombre
      Et de ses bijoux précieux,

Sur la table de nuit, comme une renoncule,
      Repose; et, vide de pensers,
Un regard vague et blanc comme le crépuscule
      S'échappe des yeux révulsés.

CX

A MARTYR

Sketch by an Unknown Master.

Amid flasks, lamé fabrics
     And voluptuous furnishings,
Marbles, paintings, perfumed dresses
     That trail in sumptuous folds,

In a warm room where, like a hothouse,
     The air is dangerous and fatal,
Where wilting bouquets in their caskets of glass
     Exhale their last breath,

A headless cadaver pours, like a river,
     Upon the saturated pillow
A vivid red blood, which the canvas drinks
     With the avidity of a meadow.

Like unto pale visions engendered by shadow
     And which fasten our eyes,
The head, with the heap of its dark mane
     And of its precious jewels,

On the night table, like a ranunculus,
     Rests; and, void of thoughts,
A gaze vague and white as twilight
     Escapes the rolled back eyes.

Sur le lit, le tronc nu sans scrupules étale
   Dans le plus complet abandon
La secrète splendeur et la beauté fatale
   Dont la nature lui fit don;

Un bas rosâtre, orné de coins d'or, à la jambe,
   Comme un souvenir est resté;
La jarretière, ainsi qu'un œil secret qui flambe,
   Darde un regard diamanté.

Le singulier aspect de cette solitude
   Et d'un grand portrait langoureux,
Aux yeux provocateurs comme son attitude,
   Révèle un amour ténébreux,

Une coupable joie et des fêtes étranges
   Pleines de baisers infernaux,
Dont se réjouissait l'essaim des mauvais anges
   Nageant dans les plis des rideaux;

Et cependant, à voir la maigreur élégante
   De l'épaule au contour heurté,
La hanche un peu pointue et la taille fringante
   Ainsi qu'un reptile irrité,

Elle est bien jeune encor! — Son âme exaspérée
   Et ses sens par l'ennui mordus
S'étaient-ils entr'ouverts à la meute altérée
   Des désirs errants et perdus?

L'homme vindicatif que tu n'as pu, vivante,
   Malgré tant d'amour, assouvir,
Combla-t-il sur ta chair inerte et complaisante
   L'immensité de son désir?

Upon the bed, the naked torso shamelessly flaunts
  With total abandon
The secret splendor of its fatal beauty
  By nature endowed;

A roseate stocking, adorned with gold clocks, on her leg,
  Stayed like a memory;
The garter, like a covert eye ablaze,
  Darts a diamantine gaze.

The peculiar aspect of that solitude
  And of so languorous a large portrait,
As provocative to the eyes as her posture,
  Reveals a tenebrous love,

A guilty pleasure and strange revels
  Full of infernal embraces,
In which the swarm of fallen angels would rejoice
  Swimming in the folds of the curtains.

And yet, examining the elegant slimness
  Of the shoulder's sharp contour,
The hip a bit pointed and the waist taut
  Like an agitated reptile,

She is still quite young! —Her exasperated soul
  And senses gnawed by ennui
Had they laid themselves open to the thirsty pack
  Of lost and wandering desires?

The vindictive man you could not, while alive,
  Despite such love, satiate,
Did he satisfy upon your inert and complaisant flesh
  The immensity of his desire?

Réponds, cadavre impur! et par tes tresses roides
    Te soulevant d'un bras fiévreux,
Dis-moi, tête effrayante, a-t-il sur tes dents froides
    Collé les suprêmes adieux?

— Loin du monde railleur, loin de la foule impure,
    Loin des magistrats curieux,
Dors en paix, dors en paix, étrange créature,
    Dans ton tombeau mystérieux;

Ton époux court le monde, et ta forme immortelle
    Veille près de lui quand il dort;
Autant que toi sans doute il te sera fidèle,
    Et constant jusques à la mort.

Answer, unclean cadaver! and by your stiff braids
      Lifting you in a feverish embrace,
Tell me, frightful head, with his cold teeth
      Did he stamp his final farewells?

—Far from the jeering world, far from the filthy rabble,
      Far from prying magistrates,
Rest in peace, rest in peace, strange creature,
      In your mysterious tomb;

Your husband roams the world, and your immortal form
      Watches over him as he sleeps;
No less than you he will doubtless be faithful,
      And true unto death.

LESBOS

Mère des jeux latins et des voluptés grecques,
Lesbos, où les baisers, languissants ou joyeux,
Chauds comme les soleils, frais comme les pastèques,
Font l'ornement des nuits et des jours glorieux;
Mère des jeux latins et des voluptés grecques,

Lesbos, où les baisers sont comme les cascades
Qui se jettent sans peur dans les gouffres sans fonds,
Et courent, sanglotant et gloussant par saccades,
Orageux et secrets, fourmillants et profonds;
Lesbos, où les baisers sont comme les cascades!

Lesbos, où les Phrynés l'une l'autre s'attirent,
Où jamais un soupir ne resta sans écho,
À l'égal de Paphos les étoiles t'admirent,
Et Vénus à bon droit peut jalouser Sapho!
Lesbos où les Phrynés l'une l'autre s'attirent,

Lesbos, terre des nuits chaudes et langoureuses,
Qui font qu'à leurs miroirs, stérile volupté!
Les filles aux yeux creux, de leur corps amoureuses,
Caressent les fruits mûrs de leur nubilité;
Lesbos, terre des nuits chaudes et langoureuses,

Laisse du vieux Platon se froncer l'œil austère;
Tu tires ton pardon de l'excès des baisers,
Reine du doux empire, aimable et noble terre,
Et des raffinements toujours inépuisés.
Laisse du vieux Platon se froncer l'œil austère.

LESBOS

Mother of Latin games and Greek pleasures,
Lesbos, where kisses, languid or joyous,
Hot as suns, fresh as watermelons,
Ornament the nights and the glorious days;
Mother of Latin games and Greek pleasures,

Lesbos, where kisses are like cascades
That pour fearlessly into bottomless chasms,
And flow, heaving with sobs and guffaws,
Thunderous and secret, afroth and profound;
Lesbos, where kisses are like cascades!

Lesbos, where one to another the Phrynes are drawn,
Where a sigh never rests without echo,
In the eyes of the stars you are equal to Paphos,
And Venus is right to be jealous of Sappho!
Lesbos, where one to another the Phrynes are drawn,

Lesbos, land of hot and languorous nights,
Which make before mirrors, sterile pleasure!
The hollow-eyed girls, their own bodies' beloveds,
Caress the ripe fruits of their nubility;
Lesbos, land of hot and languorous nights,

Let old Plato furrow his austere eye;
By excess of kisses you earn your pardon,
Queen of the gentle empire, beloved and noble land,
And of endlessly inexhaustible refinements.
Let old Plato furrow his austere eye.

Tu tires ton pardon de l'éternel martyre,
Infligé sans relâche aux cœurs ambitieux,
Qu'attire loin de nous le radieux sourire
Entrevu vaguement au bord des autres cieux!
Tu tires ton pardon de l'éternel martyre!

Qui des Dieux osera, Lesbos, être ton juge
Et condamner ton front pâli dans les travaux,
Si ses balances d'or n'ont pesé le déluge
De larmes qu'à la mer ont versé tes ruisseaux?
Qui des Dieux osera, Lesbos, être ton juge?

Que nous veulent les lois du juste et de l'injuste?
Vierges au cœur sublime, honneur de l'archipel,
Votre religion comme une autre est auguste,
Et l'amour se rira de l'Enfer et du Ciel!
Que nous veulent les lois du juste et de l'injuste?

Car Lesbos entre tous m'a choisi sur la terre
Pour chanter le secret de ses vierges en fleurs,
Et je fus dès l'enfance admis au noir mystère
Des rires effrénés mêlés aux sombres pleurs;
Car Lesbos entre tous m'a choisi sur la terre.

Et depuis lors je veille au sommet de Leucate,
Comme une sentinelle à l'œil perçant et sûr,
Qui guette nuit et jour brick, tartane ou frégate,
Dont les formes au loin frissonnent dans l'azur;
Et depuis lors je veille au sommet de Leucate

Pour savoir si la mer est indulgente et bonne,
Et parmi les sanglots dont le roc retentit
Un soir ramènera vers Lesbos, qui pardonne,
Le cadavre adoré de Sapho, qui partit
Pour savoir si la mer est indulgente et bonne!

You earn your pardon by eternal martyrdom,
Ruthlessly inflicted upon ambitious hearts,
We are drawn from afar by the radiant smile
Vaguely glimpsed at the edge of other skies!
You earn your pardon by eternal martyrdom!

Who would dare be your judge, Lesbos, among the Gods?
And condemn your brow made pallid by toil,
If their scales of gold had not weighed the flood
Of tears poured into the sea by your streams?
Who would dare be your judge, Lesbos, among the Gods?

What have we to do with right and wrong?
Virgins of the sublime heart, honor of the archipelago,
Your religion is august as any other,
And love will laugh at Hell and at Heaven!
What have we to do with right and wrong?

For Lesbos chose me among all of the earth
To sing the secret of her virgins in flower,
And as a child I was inducted into the black mystery
Of frenzied laughs mingled with somber tears;
For Lesbos chose me among all of the earth.

And since then I keep watch on Leucate's peak,
Like a sentinel with sure and piercing eye,
Who looks out night and day for brig, tartane or frigate,
Whose distant shapes shiver in the azure;
And since then I keep watch on Leucate's peak

To learn if the sea is indulgent and kind,
And among the sobs that resound from the rock
Will bring back one evening to Lesbos, who pardons,
The adored cadaver of Sappho, departed
To learn if the sea is indulgent and kind!

De la mâle Sapho, l'amante et le poète,
Plus belle que Vénus par ses mornes pâleurs!
— L'œil d'azur est vaincu par l'œil noir que tachette
Le cercle ténébreux tracé par les douleurs
De la mâle Sapho, l'amante et le poète!

— Plus belle que Vénus se dressant sur le monde
Et versant les trésors de sa sérénité
Et le rayonnement de sa jeunesse blonde
Sur le vieil Océan de sa fille enchanté;
Plus belle que Vénus se dressant sur le monde!

— De Sapho qui mourut le jour de son blasphème,
Quand, insultant le rite et le culte inventé,
Elle fit son beau corps la pâture suprême
D'un brutal dont l'orgueil punit l'impiété
De celle qui mourut le jour de son blasphème.

Et c'est depuis ce temps que Lesbos se lamente,
Et, malgré les honneurs que lui rend l'univers,
S'enivre chaque nuit du cri de la tourmente
Que poussent vers les cieux ses rivages déserts.
Et c'est depuis ce temps que Lesbos se lamente!

Of manly Sappho, lover and poet,
In her mournful pallor more lovely than Venus!
—Blue eye vanquished by black eye ringed
With the tenebrous circle traced by sorrows
Of manly Sappho, lover and poet!

—More lovely than Venus rising over the world
And pouring the treasures of her serenity
And the radiance of her blonde youth
Upon old Ocean by his daughter enchanted;
More lovely than Venus rising over the world!

—Of Sappho who died on her blasphemous day,
When, flouting rite and concocted cult,
She made her beautiful body the final pasture
Of a brute who pridefully punished the impiety
Of she who died on her blasphemous day.

And it is ever since then that Lesbos laments,
And, in spite of the honors the universe pays her,
She gets drunk every night on the cry of torment
Raised to the heavens by her deserted shores.
And it is ever since then that Lesbos laments!

FEMMES DAMNÉES

Delphine et Hippolyte

À la pâle clarté des lampes languissantes,
Sur de profonds coussins tout imprégnés d'odeur,
Hippolyte rêvait aux caresses puissantes
Qui levaient le rideau de sa jeune candeur.

Elle cherchait, d'un œil troublé par la tempête,
De sa naïveté le ciel déjà lointain,
Ainsi qu'un voyageur qui retourne la tête
Vers les horizons bleus dépassés le matin.

De ses yeux amortis les paresseuses larmes,
L'air brisé, la stupeur, la morne volupté,
Ses bras vaincus, jetés comme de vaines armes,
Tout servait, tout parait sa fragile beauté.

Étendue à ses pieds, calme et pleine de joie,
Delphine la couvait avec des yeux ardents,
Comme un animal fort qui surveille une proie,
Après l'avoir d'abord marquée avec les dents.

Beauté forte à genoux devant la beauté frêle,
Superbe, elle humait voluptueusement
Le vin de son triomphe, et s'allongeait vers elle,
Comme pour recueillir un doux remercîment.

Elle cherchait dans l'œil de sa pâle victime
Le cantique muet que chante le plaisir,
Et cette gratitude infinie et sublime
Qui sort de la paupière ainsi qu'un long soupir.

DAMNED WOMEN

Delphine and Hippolyta

In the pale light of languishing lamps,
Upon deep cushions pregnant with perfume,
Hippolyta dreamed of the potent caresses
That had lifted the curtain of her youthful candor.

She was seeking, with tempest troubled eye,
The already distant sky of her naïveté,
As does a traveler who turns his head
Toward the bygone blue horizons of morning.

The lazy tears of her deadened eyes,
The broken air, the stupor, the dreary indulgence,
Her vanquished arms, flung down like vain weapons,
All served, all embellished her fragile beauty.

Stretched at her feet, calm and full of joy,
Delphine brooded on her with ardent eyes,
Like a powerful animal that surveys its prey,
Having already marked it with its teeth.

Strong beauty kneeling before beauty frail,
Superb, she voluptuously sniffed
The wine of her conquest, and inclined toward her,
As if to collect a sweet token of thanks.

She sought in her pale victim's eye
The silent canticle that pleasure sings,
And that infinite and sublime gratitude
Expressed by the eyelid like a long sigh.

— « Hippolyte, cher cœur, que dis-tu de ces choses?
Comprends-tu maintenant qu'il ne faut pas offrir
L'holocauste sacré de tes premières roses
Aux souffles violents qui pourraient les flétrir?

« Mes baisers sont légers comme ces éphémères
Qui caressent le soir les grands lacs transparents,
Et ceux de ton amant creuseront leurs ornières
Comme des chariots ou des socs déchirants;

« Ils passeront sur toi comme un lourd attelage
De chevaux et de bœufs aux sabots sans pitié...
Hippolyte, ô ma sœur! tourne donc ton visage,
Toi, mon âme et mon cœur, mon tout et ma moitié,

« Tourne vers moi tes yeux pleins d'azur et d'étoiles!
Pour un de ces regards charmants, baume divin,
Des plaisirs plus obscurs je lèverai les voiles
Et je t'endormirai dans un rêve sans fin! »

Mais Hippolyte alors, levant sa jeune tête:
— « Je ne suis point ingrate et ne me repens pas,
Ma Delphine, je souffre et je suis inquiète,
Comme après un nocturne et terrible repas.

« Je sens fondre sur moi de lourdes épouvantes
Et de noirs bataillons de fantômes épars,
Qui veulent me conduire en des routes mouvantes
Qu'un horizon sanglant ferme de toutes parts.

« Avons-nous donc commis une action étrange?
Explique, si tu peux, mon trouble et mon effroi:
Je frissonne de peur quand tu me dis: "Mon ange!"
Et cependant je sens ma bouche aller vers toi.

—"Hippolyta, dear heart, what do you have to say?
Do you now understand that you needn't offer
The sacred holocaust of your first flowers
To violent gusts that would make them wither?

"My kisses are light as the mayflies
That caress vast lucid lakes in the evening,
While those of your lover would furrow their ruts
As do chariots or ploughshares;

"They will pass over you like a massive team
Of horses and oxen with pitiless hooves...
Hippolyta, o my sister! turn then your face,
You, my heart and my soul, my part and my whole,

"Turn toward me your eyes full of stars and azure!
For one of those charming gazes, divine balm,
I will lift the veils of the darkest pleasures
And lull you to sleep in an endless dream!"

But then Hippolyta, raising her youthful head:
—"Though I am not ungrateful and do not repent,
My Delphine, I am worried and I am in pain,
As after a late and dreadful meal.

"I feel converging on me such weighty horrors
And black battalions of stray phantoms,
That would drive me down shifting streets
Enclosed on all sides by a bloody horizon.

"Have we committed a terrible act?
Explain, if you can, my discomfort and my fright:
I shiver with fear when you say: 'My angel!'
And yet I feel my mouth yearning toward you.

« Ne me regarde pas ainsi, toi, ma pensée!
Toi que j'aime à jamais, ma sœur d'élection,
Quand même tu serais une embûche dressée
Et le commencement de ma perdition! »

Delphine secouant sa crinière tragique,
Et comme trépignant sur le trépied de fer,
L'œil fatal, répondit d'une voix despotique:
— « Qui donc devant l'amour ose parler d'enfer?

« Maudit soit à jamais le rêveur inutile
Qui voulut le premier, dans sa stupidité,
S'éprenant d'un problème insoluble et stérile,
Aux choses de l'amour mêler l'honnêteté!

« Celui qui veut unir dans un accord mystique
L'ombre avec la chaleur, la nuit avec le jour,
Ne chauffera jamais son corps paralytique
À ce rouge soleil que l'on nomme l'amour!

« Va, si tu veux, chercher un fiancé stupide;
Cours offrir un cœur vierge à ses cruels baisers;
Et, pleine de remords et d'horreur, et livide,
Tu me rapporteras tes seins stigmatisés...

« On ne peut ici-bas contenter qu'un seul maître! »
Mais l'enfant, épanchant une immense douleur,
Cria soudain: « — Je sens s'élargir dans mon être
Un abîme béant; cet abîme est mon cœur!

« Brûlant comme un volcan, profond comme le vide!
Rien ne rassasiera ce monstre gémissant
Et ne rafraîchira la soif de l'Euménide
Qui, la torche à la main, le brûle jusqu'au sang.

"Don't look at me that way, you, my own mind!
You whom I love forever, my chosen sister,
Though you were an ambush lying in wait
And the beginning of my perdition!"

Delphine shaking her tragic mane,
And as if stamping an iron hoof,
Eye fatal, answered in a despotic voice:
—"Who dares speak of hell in the presence of love?

"Forever accursed be the useless dreamer
The first who wanted, out of stupidity,
Falling for a sterile and insoluble problem,
To mix honesty with matters of love!

"Whoever would unite in mystical accord
Shadow with heat, night with day,
Will never warm his paralytic body
With this red sun we call love!

"Go, if you want, look for some stupid fiancé;
Run off to give your virgin heart to his cruel kisses;
And, full of horror and regret, ashen,
You will bring me back your stigmatic breasts...

"Here on earth we may serve only one master!"
But the child, unburdening an immense pain,
Cried suddenly: —"I feel expand within my being
A gaping abyss; this abyss is my heart!

"Burning like a volcano, deep as the void!
Nothing will satisfy this groaning monster
And nothing will quench the thirst of the Fury
Who, torch in hand, boils the blood.

« Que nos rideaux fermés nous séparent du monde,
Et que la lassitude amène le repos!
Je veux m'anéantir dans ta gorge profonde
Et trouver sur ton sein la fraîcheur des tombeaux! »

— Descendez, descendez, lamentables victimes,
Descendez le chemin de l'enfer éternel!
Plongez au plus profond du gouffre, où tous les crimes,
Flagellés par un vent qui ne vient pas du ciel,

Bouillonnent pêle-mêle avec un bruit d'orage.
Ombres folles, courez au but de vos désirs;
Jamais vous ne pourrez assouvir votre rage,
Et votre châtiment naîtra de vos plaisirs.

Jamais un rayon frais n'éclaira vos cavernes;
Par les fentes des murs des miasmes fiévreux
Filtrent en s'enflammant ainsi que des lanternes
Et pénètrent vos corps de leurs parfums affreux.

L'âpre stérilité de votre jouissance
Altère votre soif et roidit votre peau,
Et le vent furibond de la concupiscence
Fait claquer votre chair ainsi qu'un vieux drapeau.

Loin des peuples vivants, errantes, condamnées,
À travers les déserts courez comme les loups;
Faites votre destin, âmes désordonnées,
Et fuyez l'infini que vous portez en vous!

"May our closed curtains divide us from the world,
And may lassitude bring us rest!
I want to disappear into the depths of your bosom
And discover upon your breast the coolness of tombs!"

—Descend, descend, lamentable victims,
Descend the path of eternal hell!
Plunge to the deepest depth of the chasm, where all crimes,
Whipped by a wind that does not blow from heaven,

Boil pell-mell with the roar of a storm.
Mad shades, sprint to the end of your desires;
Never can you satisfy your rage,
And your pleasures will breed your punishment.

Never will a bright ray illuminate your caverns;
Through clefts in the walls feverish miasmas
Percolate aflame like lanterns
And penetrate your bodies with their ghastly scents.

The stringent sterility of your enjoyment
Parches your thirst and stiffens your skin,
And the apoplectic wind of concupiscence
Flutters your flesh like an old flag.

Far from the nations of the living, wandering, condemned,
Run like wolves through the deserts;
Fulfill your destiny, disordered souls,
And flee the infinity that you carry within!

FEMMES DAMNÉES

Comme un bétail pensif sur le sable couchées,
Elles tournent leurs yeux vers l'horizon des mers,
Et leurs pieds se cherchant et leurs mains rapprochées
Ont de douces langueurs et des frissons amers.

Les unes, cœurs épris des longues confidences,
Dans le fond des bosquets où jasent les ruisseaux,
Vont épelant l'amour des craintives enfances
Et creusent le bois vert des jeunes arbrisseaux;

D'autres, comme des sœurs, marchent lentes et graves
À travers les rochers pleins d'apparitions,
Où saint Antoine a vu surgir comme des laves
Les seins nus et pourprés de ses tentations;

Il en est, aux lueurs des résines croulantes,
Qui dans le creux muet des vieux antres païens
T'appellent au secours de leurs fièvres hurlantes,
Ô Bacchus, endormeur des remords anciens!

Et d'autres, dont la gorge aime les scapulaires,
Qui, recélant un fouet sous leurs longs vêtements,
Mêlent, dans le bois sombre et les nuits solitaires,
L'écume du plaisir aux larmes des tourments.

Ô vierges, ô démons, ô monstres, ô martyres,
De la réalité grands esprits contempteurs,
Chercheuses d'infini, dévotes et satyres,
Tantôt pleines de cris, tantôt pleines de pleurs,

DAMNED WOMEN

Recumbent on the sand like pensive cattle,
They turn their eyes toward the seas' horizon,
Feet seeking feet and hands drawing near
With sweet languor and bitter quivers.

Some, hearts enamored of leisurely whispers,
Deep in the groves amid murmuring streams,
Spell out the loves of their timid childhoods
And carve the green wood of tender saplings;

Others, like nuns, walk slow and grave
Across rocks full of apparitions,
Where Saint Anthony saw erupt like lava
The bare and engorged breasts of his temptations;

There are those, by the glimmer of crumbling resin,
Who in silent hollow of old pagan caves
Ask you to succor their howling fevers,
O Bacchus, assuager of ancient regrets!

And others, breast ardent for scapulars,
Who, concealing a whip beneath their long robes,
Intermingle, in somber woods and solitary nights,
The foam of pleasure with tears of pain.

O virgins, o demons, o monsters, o martyrs,
Great spirits who scorn reality,
Seekers of the infinite, devotees and satyrs,
Now full of cries, now full of tears,

Vous que dans votre enfer mon âme a poursuivies,
Pauvres sœurs, je vous aime autant que je vous plains,
Pour vos mornes douleurs, vos soifs inassouvies,
Et les urnes d'amour dont vos grands cœurs sont pleins!

You whom my soul followed into your hell,
Poor sisters, I love you as much as I pity you,
For your dreary sorrows, your unquenchable thirsts,
And the urns of love overflowing great hearts!

LES DEUX BONNES SŒURS

La Débauche et la Mort sont deux aimables filles,
Prodigues de baisers et riches de santé,
Dont le flanc toujours vierge et drapé de guenilles
Sous l'éternel labeur n'a jamais enfanté.

Au poète sinistre, ennemi des familles,
Favori de l'enfer, courtisan mal renté,
Tombeaux et lupanars montrent sous leurs charmilles
Un lit que le remords n'a jamais fréquenté.

Et la bière et l'alcôve en blasphèmes fécondes
Nous offrent tour à tour, comme deux bonnes sœurs,
De terribles plaisirs et d'affreuses douceurs.

Quand veux-tu m'enterrer, Débauche aux bras immondes?
Ô Mort, quand viendras-tu, sa rivale en attraits,
Sur ses myrtes infects enter tes noirs cyprès?

CXII

THE TWO GOOD SISTERS

Debauchery and Death are two lovable daughters,
Prodigal with kisses and rich in health,
Loins ever virgin and draped in rags
Ever in labor to never give birth.

To the sinister poet, enemy of the family,
Favorite of hell, low-rent courtier,
Tombs and brothels disclose in their bowers
A bed in which remorse has never been.

And the fecund blasphemies of alcove and coffin
Offer in turn, like two good sisters,
Their terrible pleasures and dreadful balms.

When will you bury me, filth-armed Debauchery?
O Death, when will you come, her rival in charms,
To graft black cypress upon infected myrtle?

CXIII

LA FONTAINE DU SANG

Il me semble parfois que mon sang coule à flots,
Ainsi qu'une fontaine aux rythmiques sanglots.
Je l'entends bien qui coule avec un long murmure,
Mais je me tâte en vain pour trouver la blessure.

À travers la cité, comme dans un champ clos,
Il s'en va, transformant les pavés en îlots,
Désaltérant la soif de chaque créature,
Et partout colorant en rouge la nature.

J'ai demandé souvent à des vins captieux
D'endormir pour un jour la terreur qui me mine;
Le vin rend l'œil plus clair et l'oreille plus fine!

J'ai cherché dans l'amour un sommeil oublieux;
Mais l'amour n'est pour moi qu'un matelas d'aiguilles
Fait pour donner à boire à ces cruelles filles!

THE FOUNTAIN OF BLOOD

Sometimes it seems my blood pours out in waves,
The issue of a fountain's rhythmic sobs.
I hear the slow murmur of its flow,
But feel in vain to find the wound.

Across the city, as if through an arena,
It wends it way, turning cobbles to islands,
Quenching the thirst of every creature,
And dyeing all of nature red.

I've often asked deceptive wines
To dull for a day the enfeebling fear;
Wine clarifies the eye and hones the ear!

I sought in love a forgetful sleep;
But love for me is just a bed of nails
That's made for these cruel whores to draw a drink!

ALLÉGORIE

C'est une femme belle et de riche encolure,
Qui laisse dans son vin traîner sa chevelure.
Les griffes de l'amour, les poisons du tripot,
Tout glisse et tout s'émousse au granit de sa peau.
Elle rit à la Mort et nargue la Débauche,
Ces monstres dont la main, qui toujours gratte et fauche,
Dans ses jeux destructeurs a pourtant respecté
De ce corps ferme et droit la rude majesté.
Elle marche en déesse et repose en sultane;
Elle a dans le plaisir la foi mahométane,
Et dans ses bras ouverts, que remplissent ses seins,
Elle appelle des yeux la race des humains.
Elle croit, elle sait, cette vierge inféconde
Et pourtant nécessaire à la marche du monde,
Que la beauté du corps est un sublime don
Qui de toute infamie arrache le pardon.
Elle ignore l'Enfer comme le Purgatoire,
Et quand l'heure viendra d'entrer dans la Nuit noire,
Elle regardera la face de la Mort,
Ainsi qu'un nouveau-né, — sans haine et sans remords.

CXIV

ALLEGORY

A beautiful woman with an ample neck,
Who lets her hair flow into her wine.
The talons of love, the poisons of the brothel,
Glance off and blunt upon her granite skin.
She laughs at Death and mocks Debauchery,
Monsters whose hands, which scrape and grift,
Still show respect in their baleful games
For the stern majesty of her upright frame.
She walks as a goddess and reclines as a sultan;
In pleasure she sets a Mohammedan faith,
And with open arms, overflowing with breasts,
She calls with her eyes the human race.
She feels, she knows, this barren virgin
So necessary to the way of the world,
How sublime a gift is physical beauty
That snatches forgiveness from every infamy.
She heeds neither Hell nor Purgatory,
And when it is time to enter the black Night,
She will look into the face of Death,
As would a newborn, —no hatred and no regrets.

LA BÉATRICE

Dans des terrains cendreux, calcinés, sans verdure,
Comme je me plaignais un jour à la nature,
Et que de ma pensée, en vaguant au hasard,
J'aiguisais lentement sur mon cœur le poignard,
Je vis en plein midi descendre sur ma tête
Un nuage funèbre et gros d'une tempête,
Qui portait un troupeau de démons vicieux,
Semblables à des nains cruels et curieux.
À me considérer froidement ils se mirent,
Et, comme des passants sur un fou qu'ils admirent,
Je les entendis rire et chuchoter entre eux,
En échangeant maint signe et maint clignement d'yeux:

— « Contemplons à loisir cette caricature
Et cette ombre d'Hamlet imitant sa posture,
Le regard indécis et les cheveux au vent.
N'est-ce pas grand-pitié de voir ce bon vivant,
Ce gueux, cet histrion en vacances, ce drôle,
Parce qu'il sait jouer artistement son rôle,
Vouloir intéresser au chant de ses douleurs
Les aigles, les grillons, les ruisseaux et les fleurs,
Et même à nous, auteurs de ces vieilles rubriques,
Réciter en hurlant ses tirades publiques? »

BEATRICE

In fields of cinders, scorched, not a hint of green,
As I was complaining to nature one day,
And sharpening slowly, while roaming at random,
The dagger of my thoughts upon my heart,
At high noon I saw descend upon my head
A funereal cloud that was swollen with storm,
Which carried a horde of vicious demons,
Resembling cruel and inquisitive dwarves.
They cast a cold eye upon me,
And, like passersby admiring a madman,
I heard them laugh and whisper to themselves,
Trading winks and nudges back and forth:

—"Take a moment to consider this caricature
And this shadow of Hamlet mimicking his manner,
The indecisive gaze and the tussled hair.
Is it not a great pity to see this bon vivant,
This wretch, this out of work histrion, this joke,
Since he so artfully plays his role,
Trying to interest in the song of his sorrows
The eagles, the crickets, the streams and the flowers,
And even us, authors of these old rubrics,
By bellowing the recitation of his public tirades?"

J'aurais pu (mon orgueil aussi haut que les monts
Domine la nuée et le cri des démons)
Détourner simplement ma tête souveraine,
Si je n'eusse pas vu parmi leur troupe obscène,
Crime qui n'a pas fait chanceler le soleil!
La reine de mon cœur au regard nonpareil,
Qui riait avec eux de ma sombre détresse
Et leur versait parfois quelque sale caresse.

I could have (my pride towering as the mountains
Over the cloud and the cry of the demons)
Simply turned my sovereign head,
Had I not glimpsed among this obscene horde,
Crime which did not shake the sun!
The queen of my heart with her matchless gaze,
Who laughed with them at my somber distress
And stroked them sometimes with indecent caress.

LA MÉTAMORPHOSES DU VAMPIRE

La femme cependant, de sa bouche de fraise,
En se tordant ainsi qu'un serpent sur la braise,
Et pétrissant ses seins sur le fer de son busc,
Laissait couler ces mots tout imprégnés de musc:
— « Moi, j'ai la lèvre humide, et je sais la science
De perdre au fond d'un lit l'antique conscience.
Je sèche tous les pleurs sur mes seins triomphants,
Et fais rire les vieux du rire des enfants.
Je remplace, pour qui me voit nue et sans voiles,
La lune, le soleil, le ciel et les étoiles!
Je suis, mon cher savant, si docte aux voluptés,
Lorsque j'étouffe un homme en mes bras redoutés,
Ou lorsque j'abandonne aux morsures mon buste,
Timide et libertine, et fragile et robuste,
Que sur ces matelas qui se pâment d'émoi,
Les anges impuissants se damneraient pour moi! »

Quand elle eut de mes os sucé toute la mœlle,
Et que languissamment je me tournai vers elle
Pour lui rendre un baiser d'amour, je ne vis plus
Qu'une outre aux flancs gluants, toute pleine de pus!
Je fermai les deux yeux, dans ma froide épouvante,
Et quand je les rouvris à la clarté vivante,
À mes côtés, au lieu du mannequin puissant
Qui semblait avoir fait provision de sang,
Tremblaient confusément des débris de squelette,
Qui d'eux-mêmes rendaient le cri d'une girouette
Ou d'une enseigne, au bout d'une tringle de fer,
Que balance le vent pendant les nuits d'hiver.

METAMORPHOSES OF THE VAMPIRE

Meanwhile the woman, from her strawberry mouth,
Writhing like a snake upon the embers,
And kneading her breasts against the iron of her busk,
Let slip these words impregnated with musk:
—"Me, I have wet lips, and I know the art
Of mislaying antique conscience in the depths of a bed.
I dry all tears on my triumphant breasts,
And make the old laugh with the laughter of children.
I replace, for those who see me unveiled and naked,
The moon, the sun, the sky and the stars!
I am, my dear scholar, so versed in the pleasures,
That when I smother a man in my redoubtable arms,
Or abandon my breast to his bites,
Timid and libertine, fragile and strong,
Upon these cushions that swoon with emotion,
The powerless angels would damn themselves for me!"

When she had sucked all the marrow from my bones,
And when I turned languidly toward her
To render a lover's kiss, I saw no more
Than a sticky goatskin, filled full of pus!
I closed both my eyes, in my cold horror,
And when I opened them to the living light,
At my side, in place of the powerful mannequin
That seemed to have made provision of my blood,
There trembled confusedly the remnants of a skeleton
Which among themselves issued the shriek of a weathervane
Or of a sign, hung from an iron rail,
That sways in the wind during winter nights.

UN VOYAGE À CYTHÈRE

Mon cœur, comme un oiseau, voltigeait tout joyeux
Et planait librement à l'entour des cordages;
Le navire roulait sous un ciel sans nuages,
Comme un ange enivré d'un soleil radieux.

Quelle est cette île triste et noire? — C'est Cythère,
Nous dit-on, un pays fameux dans les chansons,
Eldorado banal de tous les vieux garçons.
Regardez, après tout, c'est une pauvre terre.

— Île des doux secrets et des fêtes du cœur!
De l'antique Vénus le superbe fantôme
Au-dessus de tes mers plane comme un arome,
Et charge les esprits d'amour et de langueur.

Belle île aux myrtes verts, pleine de fleurs écloses,
Vénérée à jamais par toute nation,
Où les soupirs des cœurs en adoration
Roulent comme l'encens sur un jardin de roses

Ou le roucoulement éternel d'un ramier!
— Cythère n'était plus qu'un terrain des plus maigres,
Un désert rocailleux troublé par des cris aigres.
J'entrevoyais pourtant un objet singulier!

Ce n'était pas un temple aux ombres bocagères,
Où la jeune prêtresse, amoureuse des fleurs,
Allait, le corps brûlé de secrètes chaleurs,
Entrebâillant sa robe aux brises passagères;

A VOYAGE TO CYTHERA

My heart, like a bird, fluttered joyfully
And hovered freely around the ropes;
The ship swayed beneath a cloudless sky,
Like an angel drunk on radiant sun.

What is this island sad and black? —It is Cythera,
They say, a country renowned in songs,
Banal Eldorado of all old bachelors.
Look, after all, it's a pitiful place.

—Isle of sweet secrets and heart's revels!
The glorious ghost of ancient Venus
Hovers over your seas like a scent,
And fills our spirits with love and languor.

Beautiful isle of green myrtle, full of flowers in bloom,
Venerated for all time by every nation,
Where the sighs of hearts in adoration
Waft like incense through a garden of roses

Or the eternal cooing of a dove!
—Cythera was no more than the most meager of lands,
A stony desert strafed by stringent cries.
Yet I caught a glimpse of a singular object!

It was not a temple amid shady groves,
Where a young priestess, lover of flowers,
Went, her body inflamed by secret fervors,
Slipping open her robe for passing breezes;

Mais voilà qu'en rasant la côte d'assez près
Pour troubler les oiseaux avec nos voiles blanches,
Nous vîmes que c'était un gibet à trois branches,
Du ciel se détachant en noir, comme un cyprès.

De féroces oiseaux perchés sur leur pâture
Détruisaient avec rage un pendu déjà mûr,
Chacun plantant, comme un outil, son bec impur
Dans tous les coins saignants de cette pourriture;

Les yeux étaient deux trous, et du ventre effondré
Les intestins pesants lui coulaient sur les cuisses,
Et ses bourreaux, gorgés de hideuses délices,
L'avaient à coups de bec absolument châtré.

Sous les pieds, un troupeau de jaloux quadrupèdes,
Le museau relevé, tournoyait et rôdait;
Une plus grande bête au milieu s'agitait
Comme un exécuteur entouré de ses aides.

Habitant de Cythère, enfant d'un ciel si beau,
Silencieusement tu souffrais ces insultes
En expiation de tes infâmes cultes
Et des péchés qui t'ont interdit le tombeau.

Ridicule pendu, tes douleurs sont les miennes!
Je sentis, à l'aspect de tes membres flottants,
Comme un vomissement, remonter vers mes dents
Le long fleuve de fiel des douleurs anciennes;

Devant toi, pauvre diable au souvenir si cher,
J'ai senti tous les becs et toutes les mâchoires
Des corbeaux lancinants et des panthères noires
Qui jadis aimaient tant à triturer ma chair.

But here as we skimmed so close to the coast
To trouble the birds with our white sails,
What we saw was a gibbet with three branches,
Carved from the sky in black, like a cypress.

Ferocious birds perched upon their prey
Destroying with rage a ripe hanged man,
Each driving, like a spade, its filthy beak
Into every bleeding recess of rot;

The eyes were two holes, and from the eroded belly
Heavy intestines poured down the thighs,
And his torturers, gorged upon gruesome delights,
Had pecked him absolutely castrated.

Below the feet, a herd of jealous quadrupeds,
Muzzle raised, circled and prowled;
One huge beast twitched among them
Like an executioner surrounded by henchmen.

Inhabitant of Cythera, child of so beautiful a sky,
Silently you suffered these insults
In expiation of your cultic infamies
And of sins that forbade you the tomb.

Ridiculous hanged man, your sufferings are mine!
I feel, at the sight of your swaying limbs,
Like vomit, that rises toward my teeth
The long river of bile flow from ancient pains;

There before you, poor devil in memory held dear,
I felt every beak and every jaw
Of the thrusting crows and the black panthers
Who once so loved to grind my flesh.

— Le ciel était charmant, la mer était unie;
Pour moi tout était noir et sanglant désormais,
Hélas! et j'avais, comme en un suaire épais,
Le cœur enseveli dans cette allégorie.

Dans ton île, ô Vénus! je n'ai trouvé debout
Qu'un gibet symbolique où pendait mon image.....
— Ah! Seigneur! donnez-moi la force et le courage
De contempler mon cœur et mon corps sans dégoût!

—The sky was lovely, the sea was smooth;
For me all was black and bloody hereafter,
Alas! for I had, as in a thick shroud,
Buried my heart in this allegory.

On your island, o Venus, I found nothing left
But a symbolic gibbet where my image was hung.....
—Ah! Lord! give me the strength and the courage
To look without loathing upon my body and my heart!

CXVII

L'AMOUR ET LE CRÂNE

Vieux Cul-de-Lampe

L'Amour est assis sur le crane
           De l'Humanité,
Et sur ce trône le profane,
           Au rire effronté,

Souffle gaiement des bulles rondes
           Qui montent dans l'air,
Comme pour rejoindre les mondes
           Au fond de l'éther.

Le globe lumineux et frêle
           Prend un grand essor,
Crève et crache son âme grêle
           Comme un songe d'or.

J'entends le crâne à chaque bulle
           Prier et gémir:
— « Ce jeu féroce et ridicule,
           Quand doit-il finir?

« Car ce que ta bouche cruelle
           Éparpille en l'air,
Monstre assassin, c'est ma cervelle,
           Mon sang et ma chair! »

CXVII

LOVE AND THE SKULL

An Old Colophon

Love sits upon the skull
      Of Humanity
And on this throne he profanes,
      With insolent laughter,

Gaily blows round bubbles
      Which climb in the air
As if to rejoin worlds
      In the depths of the ether.

The luminous and frail globe
      Soaring on high,
Bursts and sprays its slender soul
      Like a golden dream.

With every bubble I hear the skull
      Plead and groan:
—"This ferocious and ridiculous game,
      When will it end?

"What your cruel mouth
      Scatters in the air,
Murderous monster, is my brain,
      My flesh and my blood!"

RÉVOLTE

REVOLT

LE RENIEMENT DE SAINT PIERRE

Qu'est-ce que Dieu fait donc de ce flot d'anathèmes
Qui monte tous les jours vers ses chers Séraphins?
Comme un tyran gorgé de viande et de vins,
Il s'endort au doux bruit de nos affreux blasphèmes.

Les sanglots des martyrs et des suppliciés
Sont une symphonie enivrante sans doute,
Puisque, malgré le sang que leur volupté coûte,
Les cieux ne s'en sont point encore rassasiés!

— Ah! Jésus, souviens-toi du Jardin des Olives!
Dans ta simplicité tu priais à genoux
Celui qui dans son ciel riait au bruit des clous
Que d'ignobles bourreaux plantaient dans tes chairs vives,

Lorsque tu vis cracher sur ta divinité
La crapule du corps de garde et des cuisines,
Et lorsque tu sentis s'enfoncer les épines
Dans ton crâne où vivait l'immense Humanité;

Quand de ton corps brisé la pesanteur horrible
Allongeait tes deux bras distendus, que ton sang
Et ta sueur coulaient de ton front pâlissant,
Quand tu fus devant tous posé comme une cible,

Rêvais-tu de ces jours si brillants et si beaux
Où tu vins pour remplir l'éternelle promesse,
Où tu foulais, monté sur une douce ânesse,
Des chemins tout jonchés de fleurs et de rameaux,

SAINT PETER'S DENIAL

What does God do with the wave of anathemas
That daily ascends toward his dear Seraphim?
Like a tyrant gorged with meat and wine,
He nods off to the soothing sound of frightful blasphemies.

The sobs of martyrs and of supplicants
Must be an intoxicating symphony,
Since, despite the blood paid out for their pleasure,
The heavens are not yet satisfied!

—Ah! Jesus, recall the Garden of Olives!
In your humility you prayed upon your knees
To he on high who laughed to hear the nails
Ignoble hangmen drove into your living flesh,

When you saw them spit on your divinity
The rabble of guards and scullions,
And when you felt the thorns sink
Into your skull where lived immense Humanity;

When the horrible weight of your broken body
Stretched your two distended arms, when your blood
And sweat flowed from your pallid brow,
When you were set before them all like a target,

Did you dream of the days so beautiful and bright
When you came to fulfill the eternal promise,
When you trod, mounted on a gentle donkey,
The paths all strewn with flowers and with palms,

Où, le cœur tout gonflé d'espoir et de vaillance,
Tu fouettais tous ces vils marchands à tour de bras,
Où tu fus maître enfin? Le remords n'a-t-il pas
Pénétré dans ton flanc plus avant que la lance?

— Certes, je sortirai, quant à moi, satisfait
D'un monde où l'action n'est pas la sœur du rêve;
Puissé-je user du glaive et périr par le glaive!
Saint Pierre a renié Jésus... il a bien fait!

When, heart full of hope and valor,
With all your might you flayed the vile merchants,
When you were master, that is? Did regret not
Penetrate your side more deeply than the spear?

—Yes, I will take leave, satisfied, for my part
From a world where action is no sister of dream;
May I wield the sword and perish by the sword!
Saint Peter denied Jesus... rightly so!

ABEL ET CAÏN

I

Race d'Abel, dors, bois et mange;
Dieu te sourit complaisamment.

Race de Caïn, dans la fange
Rampe et meurs misérablement.

Race d'Abel, ton sacrifice
Flatte le nez du Séraphin!

Race de Caïn, ton supplice
Aura-t-il jamais une fin?

Race d'Abel, vois tes semailles
Et ton bétail venir à bien;

Race de Caïn, tes entrailles
Hurlent la faim comme un vieux chien.

Race d'Abel, chauffe ton ventre
À ton foyer patriarcal;

Race de Caïn, dans ton antre
Tremble de froid, pauvre chacal!

Race d'Abel, aime et pullule!
Ton or fait aussi des petits.

ABEL AND CAIN

I

Race of Abel, sleep, eat and drink;
God smiles on you complacently.

Race of Cain, in filth
Crawl and perish miserably.

Race of Abel, your sacrifice
Flatters the nose of the Seraphim!

Race of Cain, your torture
Will it never end?

Race of Abel, see how your seeds
And your cattle prosper;

Race of Cain, your entrails
Howl with hunger like an old dog.

Race of Abel, warm your belly
At your patriarchal hearth;

Race of Cain, within your den
Tremble with cold, poor jackal!

Race of Abel, be fruitful and multiply!
Even your gold has descendants.

Race de Caïn, cœur qui brûle,
Prends garde à ces grands appétits.

Race d'Abel, tu croîs et broutes
Comme les punaises des bois!

Race de Caïn, sur les routes
Traîne ta famille aux abois.

II

Ah! race d'Abel, ta charogne
Engraissera le sol fumant!

Race de Caïn, ta besogne
N'est pas faite suffisamment;

Race d'Abel, voici ta honte:
Le fer est vaincu par l'épieu!

Race de Caïn, au ciel monte,
Et sur la terre jette Dieu!

Race of Cain, of burning heart,
Beware of these great appetites.

Race of Abel, grow and graze
Like woodlice upon timber!

Race of Cain, down the streets
Drag your desperate family.

II

Ah! race of Abel, your carrion
Will fat the steaming soil!

Race of Cain, your work
Is not yet done;

Race of Abel, here is your shame:
The iron is vanquished by the spear!

Race of Cain, ascend to heaven,
And cast God down to earth.

LES LITANIES DE SATAN

Ô toi, le plus savant et le plus beau des Anges,
Dieu trahi par le sort et privé de louanges,

Ô Satan, prends pitié de ma longue misère!

Ô Prince de l'exil, à qui l'on a fait tort,
Et qui, vaincu, toujours te redresses plus fort,

Ô Satan, prends pitié de ma longue misère!

Toi qui sais tout, grand roi des choses souterraines,
Guérisseur familier des angoisses humaines,

Ô Satan, prends pitié de ma longue misère!

Toi qui, même aux lépreux, aux parias maudits,
Enseignes par l'amour le goût du Paradis,

Ô Satan, prends pitié de ma longue misère!

Ô toi qui de la Mort, ta vieille et forte amante,
Engendras l'Espérance, — une folle charmante!

Ô Satan, prends pitié de ma longue misère!

Toi qui fais au proscrit ce regard calme et haut
Qui damne tout un peuple autour d'un échafaud,

Ô Satan, prends pitié de ma longue misère!

THE LITANIES OF SATAN

O thou, most cunning and most beautiful of Angels,
God betrayed by fate and deprived of praises,

O Satan, take pity upon my tedious misery!

O Prince of exile, to whom was done wrong,
And whom, vanquished, rises ever the stronger,

O Satan, take pity upon my tedious misery!

Thou who knows all, great king of the underworld,
Genial healer of human anguish,

O Satan, take pity upon my tedious misery!

Thou who, even to lepers, to accursed pariahs,
Imparts through love the taste of Paradise,

O Satan, take pity upon my tedious misery!

O thou who with Death, old and potent lover,
Begot Hope, —a charming madwoman!

O Satan, take pity upon my tedious misery!

Thou who lends the outlaw that calm haughty gaze
Which damns everyone from a scaffold,

O Satan, take pity upon my tedious misery!

Toi qui sais en quels coins des terres envieuses
Le Dieu jaloux cacha les pierres précieuses,

Ô Satan, prends pitié de ma longue misère!

Toi dont l'œil clair connaît les profonds arsenaux
Où dort enseveli le peuple des métaux,

Ô Satan, prends pitié de ma longue misère!

Toi dont la large main cache les précipices
Au somnambule errant au bord des édifices,

Ô Satan, prends pitié de ma longue misère!

Toi qui, magiquement, assouplis les vieux os
De l'ivrogne attardé foulé par les chevaux,

Ô Satan, prends pitié de ma longue misère!

Toi qui, pour consoler l'homme frêle qui souffre,
Nous appris à mêler le salpêtre et le soufre,

Ô Satan, prends pitié de ma longue misère!

Toi qui poses ta marque, ô complice subtil,
Sur le front du Crésus impitoyable et vil,

Ô Satan, prends pitié de ma longue misère!

Toi qui mets dans les yeux et dans le cœur des filles
Le culte de la plaie et l'amour des guenilles,

Ô Satan, prends pitié de ma longue misère!

Thou who knows in what corners of envious lands
The jealous God hid precious stones,

O Satan, take pity upon my tedious misery!

Thou whose bright eye knows the deep armory
Where lies buried in slumber the nation of metals,

O Satan, take pity upon my tedious misery!

Thou whose vast hand hides the precipice
From the sleepwalker wandering at the edge of buildings,

O Satan, take pity upon my tedious misery!

Thou who, magically, makes supple the old bones
Of the sluggish drunkard trampled by horses,

O Satan, take pity upon my tedious misery!

Thou who, to console the frail man's suffering,
Instructs us to mix saltpetre and sulphur,

O Satan, take pity upon my tedious misery!

Thou who sets your mark, o subtle accomplice,
Upon the brow of pitiless and vile Croesus,

O Satan, take pity upon my tedious misery!

Thou who set in the eyes and the heart of women
The cult of the wound and the love of rags,

O Satan, take pity upon my tedious misery!

Bâton des exilés, lampe des inventeurs,
Confesseur des pendus et des conspirateurs,

Ô Satan, prends pitié de ma longue misère!

Père adoptif de ceux qu'en sa noire colère
Du paradis terrestre a chassés Dieu le Père,

Ô Satan, prends pitié de ma longue misère!

PRIÈRE

Gloire et louange à toi, Satan, dans les hauteurs
Du Ciel, où tu régnas, et dans les profondeurs
De l'Enfer, où, vaincu, tu rêves en silence!
Fais que mon âme un jour, sous l'Arbre de Science,
Près de toi se repose, à l'heure où sur ton front
Comme un Temple nouveau ses rameaux s'épandront!

Staff of exiles, lamp of inventors,
Confessor of hanged men and conspirators,

O Satan, take pity upon my tedious misery!

Adoptive father of those whom in black rage
From terrestrial paradise God the Father drove forth.

O Satan, take pity upon my tedious misery!

PRAYER

Glory and praise to thou, Satan, in the height
Of Heaven, where you reigned, and in the depths
Of Hell, where, vanquished, you dream in silence!
Grant that my soul one day, beneath the Tree of Knowledge,
May repose beside you, when over your brow
Its branches will spread like a new Temple.

LA MORT

DEATH

LA MORT DES AMANTS

Nous aurons des lits pleins d'odeurs légères,
Des divans profonds comme des tombeaux,
Et d'étranges fleurs sur des étagères,
Écloses pour nous sous des cieux plus beaux.

Usant à l'envi leurs chaleurs dernières,
Nos deux cœurs seront deux vastes flambeaux,
Qui réfléchiront leurs doubles lumières
Dans nos deux esprits, ces miroirs jumeaux.

Un soir fait de rose et de bleu mystique,
Nous échangerons un éclair unique,
Comme un long sanglot, tout chargé d'adieux;

Et plus tard un Ange, entrouvrant les portes,
Viendra ranimer, fidèle et joyeux,
Les miroirs ternis et les flammes mortes.

THE DEATH OF LOVERS

We will have beds suffused with delicate scents,
Divans deep as tombs,
And exotic flowers upon our shelves,
Blooming for us below more beautiful skies.

Vying to extinguish their dying warmth,
Our two hearts will be two vast torches,
Which come to reflect their double glow
Within our two spirits, these mirrors twinned.

One evening of pink and of mystical blue,
We will exchange a singular spark,
Like a long lament, charged full of farewell.

And later an Angel, parting the doors,
Will come to rekindle, faithful and joyous,
The tarnished mirrors and the dead flames.

LA MORT DES PAUVRES

C'est la Mort qui console, hélas! et qui fait vivre;
C'est le but de la vie, et c'est le seul espoir
Qui, comme un élixir, nous monte et nous enivre,
Et nous donne le cœur de marcher jusqu'au soir;

À travers la tempête, et la neige, et le givre,
C'est la clarté vibrante à notre horizon noir;
C'est l'auberge fameuse inscrite sur le livre,
Où l'on pourra manger, et dormir, et s'asseoir;

C'est un Ange qui tient dans ses doigts magnétiques
Le sommeil et le don des rêves extatiques,
Et qui refait le lit des gens pauvres et nus;

C'est la gloire des dieux, c'est le grenier mystique,
C'est la bourse du pauvre et sa patrie antique,
C'est le portique ouvert sur les Cieux inconnus!

THE DEATH OF THE POOR

It is Death that consoles, alas! and that makes us live;
It is the aim of life, and it is the only hope
Which, like an elixir, elevates and intoxicates us,
And gives us the heart to march unto evening;

Through the tempest, and the snow, and the frost,
It is the glowing light on our black horizon;
It is the renown inn written up in the book,
Where one may eat, and sleep, and sit;

It is an Angel who holds in its magnetic fingers
Sleep and the gift of ecstatic dreams,
And who makes the bed of the poor and the naked;

It is the glory of the gods, it is the mystic grain,
It is the poor man's purse and his ancient fatherland,
It is the portico open upon Heavens unknown!

CXXIII

LA MORT DES ARTISTES

Combien faut-il de fois secouer mes grelots
Et baiser ton front bas, morne caricature?
Pour piquer dans le but, de mystique nature,
Combien, ô mon carquois, perdre de javelots?

Nous userons notre âme en de subtils complots,
Et nous démolirons mainte lourde armature,
Avant de contempler la grande Créature
Dont l'infernal désir nous remplit de sanglots!

Il en est qui jamais n'ont connu leur Idole,
Et ces sculpteurs damnés et marqués d'un affront,
Qui vont se martelant la poitrine et le front,

N'ont qu'un espoir, étrange et sombre Capitole!
C'est que la Mort, planant comme un soleil nouveau,
Fera s'épanouir les fleurs de leur cerveau!

THE DEATH OF ARTISTS

How many times must I rattle my bells
And kiss your low brow, bleak caricature?
To hit the target, of mystical nature,
How many javelins, o my quiver, must be lost?

We will wear out our soul with subtle devices,
And demolish many a heavy armature,
Before we contemplate the great Creature
For whom we sob with infernal desire!

There are some who have never known their Idol,
And those sculptors damned and marked by an offense,
Who hammer themselves on the chest and the brow,

Have only one hope, strange and somber Capitol!
That Death, looming like a new sun,
Will bring to bloom the flowers of their brain!

LA FIN DE LA JOURNÉE

Sous une lumière blafarde
Court, danse et se tord sans raison
La Vie, impudente et criarde.
Aussi, sitôt qu'à l'horizon

La nuit voluptueuse monte,
Apaisant tout, même la faim,
Effaçant tout, même la honte,
Le Poète se dit: « Enfin!

« Mon esprit, comme mes vertèbres,
Invoque ardemment le repos;
Le cœur plein de songes funèbres,

« Je vais me coucher sur le dos
Et me rouler dans vos rideaux,
Ô rafraîchissantes ténèbres! »

THE END OF DAY

Beneath a pallid light
Life, impudent and shrill,
Runs, dances and writhes without reason.
Then, just as at the horizon

Voluptuous night rises,
Appeasing all, even hunger,
Effacing all, even shame,
The Poet tells himself: "At last!

"My spirit, like my vertebrae,
Pleads ardently for repose;
Heart full of funereal dreams,

"I will lie on my back
And roll myself up in your curtains,
O refreshing shadows!"

LE RÊVE D'UN CURIEUX

À F.N.

Connais-tu, comme moi, la douleur savoureuse,
Et de toi fais-tu dire: « Oh! l'homme singulier! »
— J'allais mourir. C'était dans mon âme amoureuse,
Désir mêlé d'horreur, un mal particulier;

Angoisse et vif espoir, sans humeur factieuse.
Plus allait se vidant le fatal sablier,
Plus ma torture était âpre et délicieuse;
Tout mon cœur s'arrachait au monde familier.

J'étais comme l'enfant avide du spectacle,
Haïssant le rideau comme on hait un obstacle...
Enfin la vérité froide se révéla:

J'étais mort sans surprise, et la terrible aurore
M'enveloppait. — Eh quoi! n'est-ce donc que cela?
La toile était levée et j'attendais encore.

CXXV

AN ECCENTRIC'S DREAM

To F.N.

Do you know, like me, delicious pain,
And do you make them say: "Oh! that curious man!"
—I was about to die. Within my amorous soul,
Desire mingled with horror, a peculiar malady;

Anguish and keen hope, without factious humor.
The more the fatal sand ran out,
The more stringent and delicious was my torture;
My heart entire tore itself from the familiar world.

I was like the child avid for the spectacle,
Hating the curtain as one hates an obstacle...
At last the cold truth was revealed:

I was uneventfully dead, and the terrible dawn
Enveloped me. —What! is that it?
The curtain had risen and I was still waiting.

LE VOYAGE

À Maxime Du Camp

I

Pour l'enfant, amoureux de cartes et d'estampes,
L'univers est égal à son vaste appétit.
Ah! que le monde est grand à la clarté des lampes!
Aux yeux du souvenir que le monde est petit!

Un matin nous partons, le cerveau plein de flamme,
Le cœur gros de rancune et de désirs amers,
Et nous allons, suivant le rythme de la lame,
Berçant notre infini sur le fini des mers:

Les uns, joyeux de fuir une patrie infâme;
D'autres, l'horreur de leurs berceaux, et quelques-uns,
Astrologues noyés dans les yeux d'une femme,
La Circé tyrannique aux dangereux parfums.

Pour n'être pas changés en bêtes, ils s'enivrent
D'espace et de lumière et de cieux embrasés;
La glace qui les mord, les soleils qui les cuivrent,
Effacent lentement la marque des baisers.

Mais les vrais voyageurs sont ceux-là seuls qui partent
Pour partir; cœurs légers, semblables aux ballons,
De leur fatalité jamais ils ne s'écartent,
Et, sans savoir pourquoi, disent toujours: Allons!

CXXVI

THE VOYAGE

To Maxime Du Camp

I

For the child, enamored of maps and prints,
The universe is equal to his vast appetite.
Ah! how large is the world in the lamplight!
In the eyes of memory how small is the world!

One morning we depart, brain full of flame
Heart great with rancor and bitter desires,
And we go, following the rhythm of the waves,
Our infinitude cradled by finite seas.

These, joyfully fleeing an infamous fatherland;
Others, the horrors of home, and some,
Astrologers drowned in a woman's eyes,
Tyrannical Circe of dangerous perfumes.

So as not to be turned into swine, they get drunk
With space and with light and with burning skies;
The biting frost, the bronzing sun,
Slowly effacing the mark of her kisses.

But the true voyagers are those who depart
For departure; light hearts, akin to balloons,
Never swerving from their fate,
And, say always, without knowing why: Let us go!

Ceux-là dont les désirs ont la forme des nues,
Et qui rêvent, ainsi qu'un conscrit le canon,
De vastes voluptés, changeantes, inconnues,
Et dont l'esprit humain n'a jamais su le nom!

II

Nous imitons, horreur! la toupie et la boule
Dans leur valse et leurs bonds; même dans nos sommeils
La Curiosité nous tourmente et nous roule,
Comme un Ange cruel qui fouette des soleils.

Singulière fortune où le but se déplace,
Et, n'étant nulle part, peut être n'importe où!
Où l'Homme, dont jamais l'espérance n'est lasse,
Pour trouver le repos court toujours comme un fou!

Notre âme est un trois-mâts cherchant son Icarie;
Une voix retentit sur le pont: « Ouvre l'œil! »
Une voix de la hune, ardente et folle, crie:
« Amour... gloire... bonheur! » Enfer! c'est un écueil!

Chaque îlot signalé par l'homme de vigie
Est un Eldorado promis par le Destin;
L'Imagination qui dresse son orgie
Ne trouve qu'un récif aux clartés du matin.

Ô le pauvre amoureux des pays chimériques!
Faut-il le mettre aux fers, le jeter à la mer,
Ce matelot ivrogne, inventeur d'Amériques
Dont le mirage rend le gouffre plus amer?

Those whose desires have the form of clouds,
And who dream, as a conscript of his cannon,
Of vast sensualities, shifting, unknown,
For which human mind has never had a name!

II

We imitate, horror! the top and the ball
In their spin and their bounce; even in sleep
Curiosity torments and turns us,
Like a cruel Angel who whips the suns.

Singular fortune whose goal is displaced,
And, being nowhere, may be no matter where!
Where Man, whose hope never tires,
Ever hurries in search of repose like a fool!

Our soul is a trimast in search of Icaria;
A voice resounds from the deck: "Eyes open!"
A cry from the crow's nest, ardent and crazed:
"Love... glory... happiness!" Hell! It's a reef!

Each islet at which the lookout points
Is an El Dorado promised by Destiny;
The Imagination which draws up its orgy
Finds only a reef in the light of morning.

O the poor lover of chimerical lands!
Must he be manacled, thrown in the sea,
This drunken sailor, inventing Americas
Whose mirage redoubles the bitter abyss?

Tel le vieux vagabond, piétinant dans la boue,
Rêve, le nez en l'air, de brillants paradis;
Son œil ensorcelé découvre une Capoue
Partout où la chandelle illumine un taudis.

III

Étonnants voyageurs! quelles nobles histoires
Nous lisons dans vos yeux profonds comme les mers!
Montrez-nous les écrins de vos riches mémoires,
Ces bijoux merveilleux, faits d'astres et d'éthers.

Nous voulons voyager sans vapeur et sans voile!
Faites, pour égayer l'ennui de nos prisons,
Passer sur nos esprits, tendus comme une toile,
Vos souvenirs avec leurs cadres d'horizons.

Dites, qu'avez-vous vu?

IV

                              « Nous avons vu des astres
Et des flots, nous avons vu des sables aussi;
Et, malgré bien des chocs et d'imprévus désastres,
Nous nous sommes souvent ennuyés, comme ici.

« La gloire du soleil sur la mer violette,
La gloire des cités dans le soleil couchant,
Allumaient dans nos cœurs une ardeur inquiète
De plonger dans un ciel au reflet alléchant.

« Les plus riches cités, les plus grands paysages,
Jamais ne contenaient l'attrait mystérieux
De ceux que le hasard fait avec les nuages.
Et toujours le désir nous rendait soucieux!

This elderly vagabond, trudging in sludge,
Dreams, nose in the air, of paradise bright;
With enchanted eyes he uncovers a Capua
Wherever the candle lights up a slum.

III

Astonishing voyagers! what noble stories
We read in your eyes profound as the seas!
Show us the caskets of your rich memories,
Those marvelous jewels, made of stars and of ether.

We long to travel without steam or sail!
So, to brighten the boredom of our prisons,
Spread over our minds, stretched like a canvas,
Your memories framed by horizons.

Tell, what have you seen?

IV

                              "We have seen stars
And waves; we have seen sands as well;
And, despite shocks and unforeseen disasters,
We often grew bored, just as you are here.

"The glory of the sun upon the violet sea,
The glory of cities in the setting sun,
Kindled in our hearts a restless ardor
To plunge into a sky of enticing reflections.

"The richest of cities, the grandest of landscapes,
Never contained the mysterious attraction
Of those that hazard makes out of the clouds.
And desire would always keep us alert!

« — La jouissance ajoute au désir de la force.
Désir, vieil arbre à qui le plaisir sert d'engrais,
Cependant que grossit et durcit ton écorce,
Tes branches veulent voir le soleil de plus près!

« Grandiras-tu toujours, grand arbre plus vivace
Que le cyprès? — Pourtant nous avons, avec soin,
Cueilli quelques croquis pour votre album vorace,
Frères qui trouvez beau tout ce qui vient de loin!

« Nous avons salué des idoles à trompe;
Des trônes constellés de joyaux lumineux;
Des palais ouvragés dont la féerique pompe
Serait pour vos banquiers un rêve ruineux;

« Des costumes qui sont pour les yeux une ivresse;
Des femmes dont les dents et les ongles sont teints,
Et des jongleurs savants que le serpent caresse. »

V

Et puis, et puis encore?

"—Enjoyment strengthens desire.
Desire, old tree fertilized by pleasure,
As it makes you grow and stiffens your bark,
Your branches strive more closely to see the sun!

"Will you grow forever, great tree more hardy
Than the cypress? —Even so we have, with care,
Gathered some sketches for your voracious album,
Brothers who find beautiful all that comes from afar!

"We have saluted idols with elephant trunks;
Thrones constellated with luminous gems;
Finely wrought palaces whose fairy pomp
Would be for your bankers a ruinous dream;

"Ceremonial robes to intoxicate your eyes;
Women whose teeth and nails are dyed,
Jugglers expert at charming a snake."

V

And then, and what next?

                           « Ô cerveaux enfantins!

« Pour ne pas oublier la chose capitale,
Nous avons vu partout, et sans l'avoir cherché,
Du haut jusques en bas de l'échelle fatale,
Le spectacle ennuyeux de l'immortel péché:

« La femme, esclave vile, orgueilleuse et stupide,
Sans rire s'adorant et s'aimant sans dégoût;
L'homme, tyran goulu, paillard, dur et cupide,
Esclave de l'esclave et ruisseau dans l'égout;

« Le bourreau qui jouit, le martyr qui sanglote;
La fête qu'assaisonne et parfume le sang;
Le poison du pouvoir énervant le despote,
Et le peuple amoureux du fouet abrutissant;

« Plusieurs religions semblables à la nôtre,
Toutes escaladant le ciel; la Sainteté,
Comme en un lit de plume un délicat se vautre,
Dans les clous et le crin cherchant la volupté;

« L'Humanité bavarde, ivre de son génie,
Et, folle maintenant comme elle était jadis,
Criant à Dieu, dans sa furibonde agonie:
"Ô mon semblable, ô mon maître, je te maudis!"

« Et les moins sots, hardis amants de la Démence,
Fuyant le grand troupeau parqué par le Destin,
Et se réfugiant dans l'opium immense!
— Tel est du globe entier l'éternel bulletin. »

VI

　　　　　　　"O childish brains!

"So as not to forget the capital thing,
　Everywhere we saw, without even looking,
　From the top to the bottom on the ladder of fate,
　The dull spectacle of immortal sin:

"Woman, vile slave, conceited and stupid,
　Tirelessly in love with herself and humorlessly self-adoring;
　Man, gluttonous tyrant, lewd, callous and covetous,
　Slave of the slave and stream in the sewer;

"The hangman who revels, the martyr who sobs;
　The feast that is seasoned and perfumed with blood;
　The poison of power enervating the despot,
　And the masses enamored of the mind-numbing whip;

"Many religions resemble our own,
　All are ladders to heaven; Saintliness,
　As a delicate wallows in a feather bed,
　Seeks pleasure in hairshirt and nails;

"Blowhard Humanity, drunk on its genius,
　And, crazy now as it was long ago,
　Cries out to God, in its furious agony:
　'O my likeness, o my master, I damn you to hell!'

"And the less stupid, steadfast lovers of Dementia,
　Fleeing the great herd penned by Destiny,
　And seeking refuge in boundless opium!
　—Such is the eternal bulletin of the whole globe."

VII

Amer savoir, celui qu'on tire du voyage!
Le monde, monotone et petit, aujourd'hui,
Hier, demain, toujours, nous fait voir notre image:
Une oasis d'horreur dans un désert d'ennui!

Faut-il partir? rester? Si tu peux rester, reste;
Pars, s'il le faut. L'un court, et l'autre se tapit
Pour tromper l'ennemi vigilant et funeste,
Le Temps! Il est, hélas! des coureurs sans répit,

Comme le Juif errant et comme les apôtres,
À qui rien ne suffit, ni wagon ni vaisseau,
Pour fuir ce rétiaire infâme; il en est d'autres
Qui savent le tuer sans quitter leur berceau.

Lorsque enfin il mettra le pied sur notre échine,
Nous pourrons espérer et crier: En avant!
De même qu'autrefois nous partions pour la Chine,
Les yeux fixés au large et les cheveux au vent,

Nous nous embarquerons sur la mer des Ténèbres
Avec le cœur joyeux d'un jeune passager.
Entendez-vous ces voix, charmantes et funèbres,
Qui chantent: « Par ici! vous qui voulez manger

« Le Lotus parfumé! c'est ici qu'on vendange
Les fruits miraculeux dont votre cœur a faim;
Venez vous enivrer de la douceur étrange
De cette après-midi qui n'a jamais de fin? »

À l'accent familier nous devinons le spectre;
Nos Pylades là-bas tendent leurs bras vers nous.
« Pour rafraîchir ton cœur nage vers ton Électre! »
Dit celle dont jadis nous baisions les genoux.

VII

Bitter knowledge, that one draws from the voyage!
The world, monotonous and small, today,
Yesterday, tomorrow, always, makes us see our own image:
An oasis of horror in a desert of ennui!

Must we go? stay? If you would stay, stay;
Go, if you must. The one runs off, the other hides
Misleading the lugubrious and vigilant enemy,
Time! There are, alas! some who run without rest,

Like the wandering Jew and like the Apostles,
For whom nothing suffices, neither wagon nor vessel,
To flee this infamous retiarius; there are others
Who know how to kill him before leaving their cradle.

When he finally puts his boot on our spine,
We may hope and cry out: Onward!
Just as of old we departed for China,
Eyes set to sea and hair blown in the wind,

We will load ourselves onto the sea of Shadows
With the joyful heart of a youthful passenger.
Can you hear those voices, charming and funereal,
Which sing: "This way! Those who would eat

"The scented Lotus! it is here that one harvests
The miraculous fruits for which your heart hungers;
Won't you drink of the exotic ease
Of this afternoon that will never end?"

By familiar accents we divine the specter;
Over there our Pylades hold out their arms.
"To refresh your heart swim toward your Electra!"
Says she whose knees we kissed long ago.

VIII

Ô Mort, vieux capitaine, il est temps! levons l'ancre!
Ce pays nous ennuie, ô Mort! Appareillons!
Si le ciel et la mer sont noirs comme de l'encre,
Nos cœurs que tu connais sont remplis de rayons!

Verse-nous ton poison pour qu'il nous réconforte!
Nous voulons, tant ce feu nous brûle le cerveau,
Plonger au fond du gouffre, Enfer ou Ciel, qu'importe?
Au fond de l'Inconnu pour trouver du *nouveau*!

VIII

O Death, ancient captain, it's time! weigh anchor!
This country bores us, o Death! Cast off!
If the sky and the sea are as black as ink,
Our hearts as you know are replete with sunbeams!

Pour us your poison to make us feel better!
We long, so this fire burns the brain,
To plunge to the bottom of the abyss, Hell or Heaven, who cares?
To the bottom of the Unknown to discover the *new*!

Table des matières

Les Fleurs du Mal [1861]

TABLEAUX PARISIENS

LE VIN

RÉVOLTE

LA MORT